Bad Blood

RaceB4Race

RACEB4RACE: CRITICAL RACE STUDIES OF THE PREMODERN

Geraldine Heng and Ayanna Thompson, series editors

A complete list of books in the series is available from the publisher.

Bad Blood

Staging Race Between Early
Modern England and Spain

Emily Weissbourd

PENN

UNIVERSITY OF PENNSYLVANIA PRESS

PHILADELPHIA

Published by
University of Pennsylvania Press
Philadelphia, Pennsylvania 19104-4112
www.upenn.edu/pennpress

Printed in the United States of America on acid-free paper
10 9 8 7 6 5 4 3 2 1

Hardcover ISBN: 978-1-5128-2290-8
Ebook ISBN: 978-1-5128-2289-2

Library of Congress Cataloging-in-Publication Data

Names: Weissbourd, Emily, author.
Title: Bad blood : staging race between early modern
England and Spain / Emily Weissbourd.
Other titles: Raceb4race.
Description: 1st edition. | Philadelphia : University of
Pennsylvania Press, [2023] | Series: RaceB4Race :
critical race studies of the premodern | Includes
bibliographical references and index.
Identifiers: LCCN 2022048762 |
ISBN 9781512822908 (hardcover)
Subjects: LCSH: English literature—Early modern, 1500–
1700—History and criticism. | Race in literature. | Spanish
literature—Classical period, 1500-1700—History and
criticism. | Black people in literature. | Slavery in literature.
Classification: LCC PR408.R34 W45 2023 |
DDC 514/.6—dc25/eng/20220934
LC record available at https://lccn.loc.gov/2022048762

CONTENTS

Introduction

Race and the Idea of Spain in Early
Modern English Studies

In July 2021, as I was completing this book, I spotted an unexpectedly relevant article in the *New York Times*. The headline read "Spain Pledged Citizenship to Sephardic Jews. Now They Feel Betrayed."[1] The article details the failures of a Spanish government program that offered Spanish citizenship for the descendants of Sephardic Jews expelled from Spain in 1492. Applicants were asked to present genealogy charts to prove that they had at least one Jewish ancestor expelled "during the Inquisition." The article begins with an anecdote about a retired woman in Albuquerque who created "a vast genealogical chart going back nearly 1,100 years, which included three ancestors who were tied to the Spanish Inquisition," and whose claim was rejected. Read through the lens of my academic training, these elaborate genealogies uncannily echoed documents filling Spanish archives that display elaborate genealogies to demonstrate the *absence* of any such Jewish ancestor. As the article continues, it describes a Venezuelan family whose petition was also denied, who hoped to emigrate to Spain to escape a Venezuelan city "crippled by economic instability and deadly gangs."

Oddly, questions about a much earlier *New York Times* article framed my approach to this project at its beginnings. This earlier piece, from December 2008, ran under the headline "Gene Test Shows Spain's Jewish and Muslim Mix."[2] It described a study based in England and Barcelona in which scientists used the Y chromosomes of Spaniards to determine that roughly 20 percent of Spanish men bear the chromosomal signature of Sephardic Jews, while 11 percent bear that of the Arab and Berber army that invaded Spain in 711.[3] The article presented these findings as scientific "proof" that many Jews and Muslims in medieval and early modern Spain converted to Christianity and integrated with the Christian population, whether because of religious conviction or out of necessity in the face of persecution or expulsion. It then described the study's significance: "The finding bears on two different versions of Spanish history. . . . [The first] holds that Spanish civilization is Catholic and other influences are foreign; the other sees Spain as having been enriched by drawing from all three of its historical cultures, Catholic, Jewish and Muslim."

Taken together, these articles offer a distilled portrait of Spain's place in Anglo-American representations of normative identities. In 2008, a U.S. newspaper ran an article about a study based in England as well as Barcelona, thus implicitly adopting Spain as a site of alterity to be investigated within the Anglosphere. In 2021, the same paper ran an article focused on "reparations" for the Inquisition, described as "one of the darkest chapters of [Spain's] history," without registering the irony of the Venezuelan family's attempt to use Jewish ancestry to escape the legacy of colonialism. This narrative of Spain is frozen in time and space; in the 2021 article, Spanish violence is Inquisitional rather than colonial; the 2008 article notes that because the Y chromosome is transmitted without changing from father to son, "the proportions of Sephardic and Moorish ancestry detected in the present population are probably the same as those just after the 1492 expulsions."

The 2008 article is particularly illustrative of the static version of Spain that often circulates in the Anglosphere. It does not entertain the possibility of immigration to or emigration from Spain after 1492 and assumes that the present-day Sephardic and Moroccan peoples from which the study drew data have remained similarly isolated—in other words, that fathers have had sons who have had sons, and so on, without relocating. It does not take into account that Islam, unlike Judaism, is a proselytizing religion, and that conversions from Christianity to Islam and vice versa were not uncommon in the early modern Mediterranean. It is not interested in genetic markers that might link Spain's population to other places in the world. Additionally, it relies on an unmarked Spanish "Catholic identity," assumed as normative without being mentioned. In other words, no attempt is made to locate a "Catholic" Y chromosome, despite Judaism's and Islam's categorization in genetic terms. The unwritten undergirding of the piece relies on an unmarked and presumably primary identity that has been transformed by intermarriage with the descendants of Jews and Muslims. Ultimately, the article reveals far less about the history of Spain than it does about fictions of transhistorical ethnicity, of the sort that Hortense Spillers describes as embodying "nothing more than memorial time."[4]

The research presented in the article also completely elides another important demographic in early modern Spain: sub-Saharan Africans brought into early modern Iberia via the slave trade. In noting this elision, I do not assert an equivalency; numerically, Jewish and Muslim populations were far greater than those of sub-Saharan African descent.[5] It is nonetheless significant that this editorial discussing "proof" of Spain's heterogeneity is only capable of recognizing difference within a strict set of parameters, as the racialized "otherness" of Spain is here cast solely in terms of inherited religious identity. This omission is symptomatic of a larger trend in both popular culture and early modern literary studies.

Bad Blood takes this omission as its starting point, demonstrating the interconnections between representations of racialized religious difference and Blackness in early modern English and Spanish literature. The book's comparative approach illuminates the centrality of slavery, and particularly the enslavement of sub-Saharan Africans in early modern Iberia, to representations of race in both Spain and England.

The importance of early modern Spanish culture to the history of race has become axiomatic for scholars of history, literature, and critical race studies. The Spanish Inquisition's persecution of those of Jewish descent in conjunction with its "pure blood statutes," which denied privileges to those of Muslim and Jewish ancestry, have been held up as important precursors to modern-day pseudoscientific notions of race, given that discourses of blood purity discriminated against practicing Christians whose ancestors were Jewish or Muslim, and thus defined religious identity as a heritable (and thus racialized) characteristic. In English literary studies, this history is often brought to bear on characters linked with Spain who are labeled as "Jews" or "Moors"; Shakespeare's Shylock and Othello are the two most notable examples.[6]

Bad Blood both builds on and complicates this narrative, arguing that when we turn to Spain, we must consider the history of that nation's enslaved sub-Saharan African population as well as the legacy of the pure blood statutes. Further, it demonstrates that these two histories—and the discourses of race that they produce—are inextricably linked. To give just one example, on the early modern Spanish stage, Black characters achieve heroic feats and are at times represented as marrying white Spanish women. Their ability to do so, however, is explicitly justified by descriptions of them as being of "pure" descent: although they are Black, they are not descended from Jews or Moors and thus are able to integrate into white Spanish communities.

That discourses of blood and phenotype in early modern Spain inform each other might seem like a straightforward, intuitive claim. Nonetheless, it has far-reaching implications because it disrupts a widely accepted narrative of racial identities in early modern England. In recent years, critics have argued that characters labeled "Moors" on the early modern English stage, especially when such characters are linked to Spain, represent anxieties about religious conversion, and that to see such characters as signs of anti-Black discourse and the rise of race-based slavery is anachronistic. Thus, by appealing to historicism, this narrative disavows the sub-Saharan slave trade's importance to representations of race in early modern literature and culture.

In contrast to this, and precisely by more carefully historicizing the place of Spain, *Bad Blood* demonstrates that the Afro-Iberian slave trade informs representations of race in early modern English and Spanish literature, particularly drama, far more than has been recognized. It does so first by focusing on how Spanish texts that address issues of purity of blood are (mis)translated when transposed to an English context. The book then turns to a comparative analysis of representations of Blackness in early modern English and Spanish drama. Analyzing representations of Black characters (or, in Spanish, *negros*) in the Spanish *comedia* in comparison with Moors on the English Renaissance stage shows that the theaters of both countries consistently represent Black characters in the context of slavery, even when they are not explicitly described as enslaved, and at times represent Blackness as an alternative to (rather than extension of) an invisible difference of faith. I show that representations of "Moorishness" on the early modern English stage, and particularly in Shakespeare's *Othello*, are at least as attuned to the enslavement of Black Africans as they are to anxieties about "impure blood" and religious conversion.

In a special issue of *Shakespeare Quarterly* titled "Rereading Early Modern Race," editors Kim F. Hall and Peter Erickson called for early modern race studies to "expand beyond the limits of England and its colonies, providing a wider European purview that combines different linguistic and national traditions."[7] By bringing Spanish texts into dialogue with both early modern English texts and present-day scholarship on race in early modern England, *Bad Blood* first challenges established narratives about the history of race that position Spain as a site of origin for hierarchies of racialized violence, and which implicitly valorize England as innocent of such preoccupations. It then demonstrates that the Iberian Peninsula's early engagement in the enslavement of sub-Saharan Africans informs representations of Blackness in English as well as Spanish literature, as both literary traditions represent Blackness as inherently linked with slavery in the late sixteenth and early seventeenth centuries.

The Idea of Spain in Early Modern Studies

Examining the idea of Spain within early modern race studies, and early modern studies in general, provides a particularly useful example of the ways that certain engrained habits of thinking can shape our assumptions about the early modern world. This is so because Spain *already* occupies a prominent place in early modern race studies—but one that is perhaps too limited in its scope. Spain's discourses of *limpieza de sangre*, or purity of blood, have long occupied a prominent place in histories of developing racial ideologies in Europe.[8] As María Elena Martínez observed, "particularly in the literature that seeks to excavate the 'origins' of race, it has become almost commonplace to postulate that the Castilian concept of blood purity was the first racial discourse produced by the West or at least an important precursor to modern notions of difference."[9] This is so largely because Spain's pure blood statutes excluded practicing Christians who were of Jewish and Muslim descent, thereby defining religious identity as a bloodline or essence apparently impervious to conversion. The statutes thus have been understood to define Jewishness and Moorishness as racial categories rather than as religious beliefs or cultural practices.[10]

Just as Spain's pure blood statutes have become a frequent point of reference in historical studies of racial ideologies, scholars focused on representations of race in early modern English literature have also drawn on Spanish histories to elucidate representations of Jews and Moors in English texts. They have done so in part because representations of Spain in early modern English literature frequently evoke racial difference; specifically, Jews and Moors are often represented as Spanish (and, conversely, many Spaniards are represented as Jews and Moors). Barrabas, the villain of *The Jew of Malta*, betrays his Iberian origins by occasionally lapsing into Spanish, for example, meditating on the "hermoso placer de los dineros" [lovely joy of money] as he counts his coins.[11] Similarly, Portia's second suitor in *The Merchant of Venice*, after the dark-skinned "Morocco," is the Spanish prince of Aragon. The

Spanish prince serves as an intermediate figure between Morocco, whose "complexion" proves unacceptable, and the more appropriately endogamous (if less titled) Venetian, Bassanio.[12] *Othello* is also haunted by "Spanish spirits"; why else, as Eric Griffin has argued, would the villainous Iago be given a name that evokes the patron Saint of Spain, Santiago Matamoros (otherwise known as St. James the Moor-killer)?[13] In the critic Edmund Campos's succinct formulation, "one cannot pose the Jewish question in Renaissance England without posing the Spanish question as well."[14] And, as work by Barbara Fuchs and Eric Griffin has demonstrated, the same could be said of the "Moorish question."[15]

Plays including *The Jew of Malta, The Merchant of Venice,* and *Othello* (among many others) demonstrate that representations of racial difference in early modern England repeatedly evoke Spain as a site of Jewish and Moorish difference. Such representations at least partially arise in response to Spain's heterogeneous history (its Jewish population prior to the expulsions of 1492 and the legacy of Al-Andalus) and to the historical presence of *conversos* of Iberian origin in early modern London.[16] They also, though, reflect the influence of the "Black Legend," English, French, and Dutch anti-Spanish propaganda that characterized Spaniards as uniquely cruel in part because of their presumed Jewish and Moorish ancestry.[17] The racialization of Spain itself in early modern England via Black Legend discourse is treated extensively in Griffin's monograph *English Renaissance Drama and the Specter of Spain.* Griffin convincingly argues that both anti-Spanish pamphlets and early modern drama demonstrate a shift in early modern English perceptions of Spanish culture and identity, from a less-engrained cultural "ethos" to a racializing "ethnos." Whereas Griffin's study is a fundamentally English project focused on English constructions of difference, Fuchs's work addresses this dynamic from a comparative perspective.[18] Although the Black Legend is not this book's central focus, it does provide a window onto the centrality of England's anxious negotiations with Spain's preeminence in the period. The larger framework of England's self-definition in this period as anxious emulation (and simultaneous disavowal) of Spanish precedent, as articulated by Griffin and Fuchs, informs my approach to this topic.[19]

Many critics, however, have moved from one demonstrable fact—that Spain appears as a site of racial difference in the early modern English imaginary—to another, less obvious, assertion: that discourses of purity of blood within Spain serve as a point of origin for an emergent discourse of racial difference that manifests itself in these plays and other English texts. For example, in a much-cited article about Spain's relevance to longer histories of race, the historian Jerome J. Friedman asserts that "without [Spain's] pure blood laws supplementing medieval anti-Judaism and providing the foundations for a secular, biological conception of Jews, modern racial anti-Semitism could not have developed."[20] Friedman's argument, that Spain's pure blood statutes are a point of origin for "modern racial anti-Semitism," positions the statutes as setting a precedent for later racial formations.[21] This interpretation of the significance of Spain's pure blood statutes (and indeed Friedman's article in particular) has taken hold in studies of early modern English literature with Jewish and Moorish characters. For example, in an essay on *The Merchant of Venice*, Janet Adelman writes, "Jerome Friedman's account of these laws [i.e., the pure blood statutes] identifies a pattern that precisely duplicates *Merchant*'s insistence on Jessica's Jewishness just when she is most liable to be mistaken for gentle/gentile or Christian."[22] Similarly, in an essay on *Othello*, Michael Neill evokes Spanish discourses of purity of blood: "The history of the simultaneous (and largely inseparable) campaigns for purity of blood (*limpieza de sangre*) and purity of religion in Spain are only extreme symptoms of a larger European difficulty that threatened to turn a phrase such as 'Moor of Venice' into a hopeless oxymoron."[23]

Friedman, Neill, and Adelman all imply that Spanish discourses of purity of blood are central to the emergence of a widespread racialist logic that defines religion (specifically Jewishness and Moorishness) as a blood-borne essence rather than a set of beliefs and practices; Neill and Adelman specifically suggest that this is true not only for later notions of racialized anti-Semitism but also for early modern English texts. What these arguments do not address, however, is how the pure blood statutes came to be central to emergent racialist discourses outside of Spain. Friedman describes a straightforward cause-and-effect mechanism: a protoracist discourse created by Spain's pure blood statutes engenders similar discourses in other nations and in later time periods. In the context of early modern English literature, this argument is complicated by the fact that such causal relationships are difficult to trace. As M. Lindsay Kaplan argues in an essay on *The Merchant of Venice*, it is unclear how much—if at all—early modern Englishmen and -women knew about the pure blood statutes in Spain.[24]

In part because such causal mechanisms are difficult to prove, scholars of early modern English literature such as Neill and Adelman have focused less on transmission than on analogy. In other words, they argue that Spanish representations of purity of blood can help us to understand English depictions of Jewishness and Moorishness because Spain offers a more extreme example of a comparable emergent racializing discourse in England. Thus, *The Merchant of Venice* "duplicates" a Spanish notion of purity of blood in moments when Jessica's Jewish blood seems to preclude her sincere conversion to Christianity, and Othello's tragic fate is a minor manifestation of a broader European racialist logic whose most "extreme symptoms" can be found in Spain. Causality is implied—Spain appears as an original to be "duplicated," or as the most extreme case of racial discourses that then manifest elsewhere—but not explicitly attributed. Nonetheless, the articles cited above (and others) share the assumption that Spain's pure blood statutes can help us to understand representations of race in early modern English literature.

This assumption invites further scrutiny. What, more precisely, is the relationship between Spain's status as a site of racial difference in early modern England, a status secured by the Black Legend, and Spanish engagements with purity of blood?

We can begin to answer this question by turning to English translations of Spanish texts that address anxieties about impure descent. Such translations can help us to understand how racial ideologies cross national and linguistic boundaries. Because early modern Spain's ethnic and cultural heterogeneity produces a larger and more specific racial vocabulary than we find in early modern England, translators must find a way to explain Spanish terms that have no direct English equivalent. In Mateo Alemán's *Guzmán de Alfarache*, for example, a group of peasants is described as possessing *limpieza*, or pure descent. When James Mabbe translates this episode, he renders *limpieza* literally as cleanliness. Mabbe's peasants are perhaps freshly bathed, but they are not capable of laying claim to honor based on their imagined pure ancestry as they are in the Spanish original. Mabbe thus completely sidesteps (and perhaps is himself unaware of) the episode's focus on racialized questions of descent, as I discuss in detail in Chapter 2. This and other moments of mistranslation reveal how complex and often contradictory Spanish representations of race are flattened and simplified as they move into English. *Bad Blood*'s first two chapters reconsider Spain's status as an imagined site of origin for racial discourses in early modern England, suggesting that the "idea of Spain" becomes a kind of containment strategy that precludes engaging with more complex—and more troubling—histories of race and racism.

Rethinking Anachronism, Recentering Slavery:
Comparative Perspectives

Early modern race studies first emerged as a field more than twenty-five years ago, with the publication of several pathbreaking studies: Ania Loomba's *Gender, Race, Renaissance Drama* (1989), Kim F. Hall's *Things of Darkness: Economies of Race and Gender in Early Modern England* (1995), and the edited collection *Women, "Race," and Writing in the Early Modern Period* (1994). Nonetheless, the field has faced skepticism since its origins, repeatedly subjected to what Hall and Erickson have labeled a "pathological averseness to thinking about race under the guise of protecting historical difference."[25] Thanks to the sustained efforts of a number of early modern race scholars, particularly scholars of color, claims that studies of early modern race are "anachronistic" have become increasingly untenable.

It has been harder, however, to dispel the notion that Blackness and slavery were not yet connected in the English imaginary in the late sixteenth and early seventeenth centuries. It is true that England had not yet become a major player in the transatlantic slave trade in this period, and that England (unlike Spain and Portugal) did not have a legal and regulated slave trade within its borders. This does not mean, however, that England remained untouched by the rise of racialized slavery. John Hawkins infamously attempted enter into the transatlantic slave trade in 1562; his mission ended in failure, but he was granted a heraldic crest of a "demi-Moor proper bound in cord."[26] As archival research by Imtiaz M. Habib and Gustav Ungerer has shown, there was a small but visible Black population in early modern England that had arrived via the Afro-Iberian slave trade.[27] Nonetheless, even scholars that address questions of race in early modern English literature have argued that racial formations in early modern English culture were not yet informed by slavery. To give just one example, Neill asserts in the most recent Oxford edition of *Othello* that despite the assumptions made by "modern audiences . . . 'Moors' were, on balance, more likely to figure in the early seventeenth century imagination as enslavers than as slaves."[28] Neill's nod to "modern audiences" here is not incidental; rather, the gesture posits two distinct racial temporalities: the premodern, defined by religious difference and shifting alliances in the Mediterranean (and in which *Othello* resides); and the modern, dominated by what he later terms "the industrialized human market place of the Atlantic triangle." This distinction positions, in Geraldine Heng's formulation, "modernity as the time of race"—or more specifically, in this instance, modernity as the time of slavery.[29]

Thus the "idea of Spain," as discussed in the previous section, becomes evidence for a racial system revolving around religion and blood rather than color and slavery. When scholars of English literature have turned to Spain to analyze race in *Othello*, for example, they have generally discussed Spanish histories of purity of blood. By this logic, when Moors on the English stage are Spanish or otherwise linked to Spain, they become aligned with the history of Spain's Muslim and *morisco* populations. Blackness in this framework becomes an exterior sign of religious difference, thereby minimizing its connection to the history of racialized slavery. For Griffin, for example, Othello becomes a Morisco, or a convert from Islam to Christianity, who is lured into sin by the inquisitorial Spanish Iago. Although Griffin's argument that "Spanish spirits" haunt *Othello* is very convincing (and has been hugely influential in the field), it also sidesteps the current of anti-Black racism that runs through the play.[30]

Bad Blood, by contrast, uses a comparative approach to demonstrate the centrality of the emergent Afro-Iberian slave trade to representations of Blackness and Moorishness in English and Spanish texts alike. It does so not only by taking the history of racialized slavery into account, but by comparing representations of Blackness and religious difference in English literature with those found in Spanish texts. Spanish drama offers a sizeable canon of plays with Black characters, most of whom are represented as enslaved.[31] Crucially, such characters are not labeled *moros*, or Moors, but rather *negros*; the *moro* on the Spanish stage is most generally not described as dark-skinned, and their religious difference is threatening precisely because it is not readily apparent. Although thus far the "idea of Spain" has appeared as evidence of an older discursive regime in which protoracism is based in religion or blood, a comparative reading of representations of both Blackness and religious difference across English and Spanish drama—in other words, a reading that considers the *negro* as well as the *moro*—can reorient our understanding of slavery not as anachronistic but rather as integral to representations of Blackness in the early modern period.

Triangulated Whiteness

Differentiating between discourses of color and of racialized religious difference is also crucial for our understanding of the growing force of whiteness in the early modern period. A self/other or native/stranger binary has often served as the paradigmatic model of early modern discourses of race in English literature. Such binary logic, however, asks us to collapse discourses of race into each other: racialized religious difference and Blackness become conflated within the umbrella category of "other" or "stranger" while the whiteness of the Christian European appears as the normative "self," thereby evading further scrutiny. This framing also predisposes us to think about Blackness as a sign or metaphor of racialized religious difference, and to overlook how Blackness at times appears not as a sign of but rather in contrast to racialized religious difference (which, after all, poses a threat precisely because it cannot be immediately perceived).

Early modern Spanish representations of race complicate a binary model, as both literary and historical documents at times represent Blackness as a sign of the *absence* of impure descent. In the Spanish comedia, the social ascent of Black characters is enabled by explicitly presenting Blackness as a less threatening form of difference than "impure blood," in part because Blackness (unlike the "taint" of Jewish or Moorish ancestry) cannot be concealed. This dynamic triangulates Blackness, racialized religious difference, and "pure" Christian whiteness, and these categories remain in tension rather than resolving into a stable model of self and other. My focus on the differential impacts of multiple racial discourses is deeply indebted to the crucial insights of intersectional feminism, and to Michael Omi and Howard Winant's trenchant analysis of the "historical flexibility of racial meanings and categories."[32]

In Chapter 3 I propose that we can best understand early modern Spanish racial discourses by adopting a triangulated rather than binary model of racial categorization, in which "pure" Christian whiteness emerges in contradiction to the opposing categories of Blackness and purity of blood.[33] In Chapter 4, I argue that this triangulated model, though not as explicitly articulated, also informs representations of race in early modern English drama, and particularly in Shakespeare's *Othello*. Finally, Chapter 5 focuses on the triangulation of blood, Blackness, and whiteness to show how anxieties about white female characters' social and economic power are displaced onto interracial marriages between secondary characters in plays by Shakespeare and Lope de Vega.

In focusing on comparative representations of Blackness, the final three chapters of *Bad Blood* put Spanish texts in dialogue with the growing field of early modern race studies, which has thus far focused largely on English literature. In particular, Hall's paradigm for analyzing the racialization of circulating "tropes of Blackness" in early modern England is instrumental to my analysis, as is Loomba's insistence on the interpenetration of discourses of color and religion in the early modern period.[34] I adopt throughout Heng's concise definition of race as "a structural relationship for the articulation and management of human differences, rather than a substantive content," and her description of racial logic's ability to "stalk and merge with other hierarchical systems."[35] The manuscript for *Bad Blood* was completed before the publication of Urvashi Chakravarty's *Fictions of Consent*, but Chakravarty's brilliant delineation of intersections of service and slavery in early modern English texts, and of these texts' status as a "critical crucible for the conceptual architecture which generates early modern England's futures of racialized slavery," resonates with many of the claims I make here.[36] By bringing this work into dialogue with Spanish representations of Blackness and the history of the Afro-Iberian slave trade, this book offers additional concrete evidence supporting many of these critics' claims, as well as a mechanism for disentangling the complex relationship between representations of color and of religion in early modern texts.

Comparative early modern race studies remains a relatively new field, with few monographs published to date. One exception to this is Robert Hornback's *Racism and Early Blackface Comic Traditions: From the Old World to the New*. In it, Hornback focuses on blackface as a "theatergram," or a circulating theatrical convention, that appears in England, Spain, Italy, and later the United States. Hornback's reading usefully underscores connections among black-faced devils in medieval mystery plays, comic figures in early modern European theater, and minstrel shows in the eighteenth- and nineteenth-century United States. His methodology and areas of interest, however, are quite different from mine. The sheer scope of his study demands a less-sustained engagement with the culturally specific dynamics of racial tropes as they emerge in one country or another, and the changes such tropes undergo in translation. *Racism and Early Blackface Comic Traditions* does, though, share with *Bad Blood* a sustained attention to the importance of the early African slave trade to representations of race in early modern Europe.[37] Noémie Ndiaye's work has also informed my approach. Although *Bad Blood* does not share Ndiaye's focus on dance and movement as a form of "race-craft," my work shares with hers a commitment to understanding racial formations as relational, demanding "a careful examination of what is unique to the process of racialization affecting a certain ethnic group, and what is connected, portable, recyclable in that process."[38]

My approach to this project is inevitably shaped by my own subject position as a white person of Jewish descent. It began from a place of personal identification, what a clever friend of mine refers to as "me-search." I have one Jewish parent (my father, not my mother, rendering me not Jewish at all by some conservative standards) and no particular religious conviction, but nonetheless a firm sense of myself as "half-Jewish" or "culturally Jewish" or Jew-*ish*. It is perhaps not surprising, then, that I became interested in representations of Jewishness as a "bloodline" or inherent trait in the early modern period. I was also fortunate to begin my graduate study in the wake of a generation of pathbreaking scholars of color whose work centered representations of Blackness in early modern texts, including Kim F. Hall, Margo Hendricks, Sujata Iyengar, Arthur Little, Ania Loomba, Joyce MacDonald, and Ayanna Thompson, among others. Drawing on their work as I brought together early modern Spanish and English materials transformed my approach. If this book began as one form of me-search, about the long history of racialized religious identities and blood, it has ended with a different form of self-scrutiny: of the ways that white people, myself included, have often overlooked—or, more accurately, learned not to see—representations of anti-Black racism in early modern texts. It asks what energies or anxieties have prompted the desire to frame turning to religious difference, blood, and Spain as a replacement for anti-Black racism rather than a contemporaneous racial discourse.

In part, then, this book exposes a defense mechanism among scholars: an unconscious push toward engaging with a model of race that may feel less challenging or require less self-scrutiny than addressing anti-Black racism would. Scholars of critical race theory have demonstrated the ways that the trauma of the Holocaust is more carefully taught than that of slavery and its aftermath, and more frequently elicits empathy.[39] Scholarship on the idea of Spain in early modern English studies unwittingly reproduces this dynamic; the relationship between Spain's pure blood statutes and modern racialized anti-Semitism has received a great deal of critical attention, while its history with the slave trade remains understudied.

Archive, Structure, Terminology

Bad Blood focuses on texts from roughly the second half of the sixteenth century and the first half of the seventeenth century. During this period in Spain, pure blood statutes rose to prominence; the Morisco uprising (1568–71) led to a series of racially motivated policies culminating in the expulsion of the Moriscos (1606–13); and the annexation of Portugal under the Iberian

Union (1580–1640) increased the population of enslaved sub-Saharan Africans within Spain. In England, sectarian and dynastic upheaval demanded increased scrutiny of what it meant to be Christian and English alike, and of the relationship between these categories; English merchants, backed by the crown, made their first foray into the transatlantic slave trade; and England established control over its first colony, Ireland. This period also witnessed dramatic and sudden shifts in Anglo-Spanish relations, from alliance by marriage between Mary I and Philip II to enmity, and back again to an attempted rapprochement with the failed Spanish match (1614–23). In both England and Spain the emergence of market economies, grounded in imperial exploitation, began to threaten older regimes of blood.

This was also a period in which both England and Spain, uniquely in Europe and largely independently of each other, developed flourishing public theaters.[40] As both England and Spain were compelled to negotiate the boundaries of racialized belonging and exclusion, and to test and reinforce the limits of acceptable exogamy, such testing often played out in the public forum of the theater. Although I ground my readings in a range of historical and cultural texts, much of *Bad Blood* focuses on drama. This is in part because the theater, as a popular medium, allows us to see how ideologies of race are disseminated among a large mixed-class audience. More importantly, though, as Ndiaye and Thompson have argued, the embodied practices of performance are a key site for analyzing representations of race, and particularly for, as Thompson writes, "implicitly constructing an *anti-racialized identity* for the English audience."[41] Theater thus offers a particularly powerful model for understanding how the performance of difference—whether of religion, blood, or color—works to reify European identities in both England and Spain.

Chapter 1 focuses on representations of purity of blood within early modern Spain, relying on analysis of both manuscript polemics and Lope de Vega's play *La villana de Getafe* (1609–14; published 1620). In examining these texts I explore a dynamic that Christina Lee has termed the "anxiety of sameness," which "arose from the physical similarities between peoples of supposedly conflicting religious origins and inherited social ranks."[42] This approach illuminates important differences between the idea of Spain as a site of origin for racialized religious difference and the complex and multivalent reception that discourses of purity of blood received within Spain itself. I argue that playful, ironic engagements with purity of blood like those found in *La villana de Getafe* reveal that Spanish engagements with purity often focus on social performance rather than immutable inherited essence.

Chapter 2, "Translating Spain," turns from a close analysis of Spanish representations of purity of blood to English appropriations of Spanish sources on this topic: Mabbe's translation of Alemán's picaresque novel *Guzmán de Alfarache* (1623), and Middleton and Rowley's *The Spanish Gypsy* (1623), which draws on two of Cervantes's novellas, *La fuerza de la sangre* and *La gitanilla* (1613). All of these texts engage with varied—and at times overlapping—kinds of difference: Jewish, Moorish, and Gypsy "blood" and identity. The chapter argues that the heterogeneity that characterizes Spanish depictions of purity of blood generally disappears in translation; English texts do not simply adopt but rather transform these Spanish discourses, often failing to register the irony with which presumed difference has been presented. Mabbe's translations of both *Guzmán* and *The Spanish Gypsy* sidestep their Spanish source texts' emphasis on passing, instead eliding ironic representations of the notion of pure blood and representing all Spaniards as themselves exoticized others.

Bad Blood turns to representations of Blackness in Chapter 3, which demonstrates how Black protagonists achieve social success in the Spanish comedia, but in a very limited context: as characters defined by their relationship to slavery, their successes are represented as in service to the white Spanish nobility, and their value is most often represented in contradistinction to the invisible but threatening difference of impure blood. Whereas Chapter 3 examines the complex relationship among Blackness, slavery, and purity of blood in the Spanish comedia, Chapter 4, "'I Have Done the State Some Service': Moorishness and Slavery on the English Stage," explores the relevance of this dynamic to representations of race in English drama. The chapter begins with a survey of English plays written between 1590 and 1640 that include characters labeled as "Black" or as "Moors," demonstrating that while few of them are associated with Islam, the majority are associated with service or slavery. It then turns to close readings of *Othello* (1604) and *Lust's Dominion* (1599) to show how these plays engage with the slave trade more deeply than has been hitherto remarked. The research presented here thus traces parallels between the rhetoric of slavery as service in the Spanish comedia and representations of Black characters' "service to the state" in these plays' English counterparts.

The final chapter uses a comparative lens to address what has been called the "problem of the unrepresentable Black woman" in early modern drama.[43] It compares representations of enslaved Black and mixed-race characters in English and Spanish drama, with a particular focus on English drama's

representation of interracial sex as monstrous in comparison to its representation in the comedia, which contains several examples of enslaved mixed-
race ladies-in-waiting who marry white Spaniards (Lope de Vega's *Servir a
señor discreto* and *Amar, servir y esperar*). This comparison reveals the ways
that white female characters are positioned as virtuous at the expense of
female characters who are marginalized by associations with either impure
blood or Blackness.

In my discussion of racial categories in early modern texts, I have
attempted to balance fidelity to the original vocabulary of the texts themselves with avoiding the normalization and repetition of derogatory terms.
In Chapter 1, I retain the Spanish terms converso and morisco in reference
respectively to converts from Judaism and Islam and their descendants. In
these early chapters, I use the word *Moorish* specifically to designate attri-
butes related to the legacy of the Al-Andalus dynasty in Iberia. In Chapter 4,
by contrast, I use the word *Moor* as it is found in early modern English drama
as a term that denotes Blackness more often than religion or place of origin.
In Chapter 2 I have retained, with some hesitation, the term *Gypsy* rather
than replacing it with *Roma* in my discussion of the play *The Spanish Gypsy*
and the Cervantine novellas on which it is based. This is partly because the
term is so central to the play, as its title indicates. More than this, however,
the figure of the Gypsy in early modern England was associated not only with
the Roma people but also with travelers and scoundrels of English origin.
Indeed, in the play itself all the "Gypsies" turn out to be English nobles in disguise. Using *Roma* here would imply a stability and primary Roma identity
that the texts themselves do not reflect. In Chapter 5, where I discuss mixed-
race female characters on the early modern Spanish stage, I have avoided
using the Spanish word *mulata* in favor of the less freighted term *mixed-race*,
except when quoting directly from the text.

CHAPTER 1

"Pure Blood . . . Doesn't Cost a Thing"

Performing Purity of Blood

Lope de Vega's play *La villana de Getafe* [The peasant girl from Getafe] (1609–14, published 1620) offers a fascinating commentary on early modern Spanish discourses of purity of blood and their relationship to race. The play's protagonist, Inés, the eponymous peasant girl, is loved and left by an already engaged nobleman far above her station; her feckless lover, Félix, promptly returns to his wealthy and noble fiancée. To win Félix back, Inés spreads a false rumor that he is a *morisco*, or descended from Moors, and thus is of "impure" descent. The false rumor, which all the other characters immediately accept as true, prompts his fiancée to break off their engagement. At the end of the play, after a number of plot twists coordinated by Inés have run their course (described in detail below), the noble Félix decides to marry Inés after all. He justifies his choice by declaring: "Inés es limpia, ¡oh Fortuna! / que la diferencia es / el llamalla doña Inés, / que no cuesta cosa alguna" [Inés is pure-blooded, oh what fortune! The only difference will be to call her Lady Inés, which doesn't cost a thing].[1] The play foregrounds two persistent themes within early modern Spanish debates about purity of blood: the extent to which a reputation for pure (or impure) descent is fragile and socially constructed, the product of rumor and at times even slander; and the relationship between nobility of blood (*nobleza de sangre*) and purity of blood (*limpieza de sangre*).

La villana de Getafe offers a window onto the complexity inherent to discourses of purity of blood in early modern Spain. As discussed in the introduction, the significance of *limpieza de sangre* (purity of blood) to early modern Spanish culture and more broadly to the development of discourses of race in Europe has been discussed at length by historians, critical race theorists, and literary critics.² Central to these discussions are Spain's now-notorious pure blood statutes, which prohibited those of Jewish and Muslim descent from entering some universities and military orders and from occupying positions of authority in churches and local governments. Candidates for admission to these institutions were required to submit elaborate genealogies and corroborating reports from neighbors to demonstrate that they were *cristianos viejos* (Old Christians), free from the taint of Jewish or Moorish blood. Because these statutes discriminated on the basis of ancestry rather than religious practices, they have been understood to inscribe religion as a racial characteristic and thus to serve as a site of origin for discourses of race in Europe and the Americas. The pure blood statutes do indeed mark an important shift in the history of race; their reception and impact within Spain, however, reveal a more complicated history, one that engages with race as a social performance as well as an imagined immutable essence.

In this chapter, I draw on *La villana de Getafe* as a case study in the complex and ambivalent dialogue surrounding purity of blood within early modern Spain, and particularly the vexed intersections of purity and nobility of blood. Because it ends with a marriage between a pure-blooded peasant and a noble, on its surface the play validates the notion that pure blood functions as an essential characteristic. Inés is marriageable, Félix tells us, because her descent is *limpia*, or pure. In this sense the play might be seen as perpetuating a racializing discourse in which "Old Christian blood" has the power to determine one's station. On closer examination, though, the play's engagement with the notion of purity of blood is revealed to be far more ambivalent. Although at the play's end Inés's purity of blood enables her upwardly mobile marriage, the series of machinations she employs to trick her lover into that marriage rely on other characters' inability to accurately discern what kind of blood runs in the veins of whom. Counterintuitively, the play draws on representations of purity of blood in order to undermine the distinction between Old Christian and convert, and to emphasize how such presumably essential categories are in fact socially constructed. As we shall see, the ease with which the signs of Moorish descent are attributed to Old Christian characters works to parody the notion of purity of blood as an essential characteristic, ultimately exposing pure descent as "an imitation without an origin."³ Before turning to a close reading of the play, I situate it within its historical context, offering a brief overview of the history of pure blood statutes and the place of Moriscos in Spain and an analysis of manuscript polemics about purity of blood.

Purity of Blood: An Overview

Spain's pure blood statutes were a series of regulations prohibiting those of Jewish and Muslim descent from entering some universities and religious and military orders, from immigrating to Spain's colonies, and from occupying certain municipal and government posts.[4] It has proved difficult to establish what the first pure blood statute was and when it appeared. Some scholars argue that regulations prohibiting conversos and Moriscos from entrance to various institutions can be found as early as the twelfth century, and others that purity of blood was not widely required until the fifteenth century, when the city of Toledo's 1449 statute inaugurated their widespread use.[5] In any case, the statutes were firmly entrenched in many Spanish institutions by the middle of the sixteenth century.

The significance of these statutes to histories of racism in Europe is apparent: in defining religious identity as an embodied trait carried in the blood, they effectively racialize religion. After all, anyone seeking a position to which the statutes applied would have been a professed Catholic; the pure blood statutes discriminated against those whose ancestors were Muslims or Jews, not those who practiced Islam or Judaism. The statutes thus inscribe and enforce a racialized definition of religious identity in which an inconvertible Jewish or Moorish "essence" is passed from parent to child.

Although sometimes referred to as "pure blood laws" in English, this term is deceptive; in fact, the statutes were not national policy but rather local in origin, and enforced by particular institutions rather than centrally codified.[6] The requirements for purity of blood varied from one institution to the next. For example, the church of Seville's statute only required those who occupied positions there not to have parents of Jewish or Moorish backgrounds (the rule was later extended one generation to grandparents), while a stricter organization like the *colegio mayor* in Cuenca ruled that any trace of Jewish or Moorish ancestry, however slight, was enough to prevent an applicant's admission.[7] The original intent of the statutes seems to have been to exclude those who secretly practiced Judaism or Islam; after all, descendants of Jews and Muslims were more likely to have been crypto-Muslims or crypto-Jews (especially if conversion was relatively recent, for example, by the parents or grandparents of the applicant). In this case, excluding those with Jewish or Moorish blood could be seen as a safeguard against admitting apostates to positions of authority. But as the statutes increasingly stipulated that all applicants have "no trace" of Jewish or Moorish blood, from either the mother's side or the father's, no matter how remote, their significance changed. "Impure blood" was no longer an indicator of possible heresy for pragmatic reasons, but rather served as proof in and of itself of an unassimilable Jewish or Moorish essence.

The importance of theories of pure blood to developing discourses of race is undeniable. Nonetheless, their effect on racial thinking in early modern Spain is far from straightforward. As Christina Lee astutely observes, scholars have often focused on the way that Spanish pure blood discourse works to denigrate and exclude those who are different. Equally important, though, is the fact that the statutes focus not on the recognizably different or other, but rather on ferreting out difference within a putatively pure dominant group. Lee terms this phenomenon the "anxiety of sameness," suggesting that "while conspicuous religious and socio-cultural difference was certainly perturbing and unsettling, in some ways it was not as threatening to the dominant Spanish identity as the potential discovery of the arbitrariness that separated them from the undesirables of society."[8] Focusing on sameness, as Lee does, allows us to see how the statutes are used to enable or police social mobility within a dominant class as much as they are used to exclude outsiders. Lee's analysis allows us to see the inherent complexity of using the model of the pure blood statutes in readings of representations of Jewishness and Moorishness in the context of English drama.

Although scholars of English literature have most often used the history of pure blood discourse in Spain to engage with representations of outsiders (e.g., in readings of *Othello* and *The Merchant of Venice*), Lee's formulation of the "anxiety of sameness" offers an important reminder that the racialization of the already marginalized is not the primary function of pure blood discourse within Spain itself, either in historical texts or on the stage. Instead, representations of pure and impure blood in Spain focus on two related anxieties: first, that a hitherto undetectable taint of impurity could lurk in the bloodlines of anyone in the dominant class; and second, that a focus on purity rather than nobility of descent could prove a dangerous engine of social mobility. In this context, anxieties about impure blood are less relevant to Shylock and Othello, as figures already clearly marked as outsiders. Instead, a closer Shakespearean analogue might be *All's Well That Ends Well*, where anxieties about Helena's upwardly mobile marriage are expressed in the vocabulary of blood and stock that is so prevalent in the pure blood statutes.

Indeed, Spanish representations of Jewish and Moorish blood as irreversibly tainted are related to discussions of class as well as racial identity in early modern Spain. Because many Spanish nobles intermarried with wealthy converted Jews and their descendants before the statutes rose to prominence, pure blood statutes could work to exclude members of the high nobility from positions that were left open for lower-ranking, and often rural, lords, and even in some cases those of peasant ancestry, as long as they were Old Christians.[9] Thus critics of the statutes in early modern Spain often argued that accusations of impure blood were purely strategic and more connected to class identity and social mobility than to essential—and threatening—difference. *Limpieza de sangre* became another form of honor, separate from *nobleza de sangre*, to which lower gentry could lay claim in order to obtain positions for which they would have otherwise been outranked. For example, a seventeenth-century commentary on the pure blood statutes tells us:

> En España hay dos géneros de nobleza. Una mayor, que es la hidalguía, y otra menor que es la limpieza, que llamamos christianos [*sic*] viejos. Y aunque la primera de la hidalguía es más honrado de tenerla, pero muy más afrentoso es faltar la segunda: porque en España mas estimamos a un hombre pechero y limpio que a un hidalgo que no es limpio.

> [In Spain there are two kinds of nobility. One greater one, which is high rank, and another minor one, which is purity of blood, and we call those who have that Old Christians. And even though having the first, high rank, is a greater honor, it is a much greater shame to lack the second: because in Spain we hold a man who is pure-blooded and plebeian in greater esteem than a noble who is impure.][10]

The status granted by *limpieza*, or purity (as opposed to *nobleza*, or nobility) is a recurring theme in early modern Spanish literature as well. Peasants' inflated self-pride based on trumped-up claims to pure descent is the butt of satire in a variety of texts, most famously Cervantes's interlude *El retablo de las maravillas* (published 1615).[11] The interlude presents a variation on the folktale of the emperor's new clothes. The story follows a group of tricksters who arrive in a Spanish village and offer to put on a magical puppet show that only those whose ancestry has no taint of Jewish or Moorish blood, nor of illegitimacy, will be able to see. The villagers fall for the trick, with every man and woman outdoing his or her neighbor in marveling at the wonders presented—which, of course, do not exist. Interestingly, there is no revelation of deceit at the end; instead, the villagers remain duped and the tricksters plan to move on to the next town. Here, as in many other texts in the period, the rigid requirements of the pure blood statutes appear as social conventions ripe for parody rather than as evidence of an essentially different Jewish or Moorish subject. Conversely, dramas in which virtuous peasants must reclaim their honor by defeating corrupt nobles who defile it are a staple of the comedia. As Noël Salomon has demonstrated, such depictions rely on peasants' *limpieza* to justify the notion that they have "honor" they must defend.[12]

In practice, however, the clearest paper trail left by Spain's discourses of *limpieza de sangre* does not concern peasant honor but rather the nobility, and specifically the *pruebas*, or proofs, required to gain entrance into organizations with pure blood statutes. These documents illuminate the much-discussed significance of rumor as a source of profound anxiety in early modern Spanish drama in their reliance on the testimony of neighbors. They also, though, illustrate the banal and bureaucratic lived experience of working to prove purity of blood, and how easily lampooned such practices were. Submitting *pruebas* generally involved hiring an official to travel to the claimant's town of origin and then enlisting neighbors to testify to the claimant's purity of descent. Such testimonies do not make for exciting reading. They are formalized documents that essentially ask the neighbor to answer in the affirmative the following claim: I am X person and I swear and attest that the claimant is a *cristiano viejo* without the taint (*que no tiene raza*) of Jews or Moors or heretics on the side of his mother or his father since time immemorial. They do not contain personal narratives or anecdotes about the claimant, but rather are, in the simplest terms, form letters. The language of each person's testimony is generally identical, with only the names changed.[13] An applicant to a knightly order had to present a sufficient number of these petitions to the order to which he was applying to demonstrate his purity of descent. Gathering these testimonies was costly, of course, and the outcome may have said more about the goodwill of the claimant's neighbors than the putative purity of their ancestors. Indeed, they may have privileged those rich enough to buy proof of purity rather than those of less "tainted" descent.[14]

While, in theory, pure blood statutes discriminated equally against those of Moorish or Jewish ancestry, there were significant differences between the treatment of conversos and that of Moriscos in early modern Spain. Most discussion of the statutes—both in early modern Spain and in criticism of our era—focuses predominantly on conversos. This is so because conversos were far more likely to have assimilated into Old Christian Spanish society than

Moriscos were.[15] Muslims who converted to Christianity in fifteenth- and sixteenth-century Spain (and their descendants) were more likely to live in rural rather than urban areas and to stay in self-contained communities, and often continued to speak Arabic and wear traditional clothing until they were prohibited from doing so.[16] (There are, of course, a number of exceptions to the generalities I have laid out here; in Granada, some high-ranking Moriscos intermarried with local nobility, and in many towns in Spain Moriscos did assimilate into Old Christian communities.)[17] Anxieties about Moriscos in the period often focused on the possibility that they would ally with Spain's enemies, whether North African Muslims, Ottomans, or even European Protestants, functioning as a fifth column in the event of invasion, more than on their covert insinuation through intermarriage into Spanish military orders or noble bloodlines.[18]

Additionally, Moriscos ultimately suffered a far harsher fate in Spain than conversos. All Muslims were legally obliged to convert to Christianity in the decades following the fall of Granada, through a series of regulations passed between 1502 and 1526. Increasingly harsh regulations ultimately led the Moriscos of Granada to rebel against the crown (1568–71). The rebellion failed, and in its aftermath thousands of Moriscos were sold into slavery and tens of thousands were forcefully relocated all across Spain.[19] Over subsequent years increasingly harsh regulations were passed against them, culminating in their expulsion from Spain in waves from 1609 to 1614.[20] By contrast, although Jews were expelled from Spain in 1492, conversos never were.

The influence of pure blood statutes on discourses of race in early modern Spain is irrefutable. The form such influence takes, however, is far more complex than many critics have recognized, particularly those whose primary focus is not early modern Spain but rather the influence of Spanish discourses of pure blood on early modern English literature, or the larger history of racialized anti-Semitism. As we shall see in the polemics below, both early modern advocates of the statutes and their critics struggle with the truly quixotic task of attempting to quantify and demonstrate something that does not exist: a pure Spanish ancestry unchanged across centuries. Ironically, attempting to prove purity of blood exposes the phantasmic quality of the very concept of the *cristiano viejo*. Ultimately, the pure blood statutes do produce a profoundly racist discourse with far-reaching effects both for histories of race thinking and for those persecuted for the ancestry. They also, though, create a climate in which the very notion of pure blood is undermined as often as it is reified.

Purity of Blood, Race, and Class

In 1572 the Spanish Inquisition passed an ordinance prohibiting any discussion, in public or private, about purity of blood, under pain of excommunication and a fine of five hundred ducats.[21] The prohibition, however, does not seem to have been terribly effective. Instead, materials about the pure blood statutes most often circulated in manuscript. Dozens, perhaps hundreds of these manuscripts, which debate both the practical efficacy of implementing statutes and the inherent value of using purity of descent as a metric of individual worth, survive in libraries today. A note appended to a 1596 manuscript that contains a lengthy brief debating the merits of the Toledo Cathedral's 1547 pure blood statute offers a glimpse into the transmission and circulation of such accounts. The note reads:

> Trasladose en sevilla este traslado de otro que tenia el lizenziado don andres fernandez de Cordova del consejo de su magestad y su oydor en la real audenzia de sevilla y a el presente auditor en Roma de la rota sacose todo a la letra como en el estaba y la inpettiazion y bulla del papa paulo terzero no se acabo de trasladar por estar tan mal escrita que el latin no se pudo entender.

> [This transcription was transcribed in Seville from another copy belonging to the licentiate don Andrés Fernandez de Córdova of his Majesty's council and his magistrate in the royal tribunal of Seville, and who is at this time an *auditor* in Rome. Each word was copied by rote as it was written and the papal bull of Pope Paul the Third was not completely transcribed because it was so poorly written that the Latin was incomprehensible.]

The note is in Manuscript 11211 of the Biblioteca Nacional de España, part of the Duque de Osuna's collection (which the library purchased in 1884); it is written in a single sixteenth-century hand and contains two documents that address questions of purity of blood; the first page informs us that the first document in it was composed in 1596.[22]

The licentiate Andrés Fernández de Córdoba was a well-known judge in Seville. He was prominent enough to have been mentioned several times in contemporary documents as one of the founders of a charitable brotherhood devoted to relieving the lot of prisoners in Seville, the Cofradía de Nuestra Señora de la Visitación.[23] His possession of a copy of this manuscript, and the fact that a scribe copied it for someone else's collection from him, shows us that this manuscript is a copy of a copy; the text circulated among the educated and politically connected in the second half of the sixteenth century and into the seventeenth century. Although some polemics about purity of blood made it into print, many others circulated in manuscript to avoid censorship.

The texts I will discuss here were written in the second half of the sixteenth and first half of the seventeenth century. Their provenance is difficult to trace precisely, but all were part of a thriving economy of manuscript circulation in early modern Spain. Many documents that were never printed were passed from one educated man to another; indeed, many nobles kept scribes as part of their households in part to facilitate the copying of such manuscripts. As the historian Fernando Bouza describes the situation: "In the libraries of the court noblemen, it is common to find a series of miscellanea and volumes composed of various manuscripts, all of them simply the product of this process of accumulation of papers and copies that reflect the ever-changing political and cultural atmosphere which did not necessarily reach the printing press."[24] Manuscript circulation was common practice, particularly for documents of a sensitive nature, such as pure blood statute polemic. Several of the texts I describe here appear in multiple copies in the Biblioteca Nacional and the Archivo Histórico Nacional. Undoubtedly more copies exist in other archives, and many more have been lost.

These manuscripts provide crucial insight into the complexity of concepts of purity of blood in early modern Spain and how Spanish texts attempted to define blood inheritance. One of the key points of debate in such polemics is how to understand and regulate *raza*, a term that literally translates into "race" in English but has a more varied series of connotations in early modern Spain. The definition of *raza* found in Covarrubias's 1611 dictionary helps to articulate key differences as well as similarities between early modern *raza* and race as we understand it today:

> La casta de cavallos castizos, a los quales señalan con hierro para que sean conocidos. Raza en el paño, la hilaza que diferencia de los demás hilos de la trama. . . . Raza, en los linages so toma en mala parte, como tener alguna raza de moro o judio.

[The caste of purebred horses, which are marked with a brand so that
they are recognizable. *Raza* in cloth, the strand that differs from the
other threads in the weave. . . . *Raza*, in lineages is seen as a flaw, as in
having some *raza* (race or trace) of Moor or Jew.][25]

The first of these definitions applies to a breed—literally caste—of horses.
Ironically, although their purity presumably makes them exceptional, they
must be marked by a brand so that they can be distinguished from horses of
less pure descent. The second, which applies to cloth, would best be translated as *trace* or *strand*; the word describes that part of a fabric, or strand of
a weave, that differs from the rest. This second definition is as relevant as the
first to the use of *raza* as it applies to purity of purity of blood: the *raza* of Jew
or Moor is that trace or strand of different and dangerous blood that marks a
subject as impure. The connection between the image of a differently colored
thread in a cloth and an impure lineage emerges in the grammatical construction of Covarrubias's definition of *raza* as it applies to ancestry: "como
tener alguna raza de moro o judio" [to have some *raza* of Moor or Jew]. The
distinction between having (*tener*) impure ancestry and being of impure
ancestry might seem minor, but it points to the instability of the notion of
raza in the period; grammatically, *raza* appears as a flaw that one can possess
in one's ancestry rather than a thing that one *is*. This grammatical construction also appears in *pruebas* (proofs) of purity of blood, where those who
give testimony are asked to assert that the claimant "no tenga raza de moro
o judio" [does not have *raza* of Jews or Moors]. *Raza* can thus be more precisely defined as a trace of impurity or a flaw. Indeed, the term is not applied
to backgrounds with a neutral or positive valence attached to them: an Old
Christian, for example, would not be described as having "*raza de cristiano
viejo*" but rather simply as a "*cristiano viejo*."

In these manuscript polemics, defenders of the statutes draw on a familiar array of racializing tropes. One defense of Toledo's controversial 1547
statute notes that lords with thoroughbred mares breed them carefully to
ensure that their offspring are "of a good caste." If this is done with animals, should it not also be done with humans, since Jews are known to be
a "depraved and evil generation?" It then argues that if fresh water comes
from a "poisonous source" it will always carry a trace of that poison, no matter how healthy it seems, and that the descendants of heretics similarly carry
the poison of their ancestors. Another polemic asserts that descendants of
Jews and Moors imbibe evil with their mother's milk.[26] Impure descent, in

all of these instances, appears as a stain that cannot be washed off, engrained in the body.

Opponents of the statutes, by contrast, argue that their original purpose was not to identify all descendants of Jews and Moors but rather to ascertain whose conversions were false. As one anonymous tract observes, it is logical to assume that the children of practicing Jews and Moors would absorb their "defects" because of "natural imitation." Within four or six generations, however, the tract continues, any person has more than a thousand ancestors. Believing one or two "tainted" ancestors among those thousand is enough to predetermine someone to vice is "pure nonsense."[27] The tract goes on to echo one of the most common critiques of pure blood statutes: that they can only be applied to those who either are wealthy enough to buy proofs of *limpieza* or so lowborn that there are insufficient records of their ancestry across multiple generations to reveal an (inevitable) converso or Morisco ancestor.

The tensions inherent to the pure blood statutes are particularly evident in the case of the descendants of Pablo de Santa María. In 1390, a man then known as Solomon Halevi, the chief rabbi of Burgos, converted to Christianity and took the name Pablo de Santa María. He managed to transform himself from rabbi to the bishop of Burgos and Cartagena, as well as the chief court chaplain to King Enrique III of Castile and tutor to his son, the future Juan II. A noted scholar of Hebrew and Arabic and well respected even prior to his conversion, he quickly rose to a place of prominence in both the Catholic Church and the Spanish court. His choice of the surname Santa María is apparently not incidental; he is described as "descendiente del linaxe de nuestra señora fue de nazion y profesion ebreo y de noblíssima y esclarecida sangre" [descendant of the same lineage as Our Lady, he was Hebrew in nation and religion and of the noblest and most illustrious blood]. This lineage, once he and his family have been baptized, allows his siblings and children (who converted along with him before he entered the church) to intermarry with the highest ranks of the Spanish nobility.[28] Once Pablo de Santa María has undone the sin of Jewishness by converting to Christianity, he can enter the ranks of Spain's nobles because his blood is as elevated as theirs—by virtue of consanguinity with the Virgin Mary herself. One sentence presents him as "Hebrew by nation" and "of the most illustrious and noblest blood," without registering this as a contradiction.

As the pure blood statutes became more prevalent, however, the family's known Jewish ancestry seems to have posed a problem. The text I discuss below is a petition to allow the descendants of don Pablo de Santa María to be granted the privileges of Old Christians, specifically admission to military orders. It makes clear that the meaning of the family's Jewish blood has undergone a significant transformation: "Es cierto que esta familia tuvo justa posesion de novleza y vuena fama y honrra por espazio de mucho mas de zien años antes que se hiziessen estas leies y estatutos y como esta visto cuando se hizieron no habia cometido culpa ninguna." [It is true that this family was justly in possession of nobility and good reputation and honor for a space of much more than one hundred years before they made these statutes and laws, and, as can be seen, when they made them (the family) had not committed any sin whatsoever.][29] Both the history of the family itself and this text in support of that family's rights to the status of Old Christian exemplify the problems that pure blood statutes created. Several members of the family—both Don Pablo himself and his son Alonso de Cartagena—were particularly well-known members of the clergy; other family members, as the text emphasizes, had intermarried with Spain's most noble and illustrious Old Christian families. Before Jewish descent was looked on as prohibitive in and of itself, the family, "por su mucha novleza de sangre o natural todos ellos y sus hixos y descendientes fueron sienpre nonbrados tenidos y tratados justissimamente de los reies de gloriosa memoria por notorios cavalleros hixosdalgo y asi mismo de todas las personas de sus reinos" [for its great nobility of blood or nature, all of them and their children and descendants were always named, held and treated most justly as exemplary knights and noblemen, by the rulers of glorious memory and the people of their kingdoms alike].[30] However, because by 1596 most military orders required their applicants to be without a trace of Jewish or Moorish blood, the Santa María family, because of its impure ancestry, found itself excluded from honors to which those of lower rank could claim access.

The petition itself contains no indication as to its authorship. It seems likely, however, that it is a copy of some of the materials presented by a descendant of don Pablo, don Pedro Osorio de Velasco, to King Philip III. These materials are cited in a royal warrant issued by King Philip III on February 7, 1604, declaring the descendants of Pablo de Santa María to be de facto Old Christians, "capazes de tener Habitos de las Ordenes Militares y las demas honras y Officios, y de entrar en Colegios y Iglesias que requieren limpieza y calidad de christianos viejos" [eligible to wear the habits of military orders, and for other honors and offices, and to enter schools and churches that required the purity and quality of old Christians].[31] The royal brief asserts that don Pedro Ossorio de Velasco set many testimonies ("diversos memoriales") before the king in favor of his family's illustrious lineage and unfailing Christian devotion, and that for more than ten years many theologians and scholars had felt moved to support his bid for Old Christian status. The royal warrant is followed by a brief from Pope Clement VIII dated May 24, 1603, which declares that the Santa María family's Jewish origins should not be considered a dishonor or stain.[32] The petition is unsigned but is almost certainly a copy of one of the testimonies produced for the king in support of the Santa María family. There is no indication in terms of the content that it was written by don Pedro Osorio Velasco himself, but it is possible that he or another family member was involved in its writing.

In making its case, the position articulates and implicitly reifies a number of racialized categories. In representing Pablo de Santa María's family as exceptional, it excludes them from the ranks of those who should be considered part of the *raza de judios*, rather than arguing against the logic of the statutes themselves. It also uses imagery that compares Jewishness to political and geographic affiliation:

> Excluir a uno del bien comun por solo linaxe . . . seria sin duda acepzion de personas como excluirle por ser mas o menos vlanco. o por ser descendientes de franceses o ytalianos que es totalmente inpertinente de lo qual llanamente se infiere que excluir esta familia es contra justicia distrivutiva.[33]

> [To exclude someone from the common good only because of their lineage . . . would without doubt be acception of persons like excluding him for being more or less white, or for being descendants of the French, or Italians, which is totally irrelevant. From all of which it can be plainly inferred that excluding this family is against distributive justice.][34]

Here, Jewish ancestry is compared to two other qualities: national identity and, strikingly, skin color. From a legal standpoint, according to this text, exclusion based on color and national origin is not permitted. Why, it asks, should the religious profession of one's ancestors be grounds for exclusion when none of these other categories are? The passage allows us to glimpse the contours of racial categorization in early modern Spain: color, nation, and religion are all presented as characteristics one might consider grounds for exclusion, even as they are dismissed as either illegal or illogical. Crucially, whiteness is established here as a separate category from religion, a point of contrast rather than coextensive with religious difference.

More generally, the petition works by taking into account two established forms of inherited identity or blood—nobility and Jewishness—to lobby for a place of honor for the descendants of Pablo de Santa María. It upholds the notion of noble blood, which the Santa María family can lay claim to by virtue of descent from the same lineage as the Virgin Mary, and thus from a long line of Jewish kings. Simultaneously, it complicates the idea that Jewish descent should always be considered an inherited trait, or taint in the blood. It attempts to do so without completely countering pure blood statutes, arguing that those descendants of Jews who have not yet had the opportunity to prove their allegiance to Christianity—as well as those who have already demonstrated the insincerity of their conversion—should be subject to exclusion. The text thus demonstrates first the malleability of discourses of inherited identity in the way it redefines *raza*. Second, it shows how theories of noble and of impure blood come into conflict with each other. And finally, it shows that despite both this malleability and the ways in which nobility can be pressed into service to counteract Jewish descent, a definition of Jewish inheritance as a *raza*—in other words, as a trace or strand of impurity passed by blood over countless generations—has become a presence that must be engaged with in Spanish society.

The existence of a series of regulations in early modern Spain that inscribed religious difference as an inheritance produced not only what we might now call a racializing discourse but also a counter-discourse that worked to undermine such ideas. While such a theory of racialized religious difference was more clearly expressed in Spain than it was in England (among other places), the mere act of attempting to quantify descent exposes the untenability of fantasies of purity. The strategic manipulation of notions of purity, meanwhile, became a compelling topic for mockery.

Purity and Social Mobility in *La villana de Getafe*

Although the polemic discussed above focuses predominantly on fears about the hidden converso, *La villana de Getafe* frames its interrogation of the value of pure descent in the context of the Morisco. There is historical precedent for accusations of Moorish ancestry against presumed old Christians in the period. However, as the polemics discussed above suggest, anxieties about the possibility of covert converso pollution of Old Christian blood-lines was far more acute.[35] Thus the play may focus on Moorishness because doing so would have been less inflammatory—and less likely to invite censorship—than a plot revolving around accusations of Jewish descent. Indeed, as Barbara Fuchs and Israel Burshatin have demonstrated, noble Moors can appear as romantic heroes in early modern Spanish literature, even though they may also appear as debased comic figures.[36] The converso in golden age Spanish literature does not have such romanticized positive associations, and characters explicitly described as conversos are rare in the comedia. Thus Lope's choice to base accusations of impurity on Moorish descent may work to minimize the impact of the play's critique: accusations of Morisco ancestry would have been easier to present in a comic light than accusations of converso descent.

In focusing on the Morisco, the play brings together representations of purity of blood as an invisible essence with those of Moorishness as a set of racially marked behaviors and characteristics. The play's references to racial identity and the expression of imagined racial difference in body, speech, and gesture are specific to stereotypically Moorish traits.[37] These presumably apparent traits are juxtaposed, to comic effect, with the notion of impure blood as an invisible essence of which anyone could be suspect. This juxtaposition consistently undermines the notion that any number of characteristics and behaviors—not only blood but also dress, speech, and even skin color—can be reliably deciphered. In doing so, the play obliquely suggests that *limpieza* matters less as "pure" essence than it does as a social performance.

Despite its explicit engagement with questions of purity of blood, *La villana de Getafe* has received very little attention from critics in this context, in part because it does not quite align with established lines of inquiry.[38] Scholars who discuss representations of purity of blood in the Spanish comedia have often focused on the figure of the converso (or descendant from Jews) rather than the Morisco, and on tragedy rather than comedy. Scholars such as Melveena McKendrick, Georgina Dopico Black, and John Beusterien examine references to pure and tainted blood in Spain's "wife-murder dramas" to argue that anxieties about secret sexual infidelity in these plays stand in for a larger cultural fear about the instability of a reputation for pure-blooded descent.[39] Although no characters in the plays discussed by these critics are explicitly described as conversos, a jealous husband's fear of losing honor through his wife's infidelity is interpreted as a displacement of anxiety about losing honor if his impure ancestry were to come to light. The

husband's fears inevitably lead to tragedy. *La villana de Getafe* cannot easily
be read through this lens. This is so because the consequences of accusations
of impurity are comic rather than tragic in the play, because impure descent
is explicitly discussed, and because the play focuses on Moorish rather than
Jewish descent.

Neither have critics focused on representations of Moors and Moriscos
devoted much attention to the play. Studies of Moorishness on the Spanish
stage have tended to discuss the comedia's complex relationship with the
legacy of Al-Andalus, and in particular the dichotomy between representations of romanticized noble Moors and debased comic Moriscos; the social
performance of pure descent largely does not enter such discussions.[40] And
of course a play in which the characters accused of Moorish descent are all
in fact Old Christians and have been all along does not lend itself to studies
focused on representations of Moors. Fuchs does devote a few paragraphs to
La villana de Getafe in an essay on Moriscos in Spain; however, she focuses
primarily on what the play has to tell us about the historical integration of the
Moriscos and does not offer a detailed analysis of the text itself.[41]

The successful impersonation of presumably innate characteristics is central to the plot of *La villana de Getafe*. Inés, the protagonist, begins the play
as a simple peasant girl living in a town that lies on the road between Madrid
and Seville.[42] She falls in love with the nobleman don Félix de Carpio when
she sees him on the streets of Madrid, and she runs into him again when
he stops in Getafe on the way from Madrid to Seville, where he is from. He
courts her, promising marriage—and conveniently ignoring the fact that he
is already engaged to a wealthy noblewoman, doña Ana. Inés waits in Getafe
after he leaves, believing he will return for her, for more than sixteen months.
Then she hears that he is about to be married to doña Ana. Ever resourceful,
Inés sets off to Madrid to stop the marriage, which she does by working as a
maid to Ana under the assumed name Gila, and by putting on a rustic accent.
Inés's post as doña Ana's maid gives her the opportunity to write an anonymous letter claiming that Félix and his servant Lope are Moriscos and about
to be expelled from Spain. She gives this letter to doña Ana and her father,
claiming that a stranger has handed it to her. It reads simply:

> La lástima que os tengo, señora doña Ana, me ha obligado a escrib-
> iros, que este caballero con quien os casais es morisco, y ansimismo
> lo es su criado; ya se les hace la información para echallos de España.
> Su agüelo de Don Félix [sic] se llamaba Zulema y el de Lope, lacayo,

Arambel Muley, que eso del Carpio es fingido, porque con los dineros que ganó su padre a hacer melcochas en el Andalucía ha comprado la caballería que os engaña. (2.2030–35)

[The pity I have for you, Lady Ana, has obliged me to write to you. This knight whom you are going to marry is a Morisco, and so is his servant; an investigation is already underway to expel them from Spain. Don Félix's grandfather was named Zulema and the lackey, Lope's, Arambel Muley. All this about Carpio (Félix's presumed surname) is feigned, since his father bought the knighthood that deceives you now using the money he made making candies in Andalucía.][43]

This letter is sufficiently damning to prompt doña Ana and her father to break off the engagement with Félix. Soon after, however, they learn that the accusations are false. Not only is don Félix not a Morisco, but he has been granted membership to the order of the knights of Calatrava, thereby proving beyond a doubt his Old Christian status.

Unfortunately for both Ana and Inés, Félix enters into yet another engagement, this time with another rich noblewoman, doña Elena. Inés manages to interrupt this engagement by disguising herself as Elena's cousin Juan, to whom Elena was initially promised in marriage but who departed years ago for the Americas and has been presumed dead. Elena falls in love with her "cousin" (i.e., Inés dressed as a man) and breaks off her engagement with Félix. Félix decides to try to patch things up with Ana, but before he does so Inés finds him. She reminds him that her father is an "hidalgo, aunque labrador" [a gentleman, even if a laborer] (3.3019), although the play has up until this point emphasized the inequality of any match between them. Further, she creates two fictional uncles for herself, whom she claims are sending her an inheritance of forty thousand *ducados* from the Americas via Elena's cousin Juan—who is, of course, really Inés in disguise. Upon learning this latter fact, Félix promises to marry Inés. The final scene shows Félix entering with Inés on his arm, dressed as a lady (*vestido de dama*). He proudly proclaims that Inés is the daughter of a gentleman (*hidalgo*) from Getafe, that she has a dowry of forty thousand *escudos* and that they have been secretly married for two years, presumably a reference to his earlier courtship. Just at this moment, a note arrives from Elena's real cousin from the Americas, which exposes Inés's tricks. In the midst of general confusion, doña Ana clarifies the situation:

Es que en forma de sobrino
tuyo ha venido a engañarte
la señora Doña Inés
que don Félix arrogante
por codicia del dinero
con demonstraciones tales
se ha desposado con ella
que ha sido engaño notable.

[You see, the lady doña Inés came here to deceive you in the person of
your nephew, and the arrogant don Félix, coveting money, has married
her because she pretended she had it, which was a noteworthy trick.]

The damage done, Félix counters this less-than-flattering assessment of his
motives by declaring himself content with Inés's wit and beauty and resigned
to her lack of fortune. The play ends on a happy note with a series of last-
minute marriages between the supporting characters and Félix's declaration
that he is "muy dichoso" [very fortunate] in his bride (3.3421–22).

The most extensive critical discussion of *La villana de Getafe* thus far
appears in Francisco Márquez Villanueva's monumental study *Lope: Vida
y valores*. Márquez Villanueva devotes several chapters to the play, paying
particular attention to the Morisco subplot. He argues that the play is autobiographical and was Lope's literary self-defense against jokes that he was of
Moorish descent because of his fondness for writing *romances moriscos*. As
questions of purity of blood took on greater urgency in Spain, Lope found it
prudent to clarify that such jokes were not based in reality.[44] Indeed, the autobiographical aspect of the play is hard to ignore, given that the playwright
(whose full name is Félix Lope de Vega y Carpio) has created a protagonist
named Félix with the surname Carpio whose servant is called Lope. This
autobiographical element of the play seems even more plausible, as Márquez
Villanueva convincingly argues, when we take into account the popularity of Lope's romantic portrayals of noble Moors in his *romances moriscos*.
However, Márquez Villanueva also seems to assume that the play, because it
reflects on the life and works of the playwright, must therefore not work to
critique or undermine the notion of purity of blood more broadly:

¿Estaremos, pues, ante un Lope disidente en un punto tan crucial
como es la crítica y rechazo de la limpieza de sangre? El caso de *La*

villana de Getafe aclara del todo sus intenciones y permite responder con una enfática negativa. Félix prueba con facilidad su limpieza (porque el sistema funciona con eficacia) y la calumnia que comenzó aviesa termina en nada más que una broma pueril.[45]

[Do we, then, find ourselves faced with a dissident Lope on such a crucial issue as a critique and rejection of purity of blood? The case of *La villana de Getafe* completely clarifies his intentions and permits us to respond with an emphatic negative. Félix easily proves his purity (because the system functions effectively) and the calumny that began as malicious turns out to be nothing more than a puerile joke.]

Because the play ultimately affirms Félix's purity of blood, despite the false accusations leveled against him by Inés, Márquez Villanueva argues that "el blanco moral de Lope es así, muy claramente, el vicio de la murmuración y no el concepto ni las prácticas de la limpieza de sangre."[46] [The moral target of Lope is thus, very clearly, the vice of gossip and neither the concept nor the practices of purity of blood.]

In limiting his analysis to the autobiographical aspects of the play, Márquez Villanueva oversimplifies the play's engagement with the notion of purity of blood and more generally with the question of how the inheritance of physical and behavioral traits functions. The play certainly seems to reflect Lope de Vega's personal experience, as well as pointing out the dangers of giving too much credence to gossip. But these aspects of the text do not preclude it from also offering a sharp parody of theories of purity of blood. A closer examination of its plot, language, and imagery demonstrates that the play repeatedly highlights the malleability of presumably essential inherited characteristics.

This dynamic is most evident, of course, in the Morisco subplot. At the first suggestion that Félix and the servant Lope might be of Moorish origin, other characters leap to ascribe Moorish characteristics to them. Félix's intended, Ana, begins with the servant: "Que Lope morisco sea / aun lo parece en la cara" [Lope is a Moor; he even appears to be one in his face] (2.2047–48). She then moves on to her prospective husband: "Mas de espacio le mire, / no en balde la fama suena. / Morisco me ha parecido, / y aun en el hablar también" [I looked at him more closely, and rumor doesn't speak idly. He seems like a *morisco* to me, even in the way he talks] (2.2086–89). Other characters are equally unforgiving, as Ana's father claims that don Félix "tiene de moro el gesto / y aun lo parece en hablar" [has the manner of a Moor, and even seems one in the way he speaks]. Similarly, the squire Ramirez asserts of Lope, "De Lope siempre temía, / Julia, que morisco era: cara tiene de quemado" [Julia, I always feared that Lope was a *morisco*; he has a burned face] (2.2063–65). As soon as rumor—in the form of an anonymous letter—brands Lope and Félix as Moriscos, the play's other Old Christian characters lose no time in claiming that they have been able to spot signs of the characters' Moorishness all along.

The humor in this, of course, lies in the fact that Félix and Lope show no such signs and are not in fact Moriscos. The butt of the satire here is not only the power of gossip and the gullibility of Ana's family (though it is that, too) but the notion that those of Moorish descent can reliably be distinguished from Old Christians. The episode caricatures the hysteria prompted by accusations of impure descent and destabilizes the validity of such a discourse as it does so. Ideally, those who displayed Moorish characteristics would then turn out to have impure blood. Here, that process is inverted, as Félix and Lope are seen as Moorish only after they have been accused. The irony of the situation is underscored by Ana's proud assertion in the scene before the letter is discovered: "que es Don Félix la nobleza / del mundo, y celestial su gentileza" [Don Félix is the noblest in the world, and his gentility is celestial] (2.1965–66). Of course, Félix and Lope are not really Moriscos, which minimizes the subversiveness of this moment. Nonetheless, the rapidity with which Lope and Félix are retroactively marked as having been physically different all along undermines the reliability of these presumably apparent characteristics. As soon as Lope and Félix have been labeled as Moriscos, other Old Christians rush to ascribe presumably stable signs of Moorish difference to them. This eagerness suggests an instability—even an anxiety—at the heart of the discourse of purity of blood. If it is so easy to see the Old Christians Lope and Félix as Moriscos, might not the reverse be possible? That is, might not those of Moorish descent unproblematically pass themselves off as Old Christians?[47] Doña Ana's family separates itself from Félix in part to reinforce its members' own status as pure-blooded Spaniards. The play exposes that status as precarious—not, in fact, apparent at all, but rather subject to the vagaries of popular opinion. The very fact that signs of Moorishness are so unreliable implicitly destabilizes their validity as essential inherited traits, emphasizing the ways that pure descent functions as a social construction.

Further, the play makes a series of jokes at the expense of the notion of purity of blood when the servant Lope, after hearing about the allegations against his parentage, begins to enumerate spurious claims about his ancestry: "Yo he sido / el que el tocino inventó / yo los puercos engendré" [I was the one who invented ham! I am the progenitor of pork!] (2.2156–58); "vive Dios! Que deciendo / de un estornudo del Cid" [For the love of God! I descend from the Cid's sneeze] (2.2238–39); and finally "Hijo soy de un arcipreste / muy católico y fiel" [I am the son of a very faithful and Catholic archpriest] (3.2482–83). These claims to Christian ancestry primarily, and quite simply, poke fun at any obsession with pedigree. They also, though, play on conventional notions of reproduction and inheritance. Even Lope's assertions of his Old Christian status draw on monstrosity (with Lope as the father of pigs) and social deviance (as the son of a priest). Lope's jokes align with and reinforce the play's preoccupation with fictional constructions of lineage. While his assertions are patently ludicrous, they underline how tenuous claims to purity of descent are in the play.

The play also brings up interesting questions about how the inheritance of impure blood and of physical characteristics is meant to function. One of the diatribes delivered against Lope and Félix when they are believed to be Moriscos reads:

¿Pues es bien,
don Félix o calabaza,
que ande tu honor en la plaza
y que por moro te den,
y te hagan información
para que de España salgas,
y con sangres tan hidalgas
quieres mezclar tu nación
y la secta de Zulema
y el Lope cuyos abuelos
vivían de hacer buñuelos
en cuyo aceite se quema,
con Julia, que es como el Sol?
Váyanse perros a Argel
y, pues Muley Arambel,
El melcochero espanol
Fue abuelo suyo, lacayo,
Aqui jamás los pies meta . . . (2.2115–31)

[Is it good then, don Félix, or don pumpkin, that your honor should be displayed in the village square, and that they call you a Moor, and give you orders to leave Spain. And you want to mix your nation, and Zulema's sect, with such noble blood (as that of his intended). And Lope, whose grandparents made their living selling pastries, and burned themselves in the oil from them (would intermarry) with Julia, who is like the sun? Go, dogs, to Argel, and since Muley Arambel the Spanish pastry-maker was your grandfather, lackey, never set foot here again . . .]

The passage foregrounds theories of Moorish coloring and blood and their relationship to inherited identity. The darkness of the servant Lope's grandparents' skin (and presumably Lope's own) is attributed, unexpectedly, not to exposure to the sun in Africa (one common theory of the origins of Blackness) but rather to their proximity to cooking oil while baking—a profession traditionally identified with Moors and Moriscos. Darker skin here becomes the result of a certain kind of labor as well as an inherited trait. Thus darker skin is associated with Moorish coloring, but that coloring is attributed to labor which is both traditionally Moorish and a marker of lower-class status. It is also significant that only Lope, the servant, is described as swarthy when he is accused of being a Morisco; Félix, a nobleman, is never described as having a darker complexion. Finally, it is again important to keep in mind that neither Lope nor Don Félix is in fact a Morisco. Although Lope makes jokes about the swarthiness of his own complexion early in the play, it is only after Inés plants her accusatory letter that his complexion is understood to indicate Moorish ancestry.[48]

In less obvious ways, the trick Inés uses to end Félix's second engagement, to doña Elena, also exposes the ways in which "blood"—in this case, family ties—may be falsely impersonated. In order to break up this match, Inés disguises herself as Elena's cousin Juan, recently returned from the Americas. The two had been intended for each other since childhood, but the real Juan is presumed to have been lost at sea. Interestingly, the play works to emphasize the presumed blood relationship between the cousins. The first time they see each other, Inés greets him, "¿Es mi prima?" [Are you my cousin?], to which Elena replies, "Primo mio!" [My cousin!] (3.2588); and Elena affirms her devotion to "Juan" by proclaiming, "Pagais mi justa aficion / que añadió despues que os ví / primo, ese talle y valor / *a la sangre* nuevo amor" [You repay my just preference, which added new love to that which arises from blood after I saw your form and worth, cousin] (3.2691–93; italics mine).

Most conspicuously of all, Juan/Inés draws attention to Elena's continued use of the word *primo* to refer to him/her:

> *Inés:* ¿Soy vuestro marido?
> *Elena:* Si
> *Inés:* ¿Pues, por que me llamais primo? (3.2695–96)
> [*Inés:* Am I your husband?
> *Elena:* Yes
> *Inés:* Then why do you call me cousin?]

The play deliberately draws attention to the presumed blood relationship between Elena and the character she imagines to be her cousin.[49] In doing so, it highlights the ease with which Inés has been able to insert herself into a family to which she does not belong by blood. Just as Lope and Don Félix are apparently indistinguishable from Moriscos, a disguised Inés can easily pass herself off as a member of Elena's noble family—and indeed as a man. In *La villana de Getafe* the emphasis on blood ties between the lovers reminds the viewer or reader that Elena's cousin is in fact an impostor—but, nonetheless, an impostor who has managed easily to convince everyone around her that she is a part of Elena's family.

Both of Inés's stratagems, then, rely on exploiting the possibility that blood relations and impure blood alike can be manipulated. The success of her tricks begins to suggest that the importance of her status as pure-blooded at the play's ending may be another strategy to justify her marriage as much as it is a validation of the importance of purity of blood. Inés's tricks overtly rely on her ability to manipulate others' perceptions of blood-borne identity. Within this context, Félix's emphasis on Inés's purity of blood at the play's ending becomes a strategic validation of the concept of peasant honor in the interest of securing her (fictional) large dowry. As Félix says to Inés: "Con cuarenta mil escudos / Muy bien puede perdonarse / pues eres limpia, el jirón / que te ha dado el villanaje" [With forty thousand *escudos*, the blot of your peasant ancestry can easily be pardoned, since you are pure-blooded] (3.3041–44). This declaration gives a rather different valence to the line I cited at the beginning of this essay: "Inés es limpia, oh Fortuna! / que la diferencia es / el llamalla dona Inés, / que no cuesta cosa alguna" [Inés is pure-blooded, oh what fortune! The only difference will be to call her doña Inés, which doesn't cost a thing] (3.3215–18). After all, the status of Inés's purity of blood does not change over the course of the play; if her purity of blood is the reason—rather than the excuse—for a marriage between a peasant girl and the noble Félix, the two of them could have wed as soon as they met. Instead, the play emphasizes that Inés's purity of blood enables her marriage only because Félix believes, however erroneously, that she is an heiress. Further, when Félix declares himself fortunate in his choice at the end, despite Inés's lack of nobility, her Old Christian descent does not appear. Instead, he lauds her rare wit ("raro ingenio"), beauty ("hermosura") and form ("talle"). Inés's purity of blood is not a trick, as her impersonation of Elena's cousin Juan and her labeling of Félix and Lope as Moriscos are. The play does, though, suggest that Inés's purity of blood matters less because it grants her an inherent claim to a nobility of sorts than because it provides an excuse for her to marry above her station because she is believed to be extraordinarily wealthy. On multiple fronts, then, *La villana de Getafe* presents the rhetoric of inherited "blood" identity as a strategy—and particularly a strategy that enables class mobility—rather than as an accurate predictor of a character's essential nature.

In *La villana de Getafe*, purity of blood is most often deployed pragmatically to meet particular social ends. Blood difference is exposed as a particularly vulnerable category because it is so easily fictionalized. Despite repeated assertions of recognition, it proves impossible within the play to identify whether characters are of the blood Inés ascribes to them: whether that blood is Moorish, in the case of Félix and Lope, or familial, when she passes herself off as Juan. Inés's stratagems reach even further than that; she successfully impersonates a lower-class peasant when she becomes Ana's maid, and disguises herself not only as a member of Elena's family but as a man. The juxtaposition of these multiple forms of impersonation in *La villana de Getafe* highlights the complexity of discourses of pure blood in early modern Spain as one strand in a tightly woven fabric of gender, rank, and race, each of which appears alternately as a blood-borne essence and a social performance. Inés's carefully orchestrated chaos exposes the interdependency of these categories as well as highlighting just how unstable and performative they are.

Conclusion

La villana de Getafe offers just one example among many early modern Spanish texts that demonstrate the extent to which external forces—particularly questions of class identity and class mobility—influenced theories of the inheritance of both pure and impure blood. Registering these contradictions is particularly important as critics continue to turn to discourses of purity of blood as a site of origin for theories of race in early modern Europe. Further scrutiny of texts such as *La villana de Getafe* may alert us against characterizing early modern Spain as a site of origin for modern racialized anti-Semitism without engaging with the differential and heterogeneous impact of discourses of purity of blood. In fact, as we have seen, a clearly articulated rhetoric of inherited racialized difference in some ways has an effect the opposite of what we might expect. After all, a play such as *La villana de Getafe* evokes pure descent only to undermine the notion that blood might determine character. If we grant Spain's pure blood statutes a place of prominence in histories of race in early modern literature and culture, we must also engage with the way that Spanish texts such as *La villana de Getafe* depict fictions of pure descent as a social performance as much as an immutable essence.

Thus far, I have emphasized the ironic performance of purity in early modern Spanish texts as a destabilizing practice, one that exposes its own fictions even as it asserts its centrality to Spanish identity. My reading has been, for lack of a better term, optimistic, suggesting that ironic performances of impurity enable social mobility even as they make visible how fragile the fantasy of pure blood is. Equally important, however, is the fact that exposing notions of purity as fictions does not diminish their social power.

While many studies have emphasized the importance of Spain's pure blood statutes to the racialization of Jewishness and Moorishness, very little attention has been paid to the ways that these statutes also construct the *cristiano viejo*, or Old Christian, as a racialized identity. *La villana de Getafe* may be cynical in its celebration of Inés's status as "limpia" or pure, but her marriage to a nobleman on the basis of that purity also reifies the force of her status as an Old Christian. Critical studies of the *cristiano viejo* have largely examined it as a class position, but the discourse also clearly points to questions of race, as purity is determined entirely by ancestry. Its status as a racialized category has perhaps been less visible because it does not fall under broader rubrics of the other or the stranger that we are accustomed to focusing on in discussions of early modern race. Conversely, we might say that the racialization of the *cristiano viejo* has escaped notice in recent critical studies, much as whiteness often does, because it corresponds with an unmarked normative identity, although it is not predicated on color.[50] However, as I will discuss in Chapter 3, the category of the *cristiano viejo* is critical to understanding not only discourses of purity of blood in early modern Spain but also the racialization of Blackness and whiteness. Indeed, the racialization of the *cristiano viejo* is a key component of the dynamic of triangulated whiteness described in the introduction. As we shall see in Chapter 3, laying claim to pure descent to enable social mobility is a common trope in the Spanish comedia, not only for representations of lower-class characters but also for heroic Black protagonists.

As a form of normative or majority identity that rests on tenuous fictions of ancestry, the performance of purity in early modern Spain also offers a productive site of comparison for present-day discourses of whiteness, particularly in the United States. This is so because *La villana de Getafe* relies on the comic potential of cognitive dissonance. If a nobleman with the status of Don Félix can be credibly accused of being a Morisco, then the category of *cristiano viejo* can be reduced to mere social performance. But if the lowborn Inés can marry a nobleman by virtue of her purity of blood, that performance nonetheless holds tremendous cultural power. Both the flexibility and the power of the category of *cristiano viejo* are evident in early modern historical documents, particularly in the convoluted logic of the successful petition of the descendants of Pablo de Santa María/Solomon Halevi to be considered de facto Old Christians. From the perspective of the present day, the most striking aspect of these discourses of purity of blood may be that they retain their efficacy even as they are repeatedly exposed as fictions.

CHAPTER 2

Translating Spain

Purity of Blood and Orientalism in Mabbe's
Rogue and *The Spanish Gypsy*

The eponymous protagonist of Mateo Alemán's picaresque novel *Guzmán de Alfarache* (1599, 1604) frequently refers to Spain's now-notorious theories of *limpieza de sangre*, or "purity of blood," which discriminated against those with Jewish or Muslim ancestors. In one instance, Guzmán describes his penchant for self-aggrandizement: "¿Como trataré de linajes, para encajar la limpieza del mío? Cómo descubriré al otro su falta, para que quien oyere que la murmuro piense que yo no la tengo?" [How would I discourse on lineages, to highlight the purity of my own? How would I uncover the faults of another, so that all who overheard my gossip would think that I did not possess the same flaws?][1] Since the novel opens with the ignoble story of Guzmán's origins—his father is a converso, of Jewish descent, and thus Guzmán is as well—he recounts his claims to purity of blood with his tongue placed firmly in his cheek. The novel satirizes those who lay claim to pure descent by putting protestations of purity of blood in the mouth of a converso picaro, and in so doing suggests that this presumed purity functions as a social performance as well as an inconvertible essence.

The first English translation of *Guzmán*, James Mabbe's *The Rogue* (1622), changes the emphasis of these lines. Mabbe's Englished Guzmán tells us: "How often would my selfe fall a discoursing of other mens houses and their gentilitie, only of purpose to set my own Pedigree afoot, and to shew that I was a gentleman well descended? How often would I discover another mans defect, and find fault with it, and only to this end, that by taxing such a vice in another, I might be thought to be free from the same in myself?"[2] In Mabbe's translation, the specific notion of *limpieza* (as in *limpieza de sangre*) is replaced by the broader term *pedigree*, which Mabbe clarifies with the addition of the phrase "a gentleman well descended." Thus no trace remains in the English translation of the Spanish text's engagement with Jewish or Moorish descent.

This incomplete translation should not come as a surprise; after all, there was no equivalent to Spain's pure blood statutes in early modern England. Although for a reader in seventeenth-century Madrid, Guzmán's tossed-off gibe would have been familiar and easily understood, the social value of a "pure" lineage, defined as lacking any trace of Jewish or Moorish ancestry, would not have been immediately intelligible to that reader's English contemporary. Thus there is no straightforward way to translate this passage, even assuming Mabbe's awareness of the specific implications of the Spanish word *limpieza* (which literally translates as "cleanliness," and which, as we will see below, he mistranslates elsewhere). Nonetheless, Mabbe's small elision, even if accidental, is significant, providing a point of entry into a vexed issue: the relationship between Spanish discourses of purity of blood and developing discourses of racial difference in early modern England.

Whereas the previous chapter focused on representations of purity of blood within Spain, here I investigate how Spanish literary texts addressing questions of purity of blood were translated and adapted into English. In the introduction, I discuss the prominent place afforded to Spain's pure blood statutes in discussions of racialized religious difference in early modern England, demonstrating that discourses of purity of blood have been posited as a site of origin for the racialization of Jewish and Muslim descent. Such assumptions, however, invite further scrutiny. What, more precisely, is the relationship between Spain's status as a site of racial difference in early modern England, a status secured by the "Black Legend," and Spanish engagements with purity of blood? Examining how Spanish representations of purity of blood were translated and adapted into an English context can help us begin to answer this question. I focus here on two representative case studies: James Mabbe's translation of Mateo Alemán's *Guzmán de Alfarache*, and Middleton and Rowley's *The Spanish Gypsy*, a play set in Spain that takes its plot from two different novellas by Cervantes. Comparing source texts to their adaptations allows us to differentiate between two topics that have often been conflated: on the one hand, English representations of racial difference that evoke Spain; and, on the other, the complicated debates around purity of blood that so frequently emerge in early modern Spanish literature and culture. I attend in particular to how each of these texts constructs inherited identity, whether Jewish, Moorish, or "Gypsy."[3]

I begin with Mabbe's translation, explaining why the study of a now largely unread picaresque novel can inform early modern race studies. I focus on representations of purity of blood, addressing the challenges Mabbe faces when trying to explain covert references to those of impure descent to an English audience. The second section addresses the ways that Mabbe's translation Orientalizes Spain, marking it as exotically Moorish. The final section, on *The Spanish Gypsy*, shows how the English play avoids the radical instability and performativity that runs through Cervantes's novellas, instead presenting a Spain far more preoccupied with honor than the source texts it draws on. Ultimately, I argue that both of these adaptations flatten and simplify the ambivalent representations of racial difference that we find in the Spanish texts. By emphasizing these differences between source text and translation, I hope to destabilize Spain's status as a presumed site of origin for discourses of race in the period.

Purity of Blood in English Translation

As the previous chapter demonstrates, the pure blood statutes are a particularly complex site of racial discourse within Spain and are deeply imbricated in questions of class identity and mobility. How much, though, would early modern English people have known about this dynamic? As I argue in the introduction, Spanish ideologies of purity of blood have been understood to be particularly foundational to early modern theories of race. It is less clear how widely understood Spain's pure blood statutes were outside of Spain. Certainly, Spain's pure blood statutes in some way informed the Hispanophobic representation of Spaniards as a "mongrel generation."[4] As early as the mid-sixteenth century, a Spanish critic of the pure blood statutes contended that they were the source of Spain's tainted reputation in Europe: "porque en otras naciones donde se oye este division, que estos estatutos hacen luego concebir de ella, que españa está llena de herejes . . . españoles por limpios, y nobles que sean, doquieran se vaya fuera del Reyno los llaman marranos" [because in other nations when they hear of the division caused by these statutes, they then start to think that Spain is full of heretics. . . . Spaniards, no matter how pure and noble they may be, are called *marranos* wherever they go outside of the country].[5]

Indeed, the imagined impurity of Spaniards is a staple of anti-Spanish propaganda. For example, William of Orange's much-cited anti-Spanish diatribe (1581, English translation 1584) declares: "I will no more wonder at that which all the world beleeveth, to witte, that the greatest number of Spanyardes, and specially those, that counte themselves Noble men, are of the blood of the Moores and the Jewes."[6] The text suggests that presumed Spanish impurity was already common knowledge by the last quarter of the sixteenth century. Another text, Edwin Sandys's *Relation of the State of Religion* (1599, published 1605), offers an account of the Spanish Inquisition's persecution of crypto-Jews and -Muslims and asserts that "a great part of the Spanish Nobility is mixed at this day with Jewish blood."[7]

The specifics of Spain's pure blood statutes, however, particularly in relation to the vexed relationship between purity and nobility of blood, do not seem to form a part of English representations of Spain's pure blood discourse. Edmund Spenser's *View of the Present State of Ireland* (1595–96, published 1633) famously echoes the vocabulary of the pure blood statutes when describing the Spaniard as "of all the nations under heaven . . . the most mingled, the most uncertain, and most bastardly." The Spaniards, he claims, "though they therein labored much to ennoble themselves" have "scarce any drop of the old Spanish blood left in them."[8] Spenser does not, however, refer to Spanish persecution of conversos and Moriscos, either from statutes or the Inquisition. His mingled genealogy in fact takes a very different form than that found in Spain: there is no mention of Jewish descent, and Spain's mongrel heritage is derived from not only Moors but also Goths, Huns, and Vandals. In Spain, by contrast, claiming Gothic ancestry denoted special purity of descent. Because Visigothic Northern Spain was never part of Islamic Al-Andalus, it was mythologized as the origin of the purest "Old Christian" nobility.[9] Both Spenser's text and anti-Spanish propaganda represent Spaniards as "impure" but do not engage with the notion of the Old Christian as a racialized category and as a form of honor in its own right.

When English texts describe Spaniards as being of impure descent, they often reflect a vague awareness of Spain's pure blood statutes, as Spenser's use of the phrase "the old Spanish blood" suggests. But the debate, critique, and parody of notions of pure blood that are so prevalent in early modern Spanish texts are largely absent from English representations of Spain, as is Spanish texts' emphasis on purity as a social performance. The transformation of Alemán's *Guzmán* into Mabbe's *Rogue* offers an example of how this limited awareness flattens the Spanish text's complex engagement with questions of blood, honor, and identity.

Purity of Blood, Parody, and Social Mobility
in *Guzmán* and *The Rogue*

Both Alemán's Spanish *Guzmán de Alfarache* and Mabbe's translation were enormously popular when they were first published. Both texts reached—and influenced—a great number of readers. In Spanish, the first part of *Guzmán de Alfarache* was published in 1599 and the second in 1604. The book appeared in multiple editions in various cities in Spain and Portugal, as well as in Brussels, Paris, and Milan.[10] Italian, French, and German translations appeared in 1600, 1606, and 1616, respectively.[11] While no English translation appeared until 1622, the novel seems to have been reasonably well known to English readers in the Spanish original. For example, a commendatory poem to Thomas Coryate's 1611 *The Odcombian Banquet* praises Coryate's deeds as more illustrious than those of "Guzman of Spain, and Amadis of France."[12] Similarly, Sir William Cornwallis's 1616 *Essayes of Certaine Paradoxes* cites "Sr. Gusman de Alfarache" in an essay on the evils of scriveners (a topic that appears in *Guzmán* as well).[13] James Mabbe, *Guzmán*'s translator, was an Oxford scholar and Hispanist who had spent several years in Spain and produced several other noteworthy translations from Spanish over the course of his lifetime (among them Fernando de Rojas's late medieval work *La Celestina* and selections from Cervantes's *Novelas ejemplares*).

Whereas Alemán's *Guzmán de Alfarache* was issued in two volumes published five years apart, Mabbe issued parts 1 and 2 together. In preparing his translation, he also seems to have drawn on a French and an Italian version; in particular, the second part of his *Guzmán* contains sections that appear in Barrezzo Barrezi's 1615–16 Italian translation but not in the Spanish, possibly because he was unable to access the Spanish original. For the first part of *Guzmán*, on which I focus here, he appears to have translated primarily from the Spanish.[14] When the translation first appeared in 1622, it—like its Spanish predecessor—was immediately successful, appearing in a fourth edition by 1656.[15]

Despite the novel's complicated intertextual history, in his prefatory materials Mabbe presents himself as the sole intermediary between Alemán's Spanish text and his English readers. He emphasizes the fact that his text was taken from a Spanish source; the title page to the 1623 edition lists Mateo Alemán, "servant to his Catholike Majesty and born in Seville," as its author without mentioning Mabbe at all. Further, Mabbe includes a preface he has written in Spanish that he signs Don Diego Puede-Ser ("Sir James May-Be," a pun on his name). While other early modern English works, especially plays, often drew on Spanish sources without acknowledging that they had done so, Mabbe's translation emphasizes the novel's Spanish setting and his own background as a Hispanist.

In his repeated insistence on the Spanishness of his source, Mabbe's text presents a very different model of translation than that described by Barbara Fuchs in the *Poetics of Piracy*, the most extensive discussion of English appropriations from Spanish sources. Fuchs describes how English authors appropriate or "pirate" Spanish texts and reclaim them as English, or even (in the case of plays such as *Rule a Wife and Have a Wife* and *The Knight of the Burning Pestle*) "take Spain against Spain" by drawing on Spanish sources to produce anti-Spanish stories.[16] In contrast, Mabbe's translation of *Guzmán de Alfarache* does not explicitly participate in anti-Spanish discourse, nor does Mabbe himself represent his translation as an act of "piracy" (despite the fact that Ben Jonson's prefatory poem insists that Mabbe has thoroughly "Englished" the novel's protagonist).[17] To the contrary, the novel's extensive footnotes, which set out to render legible what is foreign and inaccessible about the novel's Spanish setting, repeatedly emphasize that both *The Rogue* and its rogue protagonist have not in fact been made English, but in fact are so irreducibly foreign that they require expert guidance to be properly understood. *The Rogue* differs from Mabbe's later translations of Spanish fiction in this close engagement with Spain. He does not use footnotes in his edition of selected Cervantes novellas (1640), and his English *Celestina*, *The Spanish Bawd* (1631) does not particularly emphasize the setting of its source text, despite its title. Instead, Mabbe replaces references to Christianity with classical allusions and "confuses the issue of locale, making his setting seem sometimes to be England, sometimes Spain, and sometimes a sort of classical never-never land."[18]

Mabbe may have particularly emphasized *The Rogue*'s Spanish setting because the novel was first published at a time when English readers had a vested interest in Spain. In 1622 negotiations for the proposed (and ultimately failed) "Spanish match" between Prince Charles and the Infanta María of Spain were reaching their zenith. The match had not yet dissolved and seemed imminent to many; thus, potential book buyers would have been particularly interested in learning more about the nation that was about to be linked once again to England through marriage ties.[19] Mabbe seems to have been especially attuned to such readers' interest. He includes lengthy footnotes on local history, proverbs, and etymology that consistently remind the reader of the foreignness of the novel's Spanish setting. And because the Spanish text frequently raises questions about purity of blood and its relationship to identity, Mabbe's translation must also engage with this topic. As he does so, as we shall see, Mabbe emphasizes certain representations of racial identities in his Spanish source and omits others. In the following section I turn to the aspect of Spanish discourses of race that Mabbe's translation most frequently elides: parodic representations of purity of blood as a social performance rather than as an indicator of essential worth. These omissions, while they often seem to be failures of comprehension rather than a deliberate strategy, nonetheless alter the book's depiction of racial identities. While Alemán's *Guzmán* satirizes representations of pure blood, in the English translation such destabilizing satire—and its implied critique of the value of pure blood—largely disappears.

The Spanish *Guzmán de Alfarache* is preoccupied with the significance of blood descent. Its protagonist repeatedly satirizes theories of purity of blood, hinting that he is a converso. These representations of purity of blood in *Guzmán de Alfarache* are inseparable from questions of class. Characters who emphasize their status as Old Christians are most often peasants, described by Guzmán as cruel and uncouth. And while Guzmán's own claims to nobility are tenuous at best, given his less-than-illustrious parentage, the picaro consistently represents himself as being of a more genteel background than the mule drivers and beggars with whom he rubs shoulders. More specifically, over the course of the novel Guzmán utters a series of veiled, but barbed, references to peasants' spurious claims to honor by means of purity of blood.

The significance of these references becomes more apparent when we place *Guzmán* in the context of the history of the pure blood statutes in early modern Spain. A similar attitude toward purity of blood pervades Alemán's *Guzmán de Alfarache*. Indeed, Guzmán's typically picaresque project—to make his way in the world despite the disreputable nature of his progenitors—resonates with contemporary debates about the ability of ancestry to determine character.[20] Alemán himself was of converso origin on his father's side; and, like the protagonist of his novel, he seems to have made efforts to conceal that fact, at times taking on the common Old Christian surname "de Ayala."[21] Thus it is not surprising that tacit critiques of discourses of purity of blood appear intermittently throughout. Both the Spanish novels and their English translation end with Guzmán repenting the error of his ways and embracing Christianity. Critics remain divided as to whether this reformation is meant to be understood as sincere, thereby suggesting that even a converso can achieve

Christian grace, or is a strategy to sneak the rogue's antics and the author's scathing social critique past the censors.[22]

As the novel begins, we learn that Guzmán's father's (and thus Guzmán's) ancestry is suspect. Alemán indicates this by referring to him as a *levantisco*, or Levantine. He writes: "Cuanto a lo primero, el mío y sus deudos fueron levantiscos. Vinieron a residir a Génova, donde fueron agregados a la nobleza." [In the first place, mine (i.e., my father) and his relatives were Levantine. They came to live in Genoa, where they assimilated into the nobility] (130–31). He goes on to inform the reader that Guzmán's father lends out money at interest, and that his religious devotion is held in suspicion by his neighbors. Although Alemán never states outright that Guzmán's father is a *converso*, most critics have assumed that he is (and thus, following the logic of the pure blood statutes, that Guzmán is as well).[23] Certainly, Guzmán's father is not the prototype of a pure-blooded noble Spaniard—and in Spanish, the word *levantisco* suffices to hint at a disreputable Eastern difference.

The translation struggles to make these glancing allusions to purity of blood legible to an English audience. Most simply, Mabbe must address the fact that the word *Levantine* does not have the same connotations in English that it does in Spanish. Mabbe's version reads: "First of all, I shall give you to understand, That my father, and his Kindred, were a certain kind of upstart Gentlemen, that came out of the Levant, who having no certaine abiding, came at length to reside, and settle in Genoa; where they were ingrafted into the Nobilitie, and had many large and goodly Priviledges granted unto them" (vol. 1, 44–45). He adds to this a footnote: "*Levantisco*, which is the word in the Originall, is taken for an Upstart, a Jew, or an Easterling, come from the Levant. And, *Estar de Levante*, is one that hath no set dwelling" (vol. 1, 44 n. 2). Mabbe again expands on the Spanish the next time the term *levantisco* is used. While Alemán simply refers to Guzmán's father, again, as "el levantisco," Mabbe translates the word to "this Easterling, this Jew, or this Moore" (vol. 1, 85). Mabbe ropes a number of quite different terms together as he grapples to define *levantisco*. The composite figure that emerges—possibly Jewish, possibly Moorish, definitely an upwardly mobile interloper from the East—certainly functions as a representative of social disorder. It does not, though, as it does in the Spanish text, set the scene for a staged conflict between uneducated but presumably pure-blooded peasants and those of higher but "tainted" descent like Guzmán.

While Mabbe's attempt to translate the word *levantisco* engages with questions of purity of blood, even if obscurely, associations between boorish peasants and spurious claims to pure descent often completely disappear in translation. Toward the beginning of his journey Guzmán falls prey to the wiles of an innkeeper who feeds him the meat of a young mule, telling him that it is veal; the meat makes Guzmán terribly ill. Because they are the off-spring of horses and donkeys, mules appear at times in Spanish texts as a symbol of miscegenation.[24] Thus questions of purity of blood are already a tacit presence as the mule-meat episode begins. When Guzmán discovers what he has actually eaten and uncovers the scandal of the mule being passed off as veal to the villagers and the authorities, the evocation of purity of blood becomes more explicit. The village officials and notaries appear on the scene, hoping to get to the bottom of the issue. As each argues for his own right to intervene, they turn on each other: "los unos a los otros desenterraron los abuelos, diciendo quienes fueron sus madres, y no perdonando a sus mujeres proprias y las devociones que habían tenido. Quizá que no mentían." [They dug up each other's grandparents, recounting who their mothers were, and not forgiving even their wives, and the devotions that they had performed. Maybe they weren't lying] (200). The phrase "las devociones que habían tenido" or "the devotions they had performed" explicitly evokes heretical reli-gious practices. By slandering the religion of each other's grandparents, the notaries accuse each other of having Jewish or Muslim ancestors, and those accusations are portrayed as having been motivated only by self-interest. The quarrel itself is presented as ridiculous, as a series of self-important local offi-cials strive to assert their right to manage the situation—and one measure of that ridiculousness is the villagers' reliance on flinging insults based on purity of blood (or rather lack thereof).

In the English translation, this issue simply disappears. Mabbe's version reads: "On both sides, they digg'd up their Grandfather's graves, twitting one another in the teeth with their fathers and their mothers, not sparing one another's wives, ripping up their faults, and the course of life that they led; wherein perhaps they did not lie" (vol. 1, 142). The translation transforms the bone of contention from the religious practices or *devociones* of long-buried grandparents to the much more vague "faults, and course of life that they led," a phrase that does not evoke religion at all. Similarly, directly prior to this incident, Guzmán discusses his lower-class traveling companion's inabil-ity to differentiate between mule meat and veal: "la gente rústica, grosera, no tocando a su bondad y limpieza, en materia de gusto pocas veces dis-tingue lo malo de lo bueno." [Crude, rustic folk, leaving aside their goodness and purity, can rarely distinguish between good and bad in matters of taste]

(191). Alemán's passage informs us that an untainted pedigree does not, in fact, guarantee refinement. Mabbe, by contrast, translates this as: "your rude, rustical clowns, (as a thing not belonging to their either goodness or cleanlinesse) in matters of taste can seldom distinguish ill from good" (vol. 1, 129). Mabbe translates *limpieza* literally as "cleanliness" rather than as a reference to *limpieza de sangre*.[25] While the Spanish text criticizes purity of blood as a vehicle whereby uncouth peasants may lay claim to honor, in the English translation no trace of this critique remains.

Other covert references to purity of blood, while translated more or less faithfully, lose their currency when placed in an English context. In the Spanish *Guzmán*, references to animal breeding and hybridity point to Guzmán's father's dubious origins in the book's first chapter. Guzmán's description of his father begins with an anecdote about paintings of purebred horses and ends with a description of the monster of Ravenna, a hermaphrodite human-animal hybrid. As Ryan Giles has argued, these glancing references align with early modern anti-converso rhetoric, thus covertly alluding to Guzmán's father's impure heritage and amplifying the narrator's penchant for "at times engaging in, obfuscating or obliquely warning against an 'inquisitorial' reading of his origins."[26] Mabbe translates the descriptions of the portraits of the horse and of the monster in a straightforward fashion, without providing explanatory notes. However, to an English reader not steeped in Spain's vexed and often encoded discussions of pure blood, it is unlikely that these allusions would register as an ambivalent engagement with Guzmán's converso identity; indeed, as the changes in the translation I discuss above suggest, Mabbe himself often seems to have been unaware of such subtexts.

As the examples cited above demonstrate, *Guzmán de Alfarache* does indeed reflect the prominence of discourses of purity of blood in early modern Spain. It often does so, however, in the form of a critique: *limpieza* appears in the Spanish text when either boorish peasants or the demonstrably "impure" pícaro Guzmán trumpet their origins to assert their authority—a move that Alemán inevitably holds up for ridicule. Thus the Spanish text demonstrates the complicated relationship between notions of purity of blood and emergent concepts of race in early modern Spain. Far from a totalizing protoracist discourse that enshrines inconvertible difference, discourses of purity of blood in early modern Spanish culture were a site of contestation, negotiation, and even parody. In the English translation, by contrast, such parodic engagements with purity of blood are lost in translation.

Mabbe's Maurophilia

While Mabbe's translation often elides the Spanish *Guzmán*'s critiques of purity of blood, it emphasizes another aspect of Spain's religious difference: its Moorish past and the traces of Al-Andalus that remain. This representation of Spain as a site of exotic Moorish difference is an example of the "Maurophilia" that Fuchs has described in *Exotic Nation*. Fuchs focuses on constructions of Spain's own problematic relationship with the legacy of Al-Andalus as well as on how other nations—particularly England—also racialize Spain by constructing it as a site of Moorish difference. Her study establishes the centrality of practices inherited from Al-Andalus to early modern Spanish culture as well as charting the complexity of representations of Moorishness both within and outside of early modern Spain: Moorishness is alternately demonized and romanticized, demanding a complex series of negotiations.[27] Fuchs does discuss the Spanish *Guzmán de Alfarache* in *Exotic Nation*; she does not, however, address Mabbe's translation, although it serves as a striking example of both English Maurophilia and of how Spain's more complex negotiations with Moorishness may be lost in translation.

Mabbe's investment in representing Spain as a site of exotic Moorishness appears most clearly in the interpolated "Moorish tale," or *novella morisca*, "Ozmín y Daraja." The novella recounts the amorous adventures of a noble Moorish knight, Ozmín, and his lady-love, Daraja. Daraja lives among the Christians in Spain as a prisoner of war; her fiancé, Ozmín, sneaks into Spain to find her. After overcoming numerous obstacles, the couple is united at last, at which point they convert to Christianity and remain in Spain—as do, the novella specifies, all of their descendants for many generations.

At the beginning of the novella, Ozmín is able to rejoin Daraja in Spain by posing as a gardener in the Christian household where she lives as an honored prisoner of war. When they first see each other, both lovers are so overwhelmed that they are bereft of all words. Ozmín communicates instead by crying, "watering the ground" with his tears. In the Spanish version Daraja "correspondió por la misma orden, vertiendo hilos de perlas por su rostro [replied in kind, casting strings of pearls down her cheeks] (I, 223). Mabbe's translation expands on this image, as Daraja "answered [Ozmín] in his owne language, distilling ropes of pearls in round orientall drops downe her lovely cheekes" (I, 176). Mabbe makes two small but significant changes to this passage. The most noticeable is that Daraja's tears become "orientall drops," further emphasizing her presumably Eastern charms. Less overt but still significant is the fact that Daraja here answers Ozmín "in his owne language" rather than "in the same way" or "in kind" [de la misma manera]. Gesturing to language here highlights the lovers' shared cultural background, as the Spanish passage does not.

Mabbe's use of the term "orientall drops" is lifted from a later passage within this novella. Ozmín, still in disguise as a gardener, befriends a Christian knight. The knight, sure that Ozmín is noble (though unaware that he is a Moor), informs Ozmín that he knows the latter's secret: "entiendo que abajo de aquestos terrones y conchas feas está el oro finísimo y perlas orientales." [I know that beneath those clods of earth and ugly shell is the finest of gold and Oriental pearls] (I, 243). The Christian knight goes on to swear by his faith in Christ and his knightly order that he will be Ozmín's true friend and keep his secret. As Fuchs has argued of the Spanish text, while the knight "ostensibly questions only the gardener's class identity, his language betrays a soupçon of maurophilia." Ozmín goes on to "confess the truth" to his new friend, in fact spinning an elaborate tale in which he passes himself off as a Christian nobleman who was raised by Moors. In so doing, Ozmín adds to the way the novella, in Fuchs's words, "complicates the distinctiveness of Christian and Moorish identities, emphasizing their shared culture and experience."[28]

Thus when Alemán uses the term "Oriental pearls," he does so with a certain ironic distance. A knight who swears by his allegiance to a military order (the same sort of order that excludes those of impure Jewish and Moorish blood) promises friendship to a man who may, he implies, be Moorish; Ozmín's potential Moorishness, however, does not deter the Christian knight from seeking his friendship, and he has no trouble believing that Ozmín may be of Christian blood. When Mabbe first uses the term, however, it instead emphasizes the similarity between Ozmín and Daraja, who speak the same language (that of tears as "orientall drops"), and their shared difference from Christians.

Another, more subtle Orientalizing practice runs throughout Mabbe's text. When Mabbe encounters Spanish words of Arabic origin in the Spanish novel he often fails to translate them; instead, he leaves them in Spanish and explains them in the footnotes, noting their Arabic origin. He refers to "an *Açumbre* more of wine," attaching a footnote that explains "*Açumbre* is a jar or pitcher . . . It is an Arabicke word" (vol. 1, 253), rather than simply translating the word as "pitcher." Similarly, when he names a suburb of Córdoba he describes "the suburbs, which they call the *Axarquia*," and then adds a footnote which states, "*Axarquia*, the suburbs adjoyning to Cordova. Padre Guadix says, it is so called, because it stands toward the east which is termed in the Arabick tongue, *Xarquia*" (vol. 2, 101). In the Spanish source text these words simply name objects and places; they are not marked in any way as being representative of the legacy of Al-Andalus. Their etymology may reflect that legacy, but there is no indication that they are meant to gesture toward Spain as a particularly Moorish place. In the English version these words take on an Orientalizing valence: Mabbe's decision to retain these Spanish words with Arabic roots in the English text, and to note those roots in the margins, serves as a persistent reminder of Spain's Moorish difference.[29]

Further, moments in the Spanish text that refer more generally to the distinction between Old Christians (Spaniards untainted by Jewish or Moorish blood) and New Christians (descendants of converted Jews and Moors) are at times reframed exclusively in the context of Moorishness. When Guzmán travels to Genoa in search of his father's relations, he tries to pass himself off as an Old Christian, a descendant of pure-blooded Goths. In Alemán's text he is called a "marrano" by skeptical Italians. An English audience might have been familiar with this word from John Florio's 1611 dictionary, *Queen Anne's New World of Words*, which defines *marrano* as "a nickname for Spaniards, that is, one descended of Jewes or Infidels and whose parents were never Christened, but for to save their goods will say they are Christians."[30] Interestingly, Mabbe translates the Spanish phrase *bellaco, marrano* (rogue, *marrano*) as "Villaine, Rogue, Moore, and the like" (vol. 1, 132). He then adds a footnote in which he cites the Spanish dictionary, Covarrubias's *Tesoro de la lengua castellana*, which reads: "The Spanish word is *marrano*, i.e. *Porcus unius anni. Et Judeus recenter conversus ad Christianismum, cum Hispanis, vocatur Marrano*" [*marrano*, i.e., a one-year-old pig. And a Jew recently converted to Christianity, when he is Spanish, is called a *marrano*]. Indeed, Covarrubias's definition focuses almost entirely on converts from Judaism.[31] Despite this definition, Mabbe chooses to focus on Spain's Moorish difference in the body of the text, and does not translate Covarrubias' Latin definition in the footnote. The presence of the footnote informs us that Mabbe has not simply defaulted to the term *Moor* but actively chosen it over *Jew*. *Marrano* is a multivalent term; in Spanish, it is a derogatory term applied primarily to those of Jewish—but also those of Muslim—descent; in English, as Florio's dictionary informs us, it can function as a "nickname for Spaniards" because they are tainted by Jewish and "infidel" blood. By defining *marrano* as "Moor" in the body of the text, Mabbe recasts a broader reference to religious difference and impure descent exclusively in the context of Spain's Moorish past.[32]

This is not to say that Moorishness—and even an Orientalizing Maurophilia—is not present in the Spanish novel as well as the English one. The Moorish theme of "Ozmín y Daraja" is of course very present in the Spanish source text as well as the English translation, and the Moorish protagonists' interchangeability with Christians remains true across both texts. Nonetheless, the valence of that similarity shifts as the novel moves from Spain to England. The Spanish text engages with the relationship between "noble blood" and "pure blood" in multiple registers; in the context of early modern Spain, these issues speak to the assimilation (or, conversely, exclusion) of conversos and Moriscos. In the English text, by contrast, the interchangeability of Moors and Spaniards does not suggest that nobles of all religious backgrounds are alike, but rather that Spaniards, specifically, are interchangeable with Moors. When the Spanish *Guzmán* was published, the expulsion of Spain's Moriscos—which eventually came to pass—was already a subject of debate. By allowing Ozmín and Daraja to convert to Christianity and remain (along with their descendants, the text specifies) in Spain, the text may be making a tacit argument for the continued presence of Moriscos in a more inclusive Spain.[33] In *The Rogue*, by contrast, the interpolated Moorish novella can be read, like the Arabic words set apart by footnotes, as a sign of Spain's Moorish difference.

I may appear to propose an overly simple opposition, in which the Spanish text critiques or ironizes purity of blood and the English translation elides such critiques and reifies exotic Moorish difference. The reality, of course, is far more complex. After all, Alemán's *Guzmán* itself romanticizes Spain's Moorish past, most notably in the interpolated "novella morisca" "Ozmín y Daraja," and the novel's covert critiques of purity of blood are hardly a rousing call for egalitarianism; in many cases, they serve to mock the pretenses of boorish peasants. Nonetheless, it is important to recognize two key changes in the translation. The first is that parodic representations of purity of blood, which are a recurrent theme in the Spanish text, by and large do not appear in Mabbe's *Rogue*. The second is that Moorishness and Spanishness are conflated throughout the body of Mabbe's text as they are not in Alemán's, with footnotes that repeatedly emphasize the legacy of Al-Andalus. Thus, while *Guzmán de Alfarache* represents Moorishness as a one part of Spain's history and identity, in *The Rogue*, Spain *becomes* Moorish.

"La fuerza de la sangre" and *The Spanish Gypsy*

The Spanish Gypsy is a very different sort of adaptation than *The Rogue*. It was most likely first performed in the summer of 1623, when Prince Charles had not yet returned from Spain and the outcome of the Spanish match was uncertain; it was performed again at Whitehall in November of that year, when the match had not completely dissolved but was looking increasingly unlikely.[34] It takes its plot from two of Cervantes's *Novelas ejemplares*, "La gitanilla" (The little Gypsy girl) and "La fuerza de la sangre" (The power of blood). While in a few instances the play adheres quite closely to the Spanish original, for the most part it incorporates only elements of Cervantes's storylines, linking the two stories (which are unconnected in Cervantes) and adding several subplots that are nowhere to be found in the *Novelas ejemplares*. The change in genre, from short story to play, requires more substantive shifts in plot and language than a translation from one language to another. Moreover, *The Spanish Gypsy* was not presented as an adaptation or a translation; Cervantes is not mentioned in the play or in its prefatory material. Instead, it is one of many English plays that draw on Spanish source materials for their plots without explicitly acknowledging those materials.[35] There is nothing particularly deliberate or anti-Spanish about such lack of recognition, which was common practice at the time. For example, early printed texts of *Othello* do not make reference to Cinthio's *Gli Hecatommithi*. Mabbe's *Rogue*, for all of the discussion in the commendatory poems prefacing it of its status as an improvement over the original, was understood by both its author and its readers to be a translation with the goal—at least in part—of rendering its source text accurately to speakers of another language.[36] The writers of *The Spanish Gypsy* would have had no such goal in mind. Rather, in drawing on Cervantes's novellas they were simply engaging in the customary practice of looking for tales that could be transformed into successful theatrical productions. While anyone who had read the *Novelas ejemplares* would have recognized the play's debt to them, a viewer who had not encountered them would have had no way of knowing that the play draws on Spanish texts, as well as being set in Spain. Thus, analyzing the relationship between an adaptation of this sort and its source calls for a different methodology than one might use with a (more or less) faithful translation. Rather than focusing on shifts in language and emphasis from the Spanish to the English text, I interrogate the decision to incorporate certain plot elements of the source materials and discuss to what ends this play represents Spain on the English stage.

The Spanish Gypsy was first published in 1653 (although it was performed much earlier, in 1623) with a title page listing Thomas Middleton and William Rowley as its authors; however, critical consensus thus far has been that it is a far more collaborative production. Most recently, Gary Taylor has established not only Middleton and Rowley, but also Thomas Dekker, and John Ford as the most likely group of authors. (John Fletcher has also frequently been associated with the play.) If nothing else, it is clear that one or more of the authors worked from the Spanish original. No translation of the *Novelas ejemplares* had yet appeared in English, though a French translation was available. Nonetheless, the authors seem to have worked directly from the Spanish text; the play repeatedly refers to the eponymous Gypsy girl's small size, presumably a reference to the Spanish title "la gitanilla," a diminutive of *gitana*, or Gypsy. The French translation, entitled *La belle egyptienne*, or "The beautiful Gypsy girl," makes no reference to her small stature.[37] Thus, we can compare the English text with the Spanish without assuming that its primary source was the French intermediary.

The play's intricate plot—consisting of multiple intertwined stories—demands some explanation. The play opens on a rich Spanish nobleman, Don Roderigo, who has gone "mad" with lust for a beautiful girl he sees walking with her parents. Despite his friends' disapproval, they help Roderigo to abduct the girl, Clara, whom he rapes and then returns to the street where he found her. Overcome with guilt following his deed, Roderigo deals with this—rather inexplicably—by telling his father that he is going to study in Salamanca, but really disguising himself as an Italian and joining a local band of Gypsies (in part in the hope of continuing to be close to his victim, Clara, while remaining unknown to her). Clara returns to her home and her life; her parents console her and encourage her to marry her longtime suitor, Luis. She turns him down without naming a specific reason for doing so.

In the meantime, another young Spanish nobleman, Juan, has fallen in love with the beautiful young Gypsy girl Preciosa. He asks her to marry him, and she agrees to do so only if he will become a Gypsy for two years; he promises to do so and is sworn into the Gypsy band. The troupe, as "Spanish gypsies, noble gypsies!," repeatedly assert that they are neither thieves nor scoundrels; rather, they are entertainers. Juan is not the only nobleman to join their ranks: Roderigo, in his Italian disguise, joins the same troupe of Gypsy entertainers, offering to be their playwright; and a stock comic figure, the rich young wastrel Sancho, joins them along with his servant, Soto. The troupe performs in front of Madrid's high nobility, including Roderigo's father, Don Fernando, the *corregidor* of Madrid, and Clara's parents. Don Fernando immediately recognizes his son through his disguise but decides to leave him be. Within that very scene, a messenger arrives to tell Clara's parents that their daughter has fainted and been carried to a nearby house for safety; by chance, the house belongs to Don Fernando, Roderigo's father. Clara immediately recognizes the bedroom to which she has been conveyed as the scene of her rape. She tells her story to Roderigo's father, showing as evidence a crucifix that she took from his room when she was first abducted there. Roderigo's father, appalled, begs her forgiveness and fears that his family's honor has been "stained" forever. Clara hints that he could salvage both her ruined honor and his by arranging a marriage between Roderigo and herself.

Don Fernando decides to orchestrate this marriage by inviting the Gypsy troupe (including Roderigo in disguise, of course) to perform at his house. He asks them to stage an elaborate play and demands that Roderigo play the lead part: that of a young wastrel who abuses his father's generosity. The play shows the son (played by Roderigo) as matched in marriage to a rich but old and ugly woman. The son mocks the portrait, declaring he would never wish to marry someone so ugly. At this point, Roderigo's father reveals that he knows Roderigo's true identity, and insists that he must in fact marry the ugly woman in the portrait. Roderigo asks that that he be allowed to marry instead a beautiful woman he saw in the audience; fortuitously, the woman is Clara. The two marry immediately, but once the ceremony ends Don Fernando tells his son that his new wife is "wanton." Further, Don Fernando insists, Roderigo must have committed a terrible crime to merit such punishment. Roderigo confesses to the rape, Don Fernando reveals that Clara is not in fact wanton but rather the woman he wronged, and Roderigo rejoices in his good fortune, vowing to "redeem [his] fault" (5.1.57).[38]

As the nobles are reconciled, problems arise for the play's other couple: Juan and Preciosa. Juan is imprisoned because he has injured a nobleman who falsely accused him of stealing. (Since no one knows Juan is not noble, the attack is a grave assault to the status quo.) It turns out that the attack was motivated by a Spanish noblewoman, Juana Cardocha, who herself wishes to marry Juan (though she does not know that he is a nobleman rather than a Gypsy). Juana Cardocha claims that Juan has stolen a jewel (which she in fact gave him), and he is sentenced to death both for the presumed theft and for injuring a nobleman. All the Gypsies are locked up on general suspicion. At this point, an old Gypsy woman intervenes and informs Don Fernando that she herself is his sister, long believed to have been lost at sea, and that the king of the Gypsies is really a Spanish nobleman, who was exiled for dueling many years ago. Further, Preciosa is not, in fact, a Gypsy, but Don Fernando's long-lost daughter, Costanza. Preciosa—now Costanza—petitions her father to free her lover, Juan. His true identity is revealed, along with the fact that the accusations against him are false. The two former Gypsies—now Spanish nobles—are officially promised to each other with their families' blessings, and the play ends on a note of celebration.

As discussed above, the play draws loosely on Cervantes's novellas. The story of the rape that ends in marriage comes from "La fuerza de la sangre," and the story of the beautiful Gypsy girl and noble lover comes from "La gitanilla." Nonetheless, the play deviates significantly from the stories; combining the two novellas by making the father of the Gypsy girl also the father of the rapist is the English playwrights' innovation.

The play adheres most closely to the first of its source texts, "La fuerza de la sangre," in its opening scenes. Both novella and play begin with a random act of sexual violence: the male protagonist, Roderigo (Rodolfo in Cervantes), sees a beautiful young girl, is overcome by lust, and immediately enlists his friends to abduct her.[39] In both texts, he rapes the girl, Clara (Leocadia in the Spanish), while she is unconscious and then makes a second attempt when she regains consciousness, which she successfully fends off. He leaves her alone in his room for a few minutes, at which time Clara/Leocadia opens the curtains, sees by moonlight the décor of the room as well as the garden outside, and pockets a jeweled crucifix as evidence that she has been inside the room. In all of these details, the play almost exactly echoes the novella. Even Clara's lines closely resemble Leocadia's speeches in the story:

> (Leocadia:) si es que tu alma admite género de ruego alguno, te ruego que ya que has triunfado de mi fama triunfes también de mi vida! Quitemela al momento, que no es bien que la tenga la que no tiene honra! Mira que el rigor de la crueldad que has usado conmigo en ofenderme se templará con la piedad que usarás en matarme, y asi, en un mismo punto, vendrás a ser cruel y piadoso! (79)[40]

> [If your soul will admit any sort of plea, I beg of you, now that you've triumphed over my reputation, triumph over my life, too! Take my life now; I shouldn't have it since I no longer have honor! For the cruelty you have used in defiling me will be tempered by the pity you

show in killing me, and so, in a single moment, you will prove cruel
and compassionate!]

Similarly, Clara declaims:

Be then a gentle ravisher, an honourable villain; as you have
Disrobed my youth of nature's goodliest portion,
My virgin purity, so with your sword,
Let out that blood which is infected now
By your soul-staining lust! (1.3.7–12)

The play picks up on the central conceit of Cervantes's passage: the notion
that Rodolfo/Roderigo can become a "gentle ravisher" or "cruel y piadoso" by
murdering the girl whose honor he has robbed. In both, Clara/Leocadia presents death as the best possible outcome, given that her honor has been lost,
and argues that murder in this case would be an act of mercy on Rodolfo/
Roderigo's part. In this scene, at least, the playwrights more or less transpose
the story to the stage, following its logic and order of events.

Even as the play follows the source text closely, however, we can trace several noteworthy differences. Most striking—as several critics have noted—is
the difference between the characterization of Rodolfo in the Spanish and
Roderigo in the English.[41] In Cervantes's story, Rodolfo appears as a remorseless cad; he does not speak to Leocadia throughout the abduction, fearing
that she will later be able to recognize his voice. When he attempts to rape
Leocadia a second time, she must resist him with all of her power: "con mas
fuerzas de las que su tierna edad prometían, se defendió con los pies, con las
manos, con los dientes y con la lengua" [with more strength than her tender
age promised, she defended herself with her feet, her hands, her teeth and her
speech] (81). It is only when Rodolfo becomes unaroused and tired ("frio y
cansado") in his attempts to wear her down that he ceases his onslaught and
goes to find his friends. He ultimately decides not to inform his friends of the
rape, not out of remorse but for fear they could incriminate him should he
ever be caught. A short time later, Rodolfo embarks on a long-planned trip
to Europe, "con tan poco memoria de lo que con Leocadia le había sucedido
como si nunca hubiera pasado" [with so little memory of what had happened
with Leocadia that it was as if it had never occurred] (83).

The Spanish Gypsy's Roderigo, in a complete about-face from the source,
is immediately filled with remorse for his crime.[42] Like Rodolfo (perhaps in

imitation of the novella) he initially remains silent as Clara asks that he kill her, but his silence arises not from fear of discovery but from shame.[43] Further, once he breaks his silence he offers Clara a heartfelt apology and assures her that, had he not violated her, he would have offered her marriage. Clara, too, brings up marriage several times, in a deviation from the source text. She first asks him to marry her; when he fails to respond, she asks, if he marries someone else, that he treat his wife with "constant love" to "redeem" the harm he has done to her (1.3.96–97). And while Roderigo attempts to have sex with Clara a second time, when she refuses to let him "enjoy" her "with free allowance" he immediately desists, averring "I mean no second force" (1.3.70–71, 73). Thus Roderigo, while still a villain, is not portrayed as unrelentingly callous, as Rodolfo is.[44]

The scene also differs from its source text in another critical aspect. While notions of purity of blood (and, conversely, its infection) are often associated with Spain, they appear in the English play and not in its Spanish source. When Clara asks Roderigo to kill her, she urges him to, "with your sword / Let out that blood which is infected now / By your soul-staining lust" (1.3.10–11). A few lines later, when Roderigo asks her name, she refuses, employing similar imagery: "I have washed off the leprosy that cleaves / To my just shame in true and honest tears. I must not leave a mention of my wrongs / The stain of my unspotted birth, to memory" (1.3.62–65). The scene is full of references to stained and infected blood, reminiscent of the polemics in support of pure blood statutes cited in the previous chapter. Here, however, Clara's blood is infected and her soul stained not by an impure lineage but by sexual violation.

In another divergence from the Spanish source, rape as a stain on the blood reappears later in the play. When Clara informs Roderigo's father of the rape, she does so by presenting him with an account of her suffering that she has written in her own blood, telling him, "sins are heard farthest when they cry in blood" (3.3.75). Fernando's response is to beg her pity for his "till-now untainted blood and honor" (3.3.87). Here, blood does not seem connected to inheritable qualities. One act—Roderigo's violation of Clara—stains or infects both her blood and his father's. Discourses of blood remain present in the play, but they are displaced onto a specific act—significantly, an act that can be righted. The marriage Fernando orchestrates between Clara and Roderigo is described as a "balm / To heal a wounded name," and Fernando offers to be Clara's "physician" (3.3.97–98, 100).

Such imagery of rape as a stain on blood and bloodlines is conventional in early modern English literature and thus need not necessarily be associated with Spanish notions of impure blood.[45] Nonetheless, given the play's consistent emphasis on its Spanish setting, the stain on blood produced by rape here resonates interestingly with notions of Spaniards as miscegenated, bearing both Jewish and Moorish blood. As many critics have discussed, early modern anti-Spanish propaganda consistently represents Spaniards as "a mongrell generation" and "the sinke, the puddle, and filthie heape of the most lothsome, infected and slavish people that ever yet lived on earth."[46] And while rape as a stain on blood is not equivalent to miscegenation, the two are intimately connected: in both cases, sexual congress is a threat to bloodlines. Crucially, though, in *The Spanish Gypsy*—unlike its source—Clara's rape does not lead to pregnancy. Instead, the "stain" on "blood and honor" works backward: the father's "till now untainted blood and honor" is sullied by his son's violent act, rather than future generations bearing a stain because they are the product of an illicit union. The stain on Roderigo's lineage is not represented as tainting his descendants, as is the case with the impure blood of Spaniards, derived from their presumed Moorish and Jewish ancestors. Thus, the play draws on a rhetoric of tainted blood, perhaps alluding to presumed Spanish obsessions with purity of blood and honor, but shifts its context, focusing instead on an act for which the misbehaving Roderigo can successfully atone.

Cervantes's Leocadia describes the rape in very different terms than does Clara. Unlike Clara, she does not ask Rodolfo to marry her, nor does she urge him to treat his future wife well. Instead, she asks that he kill her and then demands that he tell no one what has transpired. Clara asks this of Roderigo as well, but is less explicitly preoccupied with rumor and hearsay:

> yo te perdono la ofensa que me has hecho con sólo que me prometas y jures que, como la has cubierto en esta oscuridad, la cubrirás con perpetuo silencio sin decirla a nadie . . . Entre mí y el cielo pasarán mis quejas, sin querer que las oiga el mundo, el cual no juzga por los sucesos las cosas, sino conforme a él se la asienta en la estimación.

> [I will forgive your offense against me, if you will only promise and swear that, as you have hidden it (i.e., the offense) in darkness, you will continue to hide it in perpetual silence, not telling anyone . . . I will share my complaints with heaven, not wanting the world to hear, which judges events not by what really happened but rather by the consensus of public opinion.] (80)

Leocadia implies that rape is not her fault but that it will be perceived as such in the eyes of the world. When she returns to her parents and tells them what has transpired, her father is even more explicit:

> Y advierte, hija, que más lástima una onza de deshonra pública que una arroba de infamia secreta. Y pues puedes vivir honrada con Dios en público, no te pene de estar deshonrada contigo en secreto: la verdadera deshonra está en el pecado y la verdadera honra en la virtud. Con el dicho, con el deseo y con la obra se ofende a Dios; y pues tú, ni en dicho, ni en pensamiento, ni en hecho le has ofendido, tente por honrada, que yo por tal tendré . . .

> [Now listen, my daughter: an ounce of public dishonor causes more shame than a pound of secret infamy. And since you can live honorably in the eyes of God in public, don't let it pain you that you are secretly dishonored: true dishonor is in sin and true honor, in virtue. God can be offended by speech, desires and works; and since you have offended Him in neither thought nor deed, consider yourself honorable, as I consider you to be. . .] (84)

Despite Leocadia's initial declaration that she herself ought to die along with her ruined honor, her parents emphatically assert that she is free from sin, while acknowledging that public opinion would not be so kind. At no point does the family believe that Leocadia has committed a fault or that she has stained their honor; nonetheless, they all acknowledge the importance of keeping silent about the rape. In shifting their focus to public opinion, Leocadia's parents echo the logic of the polemics against pure blood discussed in the previous chapter. Leocadia's rape is represented as a potential source of public infamy but not a true dishonor, much as the anti-statute polemics assert that a Jewish or Muslim ancestor may harm one's reputation but does not actually indicate anything about a subject's individual worth. *The Spanish Gypsy* treats this situation quite differently. Clara's parents seek to console her, but they do not proclaim her innocence as Leocadia's parents do. Instead, they tell her that sadness is a pointless "vanity" and that they will do all they can to find the "monster" that "robbed [her] of the jewel held so precious" (2.2.19). The English play lacks the Spanish story's critique of the power of public opinion, its emphasis on honor as a public performance, and its subtle ironization of the relationship between descent and character.

Many critics have argued that early modern Spanish literature's preoccupation with the damaging effects of public opinion must be read, at least in part, as a response to Spain's pure blood statutes.[47] Rape, like impure descent, appears in the story—which is called, after all, "the power of blood"—as a source of public dishonor for which the victim is blameless. The story emphasizes Leocadia's innocence as well as the importance of keeping her violation—and the real origins of her child—a secret. Thus, while it does not overtly satirize the notion of purity of blood, as Cervantes does elsewhere (most notably in *El retablo de las maravillas*, discussed in the previous chapter), Leocadia's father's emphasis on true sin and virtue as distinct from a public stain on honor can also be read as a covert critique of discourses of purity of blood.

The other concrete issue that rises to the fore in Cervantes's text, but not in the play, is that of wealth. Leocadia's family is noble but poor, while Rodolfo's is quite rich. And Leocadia's poverty, as the story affirms on multiple occasions, renders her more vulnerable to assault and less able to seek revenge or restitution. Leocadia describes her relatives to Rodolfo: "a ser tan ricos como nobles, no fueran en mi tan desdichados" [if they were as rich as they are noble, they would not be as unfortunate in me (i.e., my fate)] (80). Clara, by contrast, comes from a wealthy family and is Roderigo's social equal; she has been courted by his best friend and indeed would have been a suitable match for Roderigo himself in marriage had he not "defiled" her first. Cervantes's text works to emphasize Rodolfo's casual cruelty: he is young, noble, wealthy, perfectly willing to exploit those less fortunate than he and completely remorseless. Further, the story emphasizes the social structures that grant Rodolfo license: his nobility and his wealth enable him to act with impunity. Leocadia's family, though noble, has no recourse to avenge their daughter's rape because they are poor. Thus, the rape in Cervantes's text can be read in part as a social critique: because of both his money and his noble blood (*sangre ilustre*), Rodolfo can indulge in casual cruelty.

Initially, nonetheless, the overall storyline of "La fuerza de la sangre" seems to validate the notion that nobility of blood is an essential characteristic transferred from parent to child. After Rodolfo goes to Italy, Leocadia bears his illegitimate son. The family passes him off as a nephew from the country. The boy is beloved by everyone he meets, in part because he shows signs of having been fathered by a nobleman ("daba señales de ser de algún noble padre engendrado" [85]). Leocadia is reunited with Rodolfo after her son is kicked by a horse in the street. The injury prompts his paternal grandfather—who is unaware of the boy's identity—to save him, because the boy's spilled blood mysteriously calls out to him. He brings the boy home, finds out who his family is, and summons them; when Leocadia recognizes the house, she tells Rodolfo's parents her story and shows them the crucifix she took from the chamber where she was raped. They believe her and engineer a marriage between her and Rodolfo. The last line of the story informs the reader that the happy ending is due to the power of blood: "permitido todo por el cielo y por *la fuerza de la sangre*, que vio derramada en el suelo el valeroso, ilustre y cristiano abuelo de Luisico." [And all this happened by the power of heaven and by the power of blood, which Luisico's valiant, illustrious and Christian grandfather saw spilled on the ground] (95). Strikingly, blood literally calls to blood here—it is the sight of it spilled on the ground that arouses a feeling of familial protectiveness in Luisico's grandfather, who is, significantly, described explicitly as Christian.

Nonetheless, a critique of such a valorization of blood is embedded in the story. The reader's initial introduction to the villain Rodolfo is: "Hasta veintidós años tendría un caballero de aquello ciudad a quien la riqueza, la sangre ilustre, la inclinación torcida y las compañias libres, le hacían hacer cosas y tener atrevemientos que desdecían de su calidad." [He was about twenty-two years old, a knight from the city whose wealth, noble blood, twisted inclination, and libertine companions had led him to do things and attempt audacities that seemed to deny his noble rank] (77). Here, "sangre ilustre," or noble blood, is one of the things that lead Rodolfo astray—presumably because of the license it allows him. Overall, Rodolfo is the weak link in any argument the story makes for blood's power to transmit essential nobility. Even when Rodolfo and Leocadia are reunited at the end, he expresses no remorse for having violated her; instead, we are told, he can barely wait until the evening is over to get her into bed with him again. Rodolfo's unbridled sensuality plays on another possible reading of "the power of blood:" blood as a synonym for the lust that drives his actions.[48] And while the boy Luisico shows every sign of having inherited nobility, he also, the reader is repeatedly informed, looks exactly like his father, whose behavior is far from noble. Thus, it is difficult to read "La fuerza de la sangre"—and especially the effusiveness of its ending— as an unequivocal endorsement of the power and durability of noble blood.[49]

It seems odd that Cervantes's chilling story of rape and redemption would serve as the central plot for a festive comedy. And whether we read Cervantes's story as symbolic of Catholic forgiveness and redemption or a biting satire on the value of "blood," the play does not use the rape plot to the same purpose as the novella.[50] Indeed, the moment in which blood exerts its power in the original—when Luisico's spilled blood calls out to his grandfather—does not appear in the play at all, since Clara does not conceive a child from her rape. As we have seen, *The Spanish Gypsy*, like "La fuerza de la sangre," repeatedly refers to blood. However, instead of the ironic representation of theories of inherent blood difference we find in the story, the play highlights rape as an act that stains the blood of the perpetrator's family as well as the victim's. And, crucially for *The Spanish Gypsy*'s representation of Spain, that "stain" turns out to be reversible. Why, then, choose the story of rape as the central plot for the play?

One answer to that question lies in the play-within-a-play that concludes the English text. The troupe of Gypsies—which the rapist Roderigo has joined, pretending to be Italian—goes to his father's house to perform. Roderigo's father, Fernando, sees through his son's disguise immediately, but feigns ignorance, and decides to use the device of a play to censure his son. He calls on the Gypsies to perform this play, which he has scripted, and demands that Roderigo play the role of the son, Lorenzo. Lorenzo, like Roderigo, has fled from home and disregarded his father's wishes. However, while Roderigo fled in shame after raping Clara, his double in the play-within-the-play is guilty of a different set of vices. Above all, Lorenzo is a wastrel, spending his family's inheritance on drinking and wenching. His first lines are:

> Old Don, whom I call father: am I thy son?
> If I be, flesh me with gold, fat me with silver!
> Had I Spain in this hand, and Portugal in this,
> Puff it should fly.—Where's the money I sent for? (4.3.55–58)

When his father refuses to give him more money, Lorenzo asks to be given a ship to go to sea. His father refuses, afraid that he will be "hanged for piracy" (4.3.76–77). Lorenzo then asks his father to buy him an office "in the West Indies" or to allow him to go to the wars. Fernando replaces Roderigo's real transgression (rape) with a rapaciousness and prodigality that echoes anti-Spanish propaganda. "Lorenzo" is avaricious, quarrelsome, and irresponsible, focused on accumulating (and spending) liquid capital (i.e., gold) rather than tending to his land; he even hyperbolically promises that he would trade all of Spain and Portugal for more wealth.

These purportedly typical Spanish vices stand in for the rape of Clara in the play-within-the-play. In doing so, they allow a new interpretation of her violation. The rape becomes, in this context, another manifestation of intemperate prodigality, a pursuit of immediate pleasure at the expense of sustainability. After all, the play repeatedly emphasizes the fact that, had she not been violated, Clara would have been an appropriate wife for Roderigo. He tells her so himself just after the rape, as we have seen, and repeats the wish that he had married her (at his father's urging) at the play's end. While in Cervantes's story Leocadia's poverty makes her an unlikely match for Rodolfo, Clara is in all ways suitable for Roderigo. The play-within-the-play aligns the waste of wealth with the waste of her virginity, suggesting that the younger generation of Spaniards—Roderigo chief among them—are guilty of an intemperate failure to sensibly cultivate both wealth and relationships: rape instead of marriage, waste instead of husbandry (in all senses of the word).

This preoccupation with land (and, conversely, the sale of land in exchange for gold) runs throughout the play. Curiously, the characters most invested in land and the husbandry of it are the Gypsies. This troupe of Gypsies makes its money not by stealing but by saving. As the father of the Gypsies enjoins, "refuse not a maravedi, a blank. Feather by feather birds build nests; grain pecked up after grain makes pullen fat . . . all bees, no drones, and our hive shall yield us honey" (2.1.49–50, 68–69). He uses a similarly bucolic message when infatuated noblemen rain money on Preciosa: "So, harvest will come in! Such sunshine days / Will bring in golden sheaves, our markets raise" (2.2.130–31). And when he describes the Gypsy trade to Roderigo, the Gypsy father connects it to the productive husbandry of land most concretely of all: "Our sports / Must be an orchard, bearing several trees / And fruits of several taste" (3.1.98–100). Finally, when Juan joins the band of Gypsies, he is asked to vow on the land: "Thy best hand lay on this turf of grass. / There thy heart lies" (4.1.34–35).

It seems paradoxical to link Gypsies—traditionally landless—with land, but of course these "Gypsies" are not really Gypsies at all but rather Spanish noblemen in disguise. Thus, they represent a version of Spanish identity that is—again, paradoxically—simultaneously more locally and less imperially oriented and less marked as conventionally (or essentially) Spanish. They—along with Fernando and Clara's parents—represent an idealized nobility, invested in careful cultivation and good governance rather than imperial ambition and the expenditure of both ancestral and newly plundered wealth.

The foibles and vices of the play's younger generation of nobles highlight the virtues of this older group. The most striking example of this is the comic character Sancho, Clara's parents' ward and by all accounts a wastrel. Sancho spends money carelessly and gambles his fine clothes away on a whim. Eventually, for a lark, he decides to join the Gypsy band and gleefully vows to sell his land to finance his adventure. When he joins the Gypsies he promises to pay for his pleasure: "Hang lands! It's nothing but trees, stones, and dirt—Old father, I have gold to keep up our stock" (3.1.85). Clara's parents fear they tempted providence to visit misfortune on their daughter because they hoped, out of "covetousness," that she would marry their ward Sancho, "that matchless piece of ignorance" (2.2.23–24). This fear again links Clara's rape to prodigality; by hoping to match her with the wastrel Sancho, her parents see themselves as having unwittingly brought about her loss of virtue.

The notion of reform—and particularly reform of vices typed as Spanish—becomes particularly interesting when we examine the play's transformation of the name of one of its protagonists: the callous youth Rodolfo in the source text is changed to the more typically Spanish Roderigo. As Eric Griffin has argued in reference to Shakespeare's *Othello*, the name Roderigo immediately calls Spain to mind as it is the Christian name of Spain's epic hero "Ruy" Diaz de Bivar, or El Cid. The name also, though, evokes an earlier Spanish Roderigo: Roderic, known as the last King of the Goths.[51] This second Roderigo enables the Moorish conquest of Spain by committing a rape. His ally, Julian of Biscay, turns against Roderic and makes an alliance with the Moors after Roderic deflowers his daughter, and so precipitates the fall of Gothic Spain. Further, Roderic appears in anti-Spanish propaganda as an originator of Spain's miscegenated status. In the 1589 anti-Spanish propaganda pamphlet *A Comparison of the English and Spanish Nation*, translated from French by Robert Ashley, a lengthy section on "the originalls of our Spaniards at this day" begins with the entrance of Moors into Spain provoked by Roderic's rape to expose the "mongrell generation" of Spaniards. He justifies this by arguing, "For even as the waters which run out of sulphur springs, have alwayes a taste of brimstone, so men carrie alwaeies imprinted in their manners, the vertuous or vicious qualitie of their ancestors."[52] The name Roderigo, then, evokes Spain as a site of inherent viciousness as well as intemperate lust. (And it is worth noting that *Othello's* Roderigo is driven by his passion, like the character in *The Spanish Gypsy*.)

As Taylor has demonstrated, *The Spanish Gypsy* evokes Spain more frequently and explicitly than any other play in the period.[53] By changing the protagonist's name to Roderigo, the play calls up a series of associations: Roderigo, as el Cid, is one of Spain's great heroes; as Roderic, King of the Goths, he is a leader who has succumbed to the prototypical Spanish vice of lust.

The play itself, though, takes a very different tactic toward Spanish difference than does this earlier pamphlet. While the tainted blood of Spaniards seems to be an immutable and inherent quality in *The Copie of the Anti-Spaniard*, the "bad blood" in the play is "healed" by Roderigo's marriage to Clara. Roderigo, as an archetypal Spaniard reminiscent of both El Cid and Roderic, is able to make amends for—and transform—his faults.

Overall, the play represents a series of "Spanish" behaviors that are seen as changeable. The younger characters, driven by lust, revenge, and prodigality, are brought back into harmony with a more temperate older generation. Griffin has charted a shift in negative English representations of Spaniards over the course of the sixteenth century as one from "ethos" to "ethnos," or from a vilification based on behavior (behavior characterized by the very rapaciousness displayed by this younger generation) to one based on an essentialized protoethnic difference.[54] We can see in *The Spanish Gypsy* a return to the characterization of a Spanish "ethos" with a particular twist. Spain's younger generation is represented as degenerate, perhaps because of the influx of wealth from its colonies and the changes that wrought in Spain's (and Europe's) culture and economy.[55] A nobler (and older) group of Spaniards attempts to restrain these youths; representations of them evoke "Spain" as a site of ancient honor and chivalry. The play intimates that once the younger generation returns to the fold—becoming obedient sons rather than rebellious wastrels—a happy ending will be possible. Further, it is these circumstances—rather than an inherent, even racialized difference—that have prompted Spaniards to behave as they do. In this way, the play can be read as ambivalent in its representation of Spain and Spaniards; it certainly pokes fun at traditionally Spanish faults but also implies that those faults can be reformed.

English Gypsies, Spanish Gypsies, and *The Spanish Gypsy*

This vision of Spaniards as apparently different in kind but in fact capable of reform is also essential to the play's most direct engagement with racialized difference: its Gypsies, and the fact that its title links Gypsies and Spain. Indeed, associations with Gypsies in early modern England culture make them a particularly apt choice for such an undoing of apparent difference. The troupe of Gypsies, all of whom are, after all, nobles in disguise, occupy a particularly liminal position in terms of racialized markers. Internal evidence from the play does not clearly indicate whether the actors would have darkened their skin to play the roles. Preciosa's much-celebrated whiteness is described as atypical, as she is termed a Gypsy "in her condition, not in her complexion" (1.5.109), suggesting that other Gypsies would not have been so pale. But the father of the Gypsies describes them as "Gypsies, but no tanned ones; no red-ochre rascals umbered with soot and bacon, as the English gypsies are that sally out upon pullen, lie in *emboscado* for a rope of onions as if they were Welsh free-booters. No, our style has higher steps to climb over: Spanish gypsies, noble gypsies!" (2.1.6–11). The speech describes Spanish Gypsies as whiter than their English counterparts, but not by birth. English Gypsies, however, according to the play, are "umbered" by cosmetics (soot and bacon) and by lying in the sun, rather than being dark-skinned by birth. The end of the speech is particularly ambivalent: are the "Spanish gypsies" noble because they are Spanish, thus valorizing Spain (or at least denigrating English Gypsies by comparison)? Or, conversely, are all Spaniards—including nobles—Gypsies? Taylor, in a recent discussion of the play, raises this question in the context of its title: "And is 'The Spanish Gypsy' meant as an oxymoron, or a tautology? Are we meant to realize that 'Spanish' and 'Gypsy' are alternative ethnic identities, or does the title deliberately and satirically mix the two?"[56] In other words, does the notion of a Spanish "noble gypsy" satirize *all* Spanish pretensions at nobility, or is the incongruity of the juxtaposition of terms meant to signal that this Gypsy performance is in fact a disguise?

The association of Spaniards with Roma in this play is complex, perhaps more complex than we have realized thus far because Roma and Spain are so tightly linked in our contemporary imaginary. The association of Roma with Spain's exoticism, though—and particularly Andalucia—is largely a nineteenth-century phenomenon.[57] While there were Roma people in Spain who were legislated against much as they were in England, early modern English texts do not describe Spain as site of difference because of them; similarly, references to "Gypsies" in early modern English texts in no way associate them with Spain. The first reference to a group of Gypsies in the British Isles comes from Scotland in 1505: King James IV of Scotland gave ten French crowns to a group of "Egyptians" led by "Anthony Gawain, Earl of little Egypt." The king also wrote a letter of introduction on their behalf to the king of Denmark.[58] Gypsies initially seem to have represented themselves as exiled nobles from Egypt, and as their name—drawn from "Egyptian"—sug-gests, that is the country they were associated with if any.

A later pamphlet, Thomas Dekker's 1609 *Lanthorne and Candle-Light*, describes this transformation of Englishmen into Gypsies or "moon men" more specifically still: "They are a people more scattered than Jews, and more hated; beggarly in apparel, barbarous in condition, beastly in behavior, and bloody if they meet advantage. A man that sees them would swear that they had all the yellow jaundice or that they were tawny Moors' bastards, for no red-ochre man carries a face of a more filthy complexion, yet are they not born so, neither has the sun burnt them so, but they are painted so, yet they are no good painters neither: for they do not make faces, but mar faces."[59] While Dekker does not specify that the "moon men" are English, he does assert, "sure I am that they never descended from the tribes of any of those people that came out of Egypt." And while they initially seem to have dark skin, their skin color is revealed to be the work of face painting. Again, they are in no way explicitly linked to Spain, although the comparison of them to both Jews and Moors may tacitly invite comparison to Spain's status as a site of both Jewish and Moorish difference.

If anything, however, Gypsies are less essentialized than Spaniards in early modern England and characterized predominantly by their changeability.[60] As Dale Randall astutely notes, speaking of Andrew Borde's description of Gypsies in his 1542 *The Fyrste Boke of the Introduction of Knowledge,* "Confusion lies near the surface . . . for it is a rare nation in which the native costume is a disguise."[61] Dark-skinned by art rather than nature, they are associated above all with English attempts to counterfeit otherness via costume and face painting. Indeed, the "noble gypsies" presented in this play perhaps most clearly gesture to the English nobility who starred in the play's predecessor: Ben Jonson's popular 1621 court masque *The Gypsies Metamorphosed,* which undoubtedly influenced Middleton's play. While the Gypsy characters in *The Spanish Gypsy* turn out to have been noble all along within the play world, in Jonson's masque real noblemen—most notably the Duke of Buckingham (Prince Charles's companion when he went to Spain to woo the infanta)—are revealed to be playing the parts of Gypsies. The Gypsies of *The Gypsies Metamorphosed* are associated with specific places within England above all. Their relationship with visible difference, marked by dark skin, is complex; they are repeatedly referred to as dark-skinned, but that seems to be because they paint their faces. One of the Gypsy leaders promises to reveal how "to change your complexion, With the noble confection / Of walnuts and hog's grease." Similarly, the play's epilogue emphasizes face painting:

> But lest it prove like wonder to the sight
> To see a gypsy, as an Ethiope, white
> Know that what dyed our faces was an ointment
> Made and laid on by Master Wolf's appointment . . . (1550–53)[62]

A complicated representation of potentially dark-skinned Gypsy "complexions" unfolds here. At first, they are characterized as dark-skinned by nature: it might be understood as miraculous to see a Gypsy turn white, as it would be to see an Ethiope whitened. (And this also is an allusion, of course, to Jonson's earlier *Masque of Blackness*.) However, unlike in *The Masque of Blackness*, there is no stagecraft meant to represent a magical transformation. In fact, the transformation is not even dramatized: we are simply told in the epilogue that the courtier's faces were made up by Master Wolf, the court apothecary. Further, as we have seen, the masque itself repeatedly refers to face paint as the agent that darkens Gypsy skin. Gypsies are certainly marked as separate from early modern England's normative community; that separation, however, is repeatedly flagged as a performance.

This emphasis on difference as superficial performance may serve as a tacit commentary on the circumstances of the Spanish match. Certainly one reading of the Gypsy subplot, as Taylor has argued, is a reflection on Prince Charles's impromptu visit to Spain to woo the infanta.[63] Indeed, the play makes at least one explicit reference to the trip, describing a foreign "jester that so late arrived at court" and fell from a horse, a reference to the escapades of the English court jester Archie Armstrong, who accompanied the prince on his journey.[64] One of the impediments to the marriage was the fact that the infanta wished to marry a Catholic, and the Spanish court hoped that Charles would convert during his visit. Spanish hopes that Charles would convert are echoed by Preciosa's demand that Juan "turn gypsy" if he wishes to marry her. In the play, however, this issue has an appropriately idealized solution: Juan ends up turning Gypsy only for a short period of time before it is revealed that Preciosa—now Costanza—must turn noble. Or, more precisely, it is revealed that all of the "Gypsies" have been noble all along. If we read this—at least in part—as an allusion to the Spanish match, it presents an idealized future in which, despite Juan's initially risky situation, the infanta turns out to have been just like English Protestants all along. This reading is supported by Noémie Ndiaye's analysis of the Gypsies' performance of English folk dances within the play, which, she argues, "whitens Gypsies choreographically."[65] Ultimately, however, the most important term in the father of the Gypsies's description of his band may be his characterization of them as noble; beneath the initially destabilizing performance of "Gypsified" difference lies the reassuring fantasy of a shared identity among nobility, regardless of national origin.

I have argued that Gypsies are not necessarily understood to be of different blood than the English. They are characterized frequently as English vagabonds who paint their faces and disguise their origins; thus their difference appears as mutable and performative. Because of this, they are in some ways ideal figures to represent the Spanish as not so different after all, at a time when the Spanish match is still a real possibility. Gypsies perform difference but are often just Englishmen (and women) in costume, just as Spaniards, though they have been represented as essentially different from the English—and even different in "blood" because of their Jewish and Moorish ancestors—may in fact be sufficiently similar to the English to enable a dynastic marriage between the countries. This notion is only reinforced by the fact that all of the play's Gypsies (unlike those in "La gitanilla") turn out to be nobles in disguise. In *The Spanish Gypsy*, a presumed blood difference turns out to be no such difference at all. And the presumed Spanish vices of prodigality and lust are shown as youthful rebellion, curbed with relative ease. Thus, rather than undermining or critiquing the notion of essential blood difference, as Cervantes's stories do, the play raises the specter of blood difference only to banish it.

Conclusion

At first glance, *The Spanish Gypsy* seems to offer a very different model for understanding Spain as a site of racialized difference than Mabbe's translation of *Guzmán de Alfarache*. Instead of consistently coding Spain as Moorish, *The Spanish Gypsy* ends with the revelation that what looks like racialized difference is merely disguise. The two English texts are similar, however, in their elision of Spain's internal heterogeneity. While in *The Spanish Gypsy*, all of the "gypsies" turn out to be nobility, in Cervantes's novella the heroine Preciosa is the only one of noble descent. While the novella depicts the Roma as one part of a heterogeneous Spanish community, in the play the entire Spanish nobility becomes, to borrow the play's term, "Gypsified," however briefly—much as Mabbe's Orientalizing textual apparatus marks all of Spain as Moorish. Both Mabbe's translation of *Guzmán de Alfarache* and *The Spanish Gypsy* engage with Spain's status as an imagined locus of impure blood. And in both examples the subtle satire of purity that runs through the Spanish text is flattened and simplified in its English adaptation. What is left in each instance is a reassuring substitute in which the uneasy testing of social performances of purity in Spanish texts is resolved into more stable categorizations.

I hope that this chapter has complicated one aspect of the "idea of Spain": the notion that Spanish discourses of race are a more extreme example of nascent racializing discourses in England. After all, in early modern Spanish literary texts such as *Guzmán de Alfarache* and the *Novelas ejemplares*, the notion that blood-borne identity has the power to determine character is at times articulated only to be undermined and held up for ridicule. While Spain's pure blood statutes are indeed significant to the development of racial ideologies, their impact on theories of race in Spain is complex and often contradictory. As we have seen, essentializing theories of "pure" descent often appear in Spanish literature in a satiric light, as an object of mockery. This mockery works to undermine as much as reinforce the validity of such categories.

Mabbe's translation elides this parodic aspect of Spanish discourses of purity of blood; curiously enough, four hundred years later, so too do critical studies of Jews and Moors in early modern English literature that draw on Spain. In the case of current scholarship, as most likely was the case with Mabbe's translation, this occlusion of satirical representations of purity of blood is not deliberate. But it is nonetheless indicative of the way Spain often figures in early modern English studies. The failure to engage with ambivalent Spanish representations of purity of blood leads to an oversimplified definition of Spain's role in the development of theories of race, a definition that itself may betray the lingering effects of the Black Legend.[66] Indeed, as we have seen, the representations of Jewish and Moorish descent in Mabbe's translation are less indebted to Spanish discourses of purity of blood than they are to Mabbe's own particularly English notion of Spain. Comparing Alemán's novel to Mabbe's translation demonstrates that—at least in this instance—Spain does not appear as a site of origin for discourses of race and blood in England. Indeed, *The Spanish Gypsy* is far more preoccupied with impure blood and ruined honor than either of the Spanish novellas it draws on, and Mabbe's English translation, with its persistent emphasis on the exotic Moorishness of Spaniards, offers a more essentializing portrayal of racialized difference.

CHAPTER 3

Blackness, Slavery, and Service in the Comedia

Don Agustín: Vaya el perro
Juan: No está el yerro
En la sangre ni el valor
Alférez: Estarálo en la color
Juan: Ser moreno no es ser perro;
Que ese nombre se le da
Á un alarbe, a un moro.
[*Don Agustín:* Get out, dog.
Juan: There is no flaw in my blood or valor
Ensign: There is in your color.
Juan: To be dark does not make me a dog. That is a name given to an
      Arab, to a Moor.][1]

The opening lines of Andrés de Claramonte's play *El valiente negro en Flandes*
[The valiant Black man in Flanders] (1612–20) outline an important characteristic of racialized vocabularies in early modern Spain. The play's protagonist, Juan de Mérida, is an enslaved Black man who wishes to join the Spanish
army. When he is dismissed as a "dog," unworthy to serve, he defends himself
by drawing on a common strategy: he may be Black, he informs the soldiers,
but he is not a Moor and thus not a dog. In other words, Juan, like Inés of *La
villana de Getafe* (discussed in Chapter 1), is "limpia," or of pure descent, and
thus worthy to lay claim to his share of the "glory" of fighting for Spain in the
Low Countries. For scholars of English literature, Juan's assertion that he is
not a Moor may be surprising; in early modern English, and particularly on
the stage, the word *Moor* is often used to denote Blackness.[2] In early modern
Spain, however, as Juan's assertion indicates, Blackness is at times presented
as evidence of the *absence* of "impure" Moorish (or Jewish) descent.[3]

This positioning of Blackness as distinct from Moorishness is not confined to literature. For example, Chloe Ireton has demonstrated that "blacks of the caste of black Christians," many of them formerly enslaved people and their descendants, were able to successfully petition to move to the Spanish Indies, as those of Jewish and Muslim descent were prohibited from doing. She discusses the successful petition of Roberto González, in which he requests permission for himself and his wife, both "free black Old Christians," to take up residence in the Spanish Indies. One of the witnesses interviewed in support of their case explains that they are "not *moriscos* because they are *atezados* [dark black complexion]."[4] For this witness, the fact that the couple is Black serves as evidence that they are not Moorish and thus merit inclusion in Spain's imperial ventures. The statement complicates many of our assumptions about the intersection of Blackness and Islam in early modern Europe, especially since most scholarship on this topic has focused on an English canon, where Blackness and religious difference are often conflated.

Although Black characters are a far more prominent presence in the Spanish comedia than in early modern English drama, these plays have received far less attention from scholars. This is largely due to institutional trends; academics interested in representations of Blackness in early modern Spanish literatures have tended to focus on Spain's colonies and the early years of the transatlantic slave trade.[5] Within Peninsular Spanish studies, debates about purity of blood have long dominated the field. Scholars focused on early modern race studies, many of whom are based in English departments, often lack the linguistic skills to work with these plays, most of which have not been translated. Spanish plays with Black characters, however, as we shall see, enrich and complicate theories of early modern Blackness that have drawn primarily on an English-language archive. This is especially true of the ways in which they almost universally link Blackness with enslavement. If the charge most frequently laid against reading slavery as racialized in the early modern period is that to do so is anachronistic, these Spanish plays—which repeatedly emphasize connections between Blackness and enslavement—offer powerful evidence that we can only assume that racialized slavery had not yet taken hold in early modern Europe if we disregard the Iberian Peninsula.

This chapter focuses on representations of Blackness in the Spanish comedia. I focus in particular on the ways in which representations of pure blood, Blackness, and whiteness are articulated in contradistinction to each other as alternately overlapping and opposing categories. Rather than collapse these categories into a binary (self/other or native/stranger), I trace how Blackness, whiteness, purity, and impurity remain in tension.[6] Representations of Black protagonists on the early modern Spanish stage rely on the consistent triangulation of the figure of the white "Old Christian," the white "New Christian" (either of Jewish or Moorish descent, and inevitably villainous), and the exemplary Black Christian, whose achievements are always represented as a form of service to benefit white Spanish Christendom. Indeed, as we shall see, representations of Blackness in the comedia are inextricable from representations of enslavement. Many plays with heroic Black protagonists dramatize the replacement of the converso or the Morisco with the *negro*, who, by virtue of being Black and often enslaved, does not challenge the supremacy of the white Old Christian. I begin with a brief overview of the history of slavery in Spain and then of representations of Blackness on the Spanish stage before turning to representations of Blackness and slavery in the comedia.

Slavery in Spain and on the Spanish Stage

In the fifteenth century Iberia's slave population underwent a fundamental transformation. Slavery had existed in Iberia throughout the Al-Andalusi dynasty and continued on both sides throughout the Christian Reconquista. Both Christians and Muslims were captured and enslaved through a system of raids, called *razzias*, conducted throughout the Mediterranean; enslaved people from a number of locations, including North Africa, Eastern Europe, and the Ottoman Empire, were also legally bought and sold within Spain.[7] Then, in 1444, Portuguese merchants brought 235 Guineans to Lisbon to be sold into slavery. The first permanent slave-trading post was established off of the coast of Mauritania in 1448. The expanding slave trade in Black Africans transformed perceptions of slavery's relationship to place of origin and phenotype. In fifteenth-century Valencia, for example, as Debra Blumenthal has documented, "the slaves directly captured in warfare progressively were outnumbered by shiploads of sub-Saharan Africans and Canary Islanders sent by Portuguese and Italian traders based in clearinghouses along the Atlantic coast."[8] As a result of this shift, "contemporaries increasingly were associating dark skin with slave status."[9]

The number of enslaved Black people in Iberia increased over the course of the sixteenth century, concentrated in Southern Spain and in port cities. By 1565 a census taken in Seville recorded 6,327 enslaved people out of a total population of 85,538, making the enslaved roughly 13.5 percent of the total population. Drawing on censuses like this and parish records, the historian Manuel Fernández Álvarez calculates that there were approximately forty-four thousand enslaved people in Spain by the end of the sixteenth century; other historians place the number as high as one hundred thousand.[10] Of course, many of those enslaved were not of sub-Saharan African origin. The enslavement of North African and Spanish Moors and Moriscos captured in battle or in raids continued throughout this period, as did the slave trade along established Mediterranean and trans-Saharan trade routes.[11] Nonetheless, the trade in sub-Saharan Africans quickly became an important part of Spain's slave economy. Extant records indicate that by the middle of the sixteenth century enslaved populations had become predominantly Black in regions with ties to Portugal or the New World, such as Extremadura and Andalucía (particularly Seville).[12] In Granada, enslaved Black Africans made up the majority of the slave population in the sixteenth century until the Morisco rebellion of 1568–71; at that time, tens of thousands of Spanish Moriscos were enslaved, completely transforming the demographics of Granada's enslaved population. In the years 1569–71, over 90 percent of the those bought and sold in Granada were Moriscos.[13]

Although sub-Saharan Africans were not the only enslaved people in sixteenth-century Spain, enslaved Black people quickly became a visible part of Spanish—and particularly Andalusian—society. For example, one sixteenth-century visitor to Seville compared the city to a chessboard with an equal number of black and white pieces.[14] Significantly, as the sub-Saharan slave trade continued to develop, the word *negro* began to appear in legal documents as a synonym for *esclavo* (slave).[15] In one particularly striking example, documentation from 1559 to 1576 regarding enslaved people working in silver mines in Guadalcanal (near Seville) repeatedly employs the term *negros de su majestad* (his majesty's Black people), seemingly automatically substituting *negro* for *esclavo*.[16] And in his 1569 *Summa de tratos y contratos* (Manual of deals and contracts), Fray Tomás de Mercado observes: "cautivar, o vender negros, u otra qualquier gente es negocio lícito" [to capture or sell Black people or any other people is a lawful business].[17] Mercado's phrasing here is telling. He does not limit his discussion of the legality of slavery to the enslavement of Black Africans, but they are his primary point of reference; he begins by mentioning *negros* before turning to "any other people." This latter point bears further consideration, because those who argue that race-based slavery did not affect discourses of race in the early modern period at times base that assumption on the fact that not all those enslaved in the period were Black, and not all Black people were enslaved. Both of these facts are manifestly true. But it is also true that most Black people in Europe in the sixteenth and seventeenth centuries were brought there via the slave trade, and further, that white Europeans, as Mercado does above, increasingly associated Blackness with slavery, and vice versa. Representations of Blackness in the comedia reinforce such associations.

Black characters first appeared on the Spanish stage in the sixteenth century as comic figures in farces, often speaking a racist faux dialect, *habla de negros*. Many of these early short plays are undated, and no doubt many more have been lost, but a handful of plays and interludes featuring stereotyped "negros" can be dated to the 1530s and 1540s.[18] Baltasar Fra Molinero's *La imagen de los negros en el teatro del Siglo de Oro* charts a progression in representations of Blackness from the *negro* of sixteenth-century interludes, who dances and speaks in dialect, to the more developed heroic protagonist of the first quarter of the seventeenth century, who speaks in standard Castilian and distinguishes himself in learning, battle, or Christian devotion—and in at least two plays, crowns his success by marrying a white Spanish noblewoman. More recently, Nicholas R. Jones has focused on a range of Black characters in both poetry and short *entremeses*, or interludes.[19] Black and mixed-race female characters appear on the stage as well, primarily as comic figures who speak in dialect. There are also, though, at least four plays—all by Lope de Vega—that feature an enslaved mixed-race character (labeled a *mulata* in the text) who speaks standard Castilian and ends the play marrying the white servant of her mistress's suitor. In short, there are dozens of plays with Black characters in the comedia, and these characters occupy a range of social positions. Unlike in English drama, which most frequently stages Blackness as the embodiment of an evil that must be destroyed or expelled from the (implicitly white) European community, the trajectory of Black characters in Spanish drama most often starts with exclusion and ends with inclusion—although the limits of such inclusion, as we shall see, are strictly imposed and anxiously revisited throughout these plays.

The limited inclusion granted for Black characters in the Spanish comedia is only achieved through the ubiquitous association of Blackness with slavery.[20] I know of only two Black characters in the early modern Spanish theater that are *not* represented as either enslaved or formerly enslaved: a prince born Black to white parents because of maternal impression, in *Virtudes vencen señales*, and a Black African prince who becomes a saint, in Lope de Vega's *El negro del mejor amo* [The slave/Black man of the greatest master] (written

1599–1603). And even in this second play, although the character himself is never enslaved, the conceit of the title and much of the language he uses following his conversion is that he has become the *"negro"* (Black man or slave) of the greatest master of all (i.e., God). The play's protagonist, Antiobo, is the prince of Argel and the son of an Ethiopian princess; at no point is he taken captive or sold into slavery.[21] However, as soon as he learns about Christianity and decides to convert, he begins to use a new vocabulary to describe himself, terming himself a humble slave to the greatest master—the Christian God. And as in the historical texts I cited above, the word he uses to term himself a slave is *negro*: "Virgen María, / en vuestras manos me pongo. / Vuestro negro quiero ser" [Virgin Mary, I place myself in your hands. I want to be your slave/Black man]; he then asserts, "soy esclavo de María!" [I am Mary's slave!] (473, 491).[22] Similarly, the protagonist of *El valiente negro en Flandés*, Juan de Mérida, must clarify after he wins his freedom: "aunque negro soy, no he sido esclavo" [although I am Black, I am not a slave] (32); his statement indicates that most will assume he is a slave because he is Black.

Of course, such Black characters would have been written by white men and performed by white men and women. Although there is more archival work to be done on this subject, it is likely that most if not all Black characters in the comedia were played by white actors in blackface makeup.[23] Records of costuming and makeup for Black characters from the sixteenth century has been found in Spanish archives.[24] And, as is true in English drama, references to cosmetics and face washing permeate these plays' imagery, providing a consistent metatheatrical reminder that the Blackness on stage is only a show. Lope de Vega's allegorical play *La limpieza no manchada* [Unstained purity] (1618) ends by acknowledging blackface as performance. The play ends with Spain, personified as a woman, receiving gifts and adoration from "India" (the so-called New World) and Ethiopia. Ethiopia, again personified as a woman, comes out accompanied by a "baile de negros" or Black dance, and Spain greets her: "aunque disfrazada vengas / te conozco, Andalucía" [even though you come disguised / I know you, Andalucía].[25] The play simultaneously voices an anxiety about cultural contamination and perhaps miscegenation and puts such worries to rest—this may look like a *baile de negros*, but it is just Andalusian Spaniards in disguise.

The governing question of this and the following chapters, then, is how Blackness is being used in these plays to produce and reinforce a fantasy of normative whiteness. As Manuel Olmedo Gobante observes in a recent article on *El valiente negro en Flandes*, analysis of heroic Black protagonists

in the comedia can be loosely grouped into two opposing camps: on one side
are those who read these plays as evidence of a culture of inclusion in early
modern Spain, or as "una critica moderada a la supremacía blanca, dentro de
los limites do lo possible" [a moderated critique of white supremacy within
the limits of possibility]; on the other side are those who see them as a reflection of white supremacy.[26] Here, I begin with the premise that these texts
reinforce white supremacy and that they simultaneously may contain pockets of resistance. My focus is less on *whether* these texts uphold or subvert
racializing ideologies than on *how* they construct Blackness in relationship
to whiteness, religious difference, and slavery, and in teasing out the power
shifts attendant on shifting representations of race.

Blackness, Moorishness, and Slavery in *Juan Latino*

Diego Ximénez de Enciso's play *Juan Latino* (1610–21) exemplifies the complicated representation of heroic Black protagonists on the Spanish stage.[27]
The play is loosely based on the life of a real person: a celebrated scholar
and former slave who wrote the Latin epic poem *Austrias Carmen* to com-
memorate the battle of Lepanto.[28] In the play, the fictional Juan Latino uses
his rhetorical prowess to attain first respect and then increasingly prominent
university positions. While Juan initially faces insult and prejudice, both
because he is Black and because he is enslaved, his eloquence and erudition
win over the nobility of Granada. Ultimately, he becomes a celebrated professor and wins the love of a clever Spanish noblewoman, Doña Ana. By the end
of the play, he has received high honors from the University of Granada and
married Doña Ana; nonetheless, he remains enslaved throughout. The story
of Juan's social ascent and integration into the Spanish nobility is counter-
poised with the fall from prominence of Don Fernando, a white nobleman of
Morisco origins and another suitor to Doña Ana. Don Fernando is persuaded
to help lead the Morisco uprising in the Alpujarras; he returns to Islam and
is ultimately killed.[29] While Juan Latino's exemplary Christian devotion and
humanist learning win him the praise of the nobility and the love of a white
Spanish woman, Don Fernando, who begins the play as a part of the Spanish
aristocracy, ends it as a faithless Moor who has been killed in battle.

Fra Molinero, whose 1995 chapter on *Juan Latino* remains the most sustained reading of the play thus far, highlights the reactionary force of Juan's
and Fernando's differing fates: "Al revés que Don Fernando, el rebelde, Juan

nunca va a cuestionar el orden social y jurídico que le mantiene en perpetua situación de marginado." [In contrast to the rebel Don Fernando, Juan will never question the social and juridical order that perpetually situates him on the margins.][30] Fra Molinero argues that the play, by highlighting Juan's unquestioning obedience in contrast to Fernando's rebellion, reinforces existing social hierarchies. The obedient enslaved Black person can occupy a limited place in Spain contingent on his continued obedience; the rebellious Morisco, however, is ultimately unassimilable. As we shall see, however, the play also questions this reactionary ideology—and particularly the logic of enslavement—even as it upholds it at the end.

The juxtaposition of Juan's ascent with the fall of the Morisco establishes Blackness as a preferable alternative to an invisible difference of faith.[31] Although some characters misread Juan's Blackness as a sign of inner perfidy, when they do they are swiftly corrected. Thus, when Carlobal engages Juan to tutor his sister, he justifies his decision:

¿No es hombre? El alma que tiene,
por ser negro ¿ha de perder,
siendo pura, algo del ser
que a lo racional conviene?
Quien a los hombres informa,
es el alma solamente;
el color es accidente. (243)

[Isn't he a man? Does his soul, as long as it is pure, lose anything that belongs to a rational being because he is Black? That which shapes a man is only the soul; his color is an accident.][32]

Juan's color appears most clearly "accidental" or irrelevant to his character when it is contrasted with his "pure" soul. Interestingly, however, the purity of his soul is one of the things that makes his color, if not accidental, then far from incidental. This is so because Juan, as a Black African, establishes his purity partly because his Blackness distinguishes him from the Morisco—a figure whose inner perfidy is threatening because it leaves no visible trace.[33]

Despite the purity of Juan's soul, the play places clear limits on his assimilation, most notably by drawing attention to his continued enslavement even as he becomes a valued professor (a particularly telling choice given that the historical Juan Latino was most likely manumitted).[34] Juan's enslavement

simultaneously enables and limits his social ascent, as his enslaver, the Duke
of Sesa, both creates a place of prestige for Juan and assigns definite limits to
that place by refusing to manumit him.

The first time Juan pleads for his liberty, the duke simply stonewalls him,
offering him increasingly large gifts but refusing to engage his request. Juan
asks, "¿soy libre?" [Am I free?] The duke responds by offering him four pages
to accompany him wherever he goes. Juan asks once more, and the duke
gives him four thousand ducats, promising that he will spend all he owns
("la hacienda mía") on Juan's behalf (227–28), but still ignores Juan's request.
At Juan's repeated urging, the duke finally suggests that they revisit the issue
if Juan wins a university position. We only learn the reason for the duke's
hesitation after Juan has won the position and petitions for his freedom once
again. The duke replies:

> no estimo en tanto el ser Duque
> de Sesa y Conde de Cabra,
> como el teneros por mío.
> ¿Qué príncipe, qué monarca
> podrá decir lo que yo?
> En vos vivirá mi fama
> más verde que en las antiguas,
> y prodigiosas hazañas
> de mis ilustres abuelos!
> No tratéis más desto, basta
> que sepáis que no es mi gusto. (314)

> [I do not value being Duke of Sesa and Count of Cabra as highly as
> I do having you for my own. What prince, what monarch, can say
> what I can? My fame will live on in you, staying greener than it would
> in the ancient and prodigious feats of my illustrious ancestors! Don't
> broach this subject again; suffice it to say that it is not my pleasure.]

Juan is at once a high-status possession, for whose deeds the duke can claim
credit, and an unexpected addition to the duke's family tree, keeping his family's name and fame alive. Juan's achievements take the place of the duke's
ancestors' as proof of the latter's honor and nobility. The duke simultaneously honors Juan, by describing him as his primary source of pride, and
contains him, refusing to allow him to exceed the bounds of his status as a

possession. This monologue places a significant limitation on the way Juan can be included in the duke's family, and by extension in a white Spanish community. Juan's status as a member in this Spanish community is contingent on his continued enslavement. As long as he is enslaved, Juan acts as an ornament to the duke's honor. But he must remain enslaved, and his accomplishments must demonstrate the duke's honor rather than his own, for his status in Spain to remain secure.

The play never resolves this balancing act between Juan's achievements and his enslavement. Instead, circumstances push Ana and Juan into eloping, as Ana must choose between running away with Juan and becoming a nun. The final words Juan speaks in the play are a request to the duke that he be allowed to embrace his new brother-in-law, Carlobal, with whom he has just reconciled. The duke grants him permission and promises to give him six thousand ducats but does not speak a word about his freedom. The play remains in a state of tension, questioning the limitations placed on Juan by his status as enslaved without removing them.

This tension around Juan's status as enslaved also appears in the rhetoric used to present Juan's position in the duke's household. Vocabularies of chattel slavery, patronage, and chivalric service are conflated when Juan and other characters attempt to articulate how, precisely, Juan fits into the Spanish nobility. When asking for his freedom, Juan prefaces his request with a compliment: "Bien sé que es mi hidalguía y preeminencia / ser esclavos de esclavos desta casa" [I know well it is to my great ennoblement and preeminence / to be a slave of the slaves of this household] (223). Juan's new brother-in-law, Carlobal, employs similar rhetoric when he finally accepts his sister's marriage to Juan. Carlobal enthuses of Juan, "aún no soy / digno de ser su esclavo" [I am not even worthy to be his slave], as he embraces his new brother-in-law (355). In what is meant to be a comedic moment, the play superimposes an elaborate vocabulary of courtly service ("I am your humble slave!" "No, I am yours!") on a reference to slavery as an economic practice; after all, Juan's status as a slave to the Duke of Sesa is quite different from how Carlobal might envision himself as a slave to Juan. Thus the play repurposes older vocabularies of service in the context of chattel slavery.

Indeed, representations of Juan's slavery as voluntary chivalric service are frequently (and uncomfortably) juxtaposed with repeated references to Juan's compromised position as enslaved. When Ana first meets Juan, she is struck by his humility, charm, and courtliness—and immediately wishes to buy him: "Téngole de mercar para la silla / o para ser lacayo de mi hermano" [I must buy him to carry my litter, or to attend on my brother] (199). As charming as Ana finds Juan as a potential possession, when he begins to court her she immediately brings up his enslavement, ordering him out of the room and evoking a notorious and brutal punishment for slaves: "agradeced que no os hice pringar" [be grateful that I did not have you burned with oil] (251); when he continues to court her, she threatens to beat him: "Estoy por daros mil palos, / ¿un negro me dice amores?" [I want to give you a thousand blows—a *negro*, speaking of love to me?] (263). Juan himself swears an oath that if he wins Ana's heart he will adorn love's walls by hanging a captive Black man on them ["adornaré tus paredes, / colgando un negro captivo] (210). The oath juxtaposes the medieval trope of the knight taken captive by love with an unsettling image that evokes the early modern sub-Saharan African slave trade. On multiple occasions the play reminds us that Juan can be bought and sold and subjected to punishments at the will of his captors. In doing so, it further complicates an already tangled web of signification around questions of slavery: it is represented as at once a form of ennobling service and a concrete and oppressive institution.

As we have seen, *Juan Latino* emphasizes the difficulties of defining the nature of its heroic Black protagonist's service. Juan not only remains a slave throughout, but the play also takes pains to repeatedly stage his failed attempts to secure his freedom. This tension around the nature of Juan's service to Spain is characteristic of Black protagonists in the comedia. On the one hand, Juan's social ascent while enslaved attempts to justify the rise of race-based slavery as a form of social good: through the benevolence of his enslaver, Juan is able to achieve fame and renown. On the other hand, once Juan's achievements become his own rather than his master's, they challenge the existing social order and thus present a threat. The play's failure to resolve this contradiction is particularly charged and may be part of the reason for its unusual final lines. The epilogue, playing on a conventional promise of a sequel, instead warns: "Aquí, sin parte segunda / esta Comedia acabamos, / porque no tuvo segundo / un negro del mundo espanto." [Here, without a second part, we will end this comedy, because this Black man, wonder of the world, had no sequel] (356). Juan can only be heroic and celebrated if he remains singular and exceptional.

No records exist to indicate that *Juan Latino* was particularly popular in its own era. It survives in only one printed edition, as part of one of the many collections of plays that circulated in Spain in the seventeenth century. There are no extant records of its performance, and no manuscript performance copies have been discovered. The ephemeral nature of such materials precludes reading too much into this archival absence—but it does, at the very least, suggest that the play wasn't wildly popular. The next play I turn to, by contrast, was a bona fide hit, with multiple reprints and records of performance in the seventeenth and eighteenth centuries. This may be because its hero, as an accomplished soldier, is an inherently more dynamic protagonist than an eminent Latinist. But it is also tempting to speculate that the fact that its protagonist, Juan de Mérida, was as far as we know fictional made him a less troubling figure to celebrate.

Blackness and Whiteness in *El valiente negro en Flandes*

The first Spanish dictionary, Sebastián de Covarrubias's much-cited 1611 *Tesoro de la lengua castellana o española*, defines *negro* as follows: "uno de los estremos de colores, opuesto a blanco, Latine niger. Negro el Etiope de color negra. Es color infausta y triste . . ." [one of the extremes of colors, the opposite of white, Latin niger. *Negro*: the Ethiopian, black in color. It is an ill-fated and sad color . . .]. The definition goes on to cite several proverbs, including "aunque negros, gente somos" [although we are black, we are people], which Covarrubias explains means "no se ha de despreciar nadie por humilde y baja que sea" [one should not discount anyone, no matter how humble and low]. The entry thus briefly defines the color black in the context of whiteness, then turns immediately to the word's use as a racialized marker of difference. The much longer definition of *blanca* (white) is—unsurprisingly—quite different. It begins: "color, significa castidad, limpieza, alegria" [color, which signifies chastity, purity, happiness]. After mentioning biblical references to whiteness and the use of white clothing in celebrations, the entry makes its only tacit reference to whiteness as a racialized identity category: "El opuesto de blanco, es negro. No se si fulano es negro ni blanco. Vale, no le conozco." [I don't know if that guy is black or white. It means I don't know him.][35]

The contrast between these two definitions resonates with Richard Dyer's seminal assessment of Blackness as "always marked as a colour (as the term 'coloured' egregiously acknowledges), and as always particularizing; whereas white is not anything really, not an identity, not a particularizing quality, because it is everything."[36] In early modern literature and culture, as a number of critics have demonstrated, the color white is freighted with associations with purity, beauty, and virtue, which become implicitly associated with whiteness as race, even as the categorization of the white body as a particular kind of racialized identity remains unstated and hidden from view.[37] In staging Blackness, however, early modern Spanish plays at times make whiteness visible.

This is particularly true of Andres de Claramonte's *El valiente negro en Flandes* [The valiant Black man in Flanders] (written 1612–26, published 1638). The play recounts the heroic exploits of the fictional Juan de Mérida, the son of an enslaved Black woman, who joins the Spanish army's campaign in the Low Countries, in spite of fierce opposition, and wins glory, nobility, and the patronage of the Duke of Alba through his military prowess. As in *Juan Latino*, a rhetoric of slavery as service pervades the play, with the protagonist consistently presenting himself as the devoted slave of the Duke of Alba, despite the fact that the protagonist is granted his freedom at the beginning of the play. *El valiente negro en Flandes* is also, though, particularly preoccupied with the relationship between Blackness and an idealized white identity, and particularly white masculinity.

The play's hero, Juan de Mérida (later renamed Juan de Alba), is the son of an enslaved Black woman renowned for her beauty. The play hints (through gossiping soldiers) but does not confirm that his father is a white Spanish nobleman, and he is referred to throughout as *negro* rather than mixed-race or *mulato*. At the beginning of the play, Juan entreats his master's daughter, Juana, for letters granting his freedom. She grants them, and Juan rushes to join the Duke of Alba's army in Flanders to fight for the Spanish in the Dutch War of Independence. At first Juan is spurned by the other soldiers because he is Black, and they refuse to believe he is not a slave. Nonetheless, he proves his worth through heroic acts of daring, capturing a spy from the enemy camp and ultimately—at the moment when Spain is about to surrender—capturing the enemy general himself, the Duke of Orange, thereby reversing the outcome of the war. In recompense the Duke of Alba takes him under his wing, transforming him from Juan de Mérida to Juan de Alba and eventually granting him nobility and a hefty yearly income. There are two extant seventeenth-century versions of the play's ending: in one of them, the play ends with Juan's marriage to his former enslaver.

Juan's courage, nobility, and humility are set against the decidedly ignoble actions of a white captain, Agustín. The play's secondary plot follows the romantic misadventures of Agustín and a noblewoman, Leonor. At the play's opening Agustín promises marriage to Leonor and takes her virginity—and then promptly runs off to war. His lack of honor is further reinforced by his continued taunting and resentment of his fellow soldier Juan, whose success in spite of his Blackness is a constant irritant to Agustín. Notably, Agustín takes Juan's place in a mission to capture an enemy spy, saying that such an important task should be reserved for a white Spanish nobleman. Agustín is too afraid, however, to complete the task. Instead, Juan, disguised as a member of the Dutch army, humiliates Agustín and exposes his cowardice before capturing two spies himself.

Meanwhile, Agustín's abandoned beloved, Leonor, disguises herself as a man and follows Agustín to win her honor back. She attaches herself to Juan, who is at first reluctant to associate with her because he believes her to be an effeminate man who is making sexual overtures toward him. Once Juan figures out the truth, he reluctantly takes on her cause. In the play's final act everyone returns to Spain, and Agustín discovers that his parents have arranged a marriage between him and Juan's former mistress, Juana. Since, as Agustín informs his friend, Juana is richer than Leonor and even more beautiful, he definitively abandons Leonor. In the play's final scene, Juan shows up at the wedding celebration with Leonor in tow. He has, at this point, received membership in a knightly order from the king and the Duke of Alba, and thus outranks both Agustín and the family to whom he was formerly enslaved. He exposes Agustín's treachery and forces him to make amends by marrying Leonor, then promises to make amends to Juana for her spoiled wedding by giving his own wealth to anyone she chooses to marry.

Thus, throughout the play Juan acts, in his own words, as "un negro que hace a los blancos / comedidos y compuestos" [a Black man who makes whites restrained and well-behaved] (84). The play repeatedly positions him as a corrective to the failures of white Spanish nobility, and particularly white masculinity. When he wins over white Spanish soldiers with his military might, he describes his role as follows: "Negro soy, que hago y digo y pongo espanto / a las que hablan, y no hacen" [I am a Black man who acts and speaks and engenders fear / in those who speak and do not act]; he goes on to clarify that he works to bring together "el decir y el hacer en blancos pechos" [speaking and doing in white hearts/chests] (61). His acts of valor are positioned as a form of service to white masculinity. Juan goads white men into acting as they ought to because he—despite being Black—is so easily able to best them. Conversely, the ability to see past Juan's Blackness and recognize his worth—that he is, in the play's terms, "un negro blanco en las obras" [a Black man who is white in his deeds] (94)—becomes a marker of the truly noble white man. Unsurprisingly, then, the characters who are most fulsome in their praise of Juan and quickest to recognize his worth are the Duke of Alba, the Duke of Orange, and the King of Spain.

On first consideration, it might seem that the play, in positioning its Black protagonist as a corrective to the shortcomings of white masculinity, might be critiquing—or at least undermining—the stability and dominance of whiteness as an identity category. It avoids doing so, however, by emphasizing two contradictory aspects of its dramatic representation of Blackness. It consistently gestures both to the impermanent and performative nature of blackface on the stage and to the ways that, offstage, Blackness functions as an ultimately undisguisable marker of difference.

When Juan takes prisoners in the enemy camp, he wears a mask and disguises himself as a Dutch soldier. It is in this guise that he fools the erring captain, Agustín. However, despite the fact that Agustín fails to recognize him, Juan consistently refers to his Blackness underneath the mask, referring to himself as a man of two faces ("hombre de dos caras") and referring to himself as "un aleman que fue dos horas que fue negro" [a German/Dutchman who was Black two hours ago] (43). Interestingly, Juan's disguise does not seem to matter to his actual mission once he has humiliated his own comrade. Having sent Agustín fleeing in terror, he removes his mask before invading the Dutch camp: "Ya soy venturoso, y puedo / ya la máscara quitarme. Véte, máscara, que ya / la inmortalidad me llama; negra ha de ser la fama / que aquesta occasion me da" [Now I am fortunate, and now I can take off the mask. Away, mask—now immortality calls me. The fame this occasion grants me must be Black] (44). Similarly, when he takes the Duke of Orange prisoner, Juan initially informs the audience that he has gone to the enemy camp with his mask; nonetheless, he announces himself to the Duke of Orange as "el de moreno color" [he of dark coloring] (70).

The mask works in part as a reminder of Juan's status as "un negro blanco en las obras." Unlike the play's only other Black character, Juan's servant Antonillo, who speaks in the racially marked Black speech or "habla de negro," Juan speaks in standard Castilian. The mask thus serves as a reminder that Juan is indistinguishable from white characters when his face is disguised, and that his color ought not to be read as an indication of baseness or servility. It also, though, gestures to the fact that his Blackness *is* in fact a sort of mask or cosmetic alteration. It works as a metatheatrical wink along the lines of Shakespeare's cross-dressing female characters, when a boy pretending to be a woman pretends to be a boy; in the Spanish play, a white man pretends to be a Black man pretending to be a white man. The mask thus serves as a reminder that an originary whiteness underpins the play's representation of Black heroism. The often-repeated formulation that Juan is really white internally and in his actions, despite his Black exterior, also underlines, in this context, the fact that Juan (or rather the actor playing him) is in fact white beneath his makeup.

Further, Juan's disguise as a white member of the opposing camp reinforces a Black/white binary while erasing national and linguistic difference. For example, Agustín expresses no surprise that his presumed enemy—really Juan in disguise—speaks in flawless Castilian (despite the fact that linguistic and cultural difference between the Spanish and the Dutch is a source of comedy elsewhere in the play). All that Juan needs to do to take on the role of Dutch spy is to hide his Blackness; once that is done, his language and nation become irrelevant. This moment tacitly aligns enemy factions as part of a larger white community from which Juan is excluded.

At the same time, the play emphasizes the status of Blackness as a fundamentally inalterable marker of difference. It does so largely through a sustained engagement with the trope of "washing the Ethiope white."[38] After Juan triumphantly deposits the captive Duke of Orange with his commander, the Duke of Alba, he abruptly excuses himself to wash. We next see him when he returns from his ablutions, lamenting:

> mas de tres cargas de leña
> he gastado en enjuagarme
> ya vengo limpio y caliente,
> mas no he podido limpiarme
> el rostro; ¿pero, que mucho
> si la mancha está en la carne? (73)

> [I have used more than three loads of firewood to clean myself. I'm now clean and warm, but I haven't been able to clean my face. But what of that, if the stain is in the flesh?]

As in the example discussed above, this moment serves as an ironic reminder that the actor playing Juan can in fact wash off the "stain" of Blackness from a presumed originary whiteness.

The speech also, though, cuts to the heart of the way that Juan's Blackness paradoxically enables his extraordinary social ascent. It is only one of many moments when Juan expresses the desire to erase his Blackness and become white, and laments the impossibility of doing so. The fact that he cannot disguise his origins, however, makes that very social ascent less threatening, because his Blackness, according to the logic of the play, will always mark him as set apart from white Spanish nobility. His service can be recognized and rewarded because his Blackness always already precludes his complete assimilation. Thus the Duke of Alba can declare that he wishes he could trade places with Juan, and the Duke of Orange can proclaim "que no fuera quien soy, y fuera el negro" [Oh that I was not who I am, and could be the *negro*] (72), precisely because such wishes are categorically impossible. This is the same dynamic that informs the constant questioning and subsequent reinforcement of Juan's enslaved status in *Juan Latino*. A limit to the Black protagonist's inclusion in a white Spanish community is anxiously tested, and that very act of testing makes it more apparent.

This emphasis on Juan de Mérida's inalterable visible difference is inextricable from another form of otherness that haunts this play, which is also present in *Juan Latino*: anxieties about purity of blood and an invisible difference of faith. Although there is no equivalent to the villainous Morisco Fernando in *El valiente negro en Flandes*, a few pointed references present Juan de Mérida in contradistinction to Moors and Jews. As discussed above, in the play's opening lines Juan responds angrily when Spanish soldiers insult him by calling him "perro," or dog (23). He responds that there is no error in his blood, and that "perro" is a term for an Arab or Moor—not for a Black man. The first scene clarifies that those who assign Juan impure status because he is Black have made a mistake and reproduces the triangulation of difference described at the opening of this chapter: white Old Christian / Black Christian / Morisco or converso.

Nonetheless, Juan will go on to label himself as a dog later in the play—"el perro de Alba." When he does so, he specifically positions himself as a protector against *Jewish* perfidy: "el perro de Alba soy; que vengan Judios." [I am the dog of Alba; let the Jews come/come and get me, Jews] (61). Juan thus appears as the visibly different protector of white Spanish nobility against a number of threats from within and without. He shames cowardly soldiers into bravery; forces unfaithful noblemen to honor their debts to white Spanish ladies; singlehandedly ensures Spanish victory in the Low Countries; and stands as a bulwark against the insidious infiltration of "impure" Jews and Muslims.

In this play, as in *Juan Latino*, Juan's status as a valued servant and protector is enabled by being couched within a pervasive discourse that links Blackness with slavery. Although Juan is manumitted at the beginning of the play, his efforts throughout are presented as a form of service. Juan consistently lays the credit for his heroism at the feet of the Duke of Alba, and describes his actions as service not to himself but to the crown and the duke. When he is offered spoils of war, his first act is to set aside jewels and money for his former enslavers, the duke and his soldiers; he takes no treasure for himself. The play's insistence on his status as a servant to the interests of white Spaniards is most apparent in the play's final scene. In forcing the dissolute captain Agustín to marry Leonor, the woman he seduced and abandoned, Juan ruins Agustín's impending nuptials with his former mistress, Juana. In recompense, he offers to get Juana any husband she chooses, and to supplement the man's income with the money he has received from the king. In one of the two versions of the play's ending, Juana chooses to marry Juan himself: "de negro, quiero que subas al dueño" [from Black man/slave, I want you to ascend to lord/master]. In accepting, Juan again positions himself as a willing slave: "vueseñoria me tenga / por su esclavo" [your ladyship will have me as your slave] (97–98). Juana contradicts this statement, saying from this day onward she will be *his* slave, and Juan simply suggests that they get married that night. Even as his marriage is negotiated, Juan is unable to position himself as a desiring subject rather than as an instrument of service to white Spanish nobility. His desire to marry Juana (or lack thereof) is irrelevant in the face of her desire, despite the fact that it is couched in the promise that he will become her master. Juana needs a husband since Agustín is no longer available, so Juan steps into his place.

Performing Black and White: *El santo negro Rosambuco*

Although I have focused thus far on Black protagonists who achieve glory in the secular realm, the most common Black hero on the early modern Spanish stage was the Black saint. There are three extant Lope de Vega plays that chronicle a Black character's conversion to Christianity and performance of miraculous deeds in service of a white Christian community: *El prodigio de Etiopía* [The prodigy of Ethiopia] (published 1645); *El negro del mejor amo*, discussed above; and *El santo negro Rosambuco de la ciudad de Palermo* [The saintly Black man Rosambuco from the city of Palermo] (published 1611–12, composed between 1598 and 1607). Another play, alternately titled *El negro del mejor amo* and *El negro del serafín* (manuscript, 1643, published 1653), has been attributed both to Antonio Mira de Amescua and to Luis Vélez de

Guevara. Despite sharing a title with Lope's *El negro del mejor amo*, it actually recounts the life of Rosambuco, later Saint Benedict of Palermo (who is, of course, the protagonist of *El santo negro Rosambuco*). To make matters still more confusing, there is another play by Rodrigo Pacheco also titled *El negro del serafín*, from 1641, which recounts the life of yet another Black saint.[39] (This play, as far as I can tell, exists only in manuscript and there is no record of it having been performed.)

This cluster of plays with similar titles suggests that the Black saint functions as a motif in the comedia. And, indeed, all of these plays follow a similar trajectory: a Black warrior (in some but not all cases a Muslim in the employ of the Turks) is captured and brought to Christendom, converts to Christianity, and subsequently performs a series of miracles before dying and ascending to heaven. In these plays, as in those discussed above, the Black protagonists are repeatedly described as white inside or white in their deeds ("blanca en las obras"), and they consistently represent themselves as humble slaves in service to God and to white Christians.

Several of these plays also, like *El valiente negro en Flandes*, minimize the potential transgression of their protagonists by emphasizing the performance of Blackness as a theatrical practice. Lope de Vega's *El santo negro Rosambuco* presents a highly fictionalized account of the conversion to Christianity and subsequent miraculous intercessions of the historical figure St. Benedict of Palermo. Benedict—who changes his name from Rosambuco when he converts to Christianity—offers an even more extreme example than Juan Latino or Juan de Mérida of a Black protagonist whose impossible—in this case literally miraculous—accomplishments are inevitably cast as acts of service to white Spanish nobility. Indeed, at the end of the play St. Benedict trades his life for that of his former enslaver, who has died in a fire. He asks that he be taken instead so that his enslaver can be brought back from the dead, and God answers his prayer. I can think of no clearer example of the instrumentalization of Black bodies in service to white subjectivity, or of an underlying romanticization of slavery as willing sacrifice.

The play also, though, persistently alludes to the theatrical performance of Blackness. A young white girl, the daughter of the viceroy, is brought to Benedict in the hope that he can free her from demonic possession. One of the ways this possession manifests is that she speaks in Black speech, or *habla de negro*. She (or the devil possessing her) first delivers racist diatribes against Benedict in standard Castilian: "Negro tiznado, modorro / de verte aqui me corro" [Stupid, stained Black man / seeing you here makes me run away]. She continues to insult him and then switches to *habla de negro*: Nenglo Angola, de donceya / querer sacar . . . no la puedas a la diabla / sacar de cuerpo negrino." [Black man from Angola, you want to take out (the devil) from the lady . . . you can't take the devil out of (her) body, little Black man] (384). An onlooker remarks of the devil possessing the girl: "Latín, Negro, y vizcaíno / y todos las lenguas habla" [Latin, Black, and Basque talk, he (the devil) speaks all languages] (384). *Vizcaíno*, like *habla de negro*, is an accent that was mimicked to intended comedic effect in early modern Spanish theater. The moment highlights difference as performance, presenting the spectacle of a man in blackface "talking white" alongside a white actress using "Black speech." Benedict is able to free the girl from demonic possession through prayer, and she returns to speaking standard Castilian.

This metatheatrical moment seems to have resonated, because Mira de Amescua picks up on it and inverts it in his play about Saint Benedict, *El negro del serafín*. In this later version, it is an enslaved Black woman, Catalina, who has been possessed, and her possession is marked by her speech shifting from *habla de negro* to standard Castilian. When Benedict successfully drives the devil from her, she returns to speaking *habla de negro*. Both plays thus emphasize Black speech as a performance put on and taken off at will by white performers. They simultaneously reify Blackness and minimize the ways in which a Black saint might be used to undermine existing hierarchies. Blackness becomes a performance, both cosmetic and linguistic, put on by white actors. Benedict is not only white inside as a saint but is also played by a white man. In a less straightforward fashion, the scenes in both plays also draw a parallel between Benedict and the female character who is possessed. This is particularly true in the later Mira de Amescua play, in which Catalina and Benedict are the only two Black characters. Just as Catalina is an instrument possessed by the devil, Benedict is an instrument through which God works miracles. By juxtaposing the two characters, and especially by making Catalina speak standard Castilian when possessed, the play underlines each character's status as instrument rather than agent.

Lope de Vega's *El santo negro Rosambuco* follows the scene of demonic possession with another metatheatrical wink to blackface. It does so through the character of Pedrisco, a priest who occupies a position in this play similar to that of the feckless Agustín in *El valiente negro en Flandes*. Resentful that a Black man has achieved fame for performing miracles, Pedrisco continually attempts to thwart and undermine Benedict. He hatches a plot to dress himself in blackface and pretend to be Benedict when the viceroy (the character whose daughter has been possessed) comes to visit. He then plans to act so oddly that the viceroy will believe that Benedict is crazy. The plan is foiled first by Benedict's unexpected return to the monastery, and then by a very peculiar divine intervention. Immediately after Benedict frees the young girl from demonic possession, Pedrisco appears onstage pretending to be Benedict and believing himself to be in blackface makeup. Miraculously, however, Pedrisco's blackface paint has been transformed into flour, so that he enters "enharinado"—whiter rather than blacker than before (386). Everyone recognizes him immediately and ask him why he is covered in flour, and Benedict gently tells the viceroy that Pedrisco is a little simple.

This moment serves, of course, as another ironic reminder of blackface as a cosmetic practice—a reminder that all Blackness in the staging of this play is a performance. It may even covertly engage with the imagined invisible evil of the converso or the Morisco who is white on the outside but morally darkened within, like the Morisco Fernando in *Juan Latino*. Pedrisco's response when he is caught out further emphasizes issues of race:

> El demonio me ha burlado
> De salvados vengo lleno.
> Pues aunque me causa espanto
> Lo que aqui me ha sucedido
> Aun no estoy buen persuadido
> de que este mandinga es santo. (387)

> [The devil has tricked me. I'm covered in bran flour. But even though what happened to me frightens me, I'm still not persuaded that this *mandingo* is a saint.]

The racist term *mandingo* is here put in the mouth of the closest thing the play has to a villain, and he is mocked for failing to recognize that a Black man might be a saint.

Although this moment might be read as pushing back against racism—Pedrisco, after all, is a fool for failing to recognize that a Black man might be a saint—his own path to redemption undermines such a straightforward interpretation. As the play nears its conclusion, Pedrisco tries to kill Benedict by poisoning his glass of water, but the glass miraculously breaks as Benedict makes the sign of the cross over it. Pedrisco confesses everything, and Benedict prevents the other brothers from punishing him, saying that

Pedrisco will also be a saint one day and asking Pedrisco to embrace him. Pedrisco's response, once again, draws on imagery associated with slavery: "ya, de hoy más, con dulces lazos / cadenas de mi alma son" [now, from today onward, with sweet knots, these (i.e., Benedict's arms) are chains of my soul] (391). None of the miraculous interventions that save Benedict from Pedrisco's schemes cause harm. They serve as a gentle chastisement while Pedrisco's apology reminds the audience that the white character's service to Benedict will never be more than a metaphor. Like Agustín in *El valiente negro en Flandes*, Pedrisco faces no punishment for his misdeeds but rather learns a lesson from his Black counterpart before being brought back into the fold.

The voluntary nature of Pedrisco's service and the easy forgiveness of his misdeeds both expose and rely upon his whiteness. They also complicate Dyer's description of whiteness, cited above, as "not anything, not a particularizing quality." When Pedrisco announces his plans to put on blackface and then emerges whitened instead, the play's audience is forced to confront— however briefly—the "particularizing quality" of whiteness. *El santo negro Rosambuco*, like *El valiente negro en Flandes*, represents Black characters as servants of and accessories to a white European commonwealth. As they do so, they both draw on and help to produce a discourse that naturalizes a connection between Blackness and enslavement. They also, though, render the construction of whiteness visible.

Blackness, Whiteness, and Miscegenation: A Textual History

As mentioned above, *El valiente negro en Flandes* has two different extant endings: one version ends with a marriage between its Black protagonist and the white noblewoman in whose household he was enslaved, and the other omits the marriage. Scholarly engagement with the two extant endings of this play illuminates how underlying assumptions about racial ideologies can shape what we allow ourselves to see in early modern texts.

The first dated print version of *El valiente negro en Flandes* is from 1638. Like *Juan Latino*, it appears in a collection of plays by various authors: *Parte treynta y uno de las mejores comedias que hasta oy han salido*, a copy of which has been digitized by Madrid's Biblioteca Nacional. In this version, the play ends with Juan's offer to Juana (his former enslaver) to fund her marriage to a man of her choosing, and goes straight from that to the concluding remarks, leaving her choice of spouse unspoken. In the eleven other extant printed versions of the play from the seventeenth and eighteenth centuries, Juana declares that her chosen husband is Juan himself, and he acquiesces. The 1638 edition is the only printed text before the nineteenth century that omits the marriage between Juan and his former mistress.[40] Nonetheless, in both scholarly analysis of the play and many recent scholarly editions, the interracial marriage that closes almost all extant versions of the play has either been ignored or treated as an afterthought. Thus it offers a compelling example of the interplay between early modern and present-day engagements with questions of race and particularly of interracial marriage, and of the intersections of philological practice and unconscious ideological bias.

First, though, it is important to note that one reason that the interracial marriage has been marginalized is largely circumstantial. The 1638 edition is the one that omits the marriage, and it is the first dated and published version; it also appears in a dated codex rather than in loose-leaf *pliegos*. Thus it has generally been assumed to be the princeps and the most authoritative, although there is no indication that Andrés de Claramonte, who died in 1626, was involved in this or any printing of his play. This 1638 version was the basis of the play's sole nineteenth-century version, published in 1888 as part of the Biblioteca de Autores Españoles series *Dramáticos contemporáneos de Lope de Vega*. And this version, with no mention of marriage at the end, is the one that several twentieth-century critics cite as their source.

In this case, then, the omission of the marriage may not indicate suppression or unconscious bias but rather the absence of a scholarly edition of a little-studied play. However, in the last quarter century three different editions have come out, all of which include the marriage as an unusual variant rather than as the most commonly found ending of the play. Two of these editions include the marriage at the end in a different typeface from the rest of the text, and add a note that it was either added later or censored from the 1638 princeps. Only Ana Ogallas Moreno's 2016 edition, available only as an e-book, discusses the predominance of the interracial marriage in early editions and includes it at the end. Even Ogallas Moreno, however, adds this endnote: "A partir de este verso, anuncio de boda entre la dama doña Juana y el que fue su criado negro. Es la sublimación de la transgresiøón, impensable en la época, ni en la realidad ni en la ficción." [From this verse onward, an announcement of the wedding between the lady Juana and the man who was her Black servant. It is the exaltation of transgression, unthinkable in the era in either reality or in fiction.][41] However, Ogallas Moreno's own careful cataloging of the multiple editions of the play that include this marriage suggest that, while it was certainly transgressive, it was far from unthinkable. On the contrary, the marriage between a Black man and white woman is centered both in *Juan Latino* and in almost all extent early versions of *El valiente negro en Flandes*.

One extant manuscript copy of *El valiente negro en Flandes* shows both that the interracial marriage that ends the play was part of the performance tradition and that it was not deemed suitable for all audiences. The Biblioteca Nacional de España contains one manuscript of a performance script of the play with signatures of censors from 1651 and 1652. This manuscript is most likely a scribal copy of a now-lost autograph. The names of several actors are written in the margins, indicating that the play was used by performers as well as given to censors to read before authorizing the play for performance. Both censors approved the play, but one seems to have made some changes, excising certain lines. Juana's decision to marry Juan is among the parts cut; the lines are struck through and the word "no" is written several times in the margin.

Making assertions about a manuscript written in several hands, as this one is, is tricky. It is possible that these lines were cut before the censor read the manuscript for reasons entirely unrelated to censorship. However, other censored manuscripts from the period follow a similar pattern—the censor strikes through passages of which he does not approve and writes "no" alongside them—so censorship seems by far the most plausible explanation. Assuming that this is the case, the manuscript tells us that by 1651, at the latest, the marriage between Juan de Mérida and his former mistress was a part of the performance tradition, but also that it generated enough controversy (or at the very least anxiety for one censor) to demand its removal for certain audiences. The print and manuscript tradition of *El valiente negro en Flandes* indicates that Juan's social ascent and marriage were seen as transgressive enough to merit censorship, but also that this theater company initially planned to include the marriage in their performance.

In sum, then, there are eleven early print versions of the play that include the interracial marriage, one version that omits it, and a single manuscript in which it was initially included and then censored. Critical discussion about the play, though, has struggled to engage with the fact that most early versions of the play end with Juan's marriage to a white woman. Fra Molinero's chapter on the play ends by arguing that Juan has been left to remain in a state of neutralizing celibacy ("celibato neutralizador") without the ability to create a lineage.[42] He adds a footnote saying "there are other versions of this comedy in which Juan de Mérida marries his former mistress," and that a colleague is writing a doctoral dissertation on the different versions of the play, but does not specify further.[43] John Beusterien also does not mention the end of the play when he discusses it in his chapter on Black protagonists in the Spanish comedia. In a section on Black saint plays, however, Beusterien asserts that "the Black . . . is an unmarriable icon . . . the Black saint is excluded from the social scene of reproduction." He appends a note to this passage: "I am also thinking of the many [sic] censored final scene versions of *El valiente negro en Flandes*. Representations of Black men married to Whites appear in the nineteenth century with the translations of *Othello*."[44]

Beusterien and Fra Molinero both acknowledge the marriage only in footnotes as they discuss the impossibility of interracial alliance on the early modern Spanish stage. Ogallas Moreno, similarly, asserts that the transgression of Juan and Juana's marriage is unthinkable for people of the era, despite cataloging the prevalence of editions in which it is included. All of these critics argue that the play serves to uphold white supremacy, and it seems that a reading that centers interracial marriage at the end is, for them, fundamentally incompatible with this approach, and thus they largely exclude it from their discussion of the play.

Indeed, thus far, critics who do foreground the interracial marriage have used it to argue that the play offers a model of racial inclusivity or a covert critique of the institution of slavery.[45] These critics assert that readings of the play that focus on white supremacy are anachronistically projecting present-day racial discourses on the past, and that the marriage offers proof that anti-Black racism had not yet taken hold in seventeenth-century Spain. To hold such a position requires turning a blind eye to the anti-Black rhetoric and romanticization of slavery as willing service that permeate the comedia, as I hope this chapter has clearly delineated. The scholarship to date seems to suggest that we must either fail to engage with the play's interracial marriage or fail to engage with the ways that the play upholds a logic of white supremacy.

Conclusion

What if, instead of reading the play's interracial marriage as an inherently progressive or liberatory gesture, we instead viewed the ending as *reinforcing* a logic of white supremacy? In this context, Juan's marriage to Juana becomes another form of service to the white Spanish community, as my earlier analysis of the play suggests. His marriage meets Juana's need for a husband while presenting him as a corrective to the errors of the feckless Agustín, and thus is very much aligned with his role throughout the play as tireless servant to the needs of the white nobility. It is particularly important that in no version of the play does Juan himself suggest that he could marry Juana, and there is no point in the play in which he indicates any erotic desire for her. Just as Juan has compensated for Agustín's cowardice on the battlefield, he here compensates for the latter's sexual profligacy in replacing him as a husband. Juan can only marry Juana because doing so meets the needs of the white nobility and the marriage plot alike.

Crucially, this dynamic relies on the unseen presence of another form of prohibited alliance: between the "pure-blooded" white Spanish woman and someone of impure descent. Juan's inclusion in Spain and marriage to Juana—like Juan Latino's marriage to Ana in the play discussed earlier—is contingent on establishing his difference from the Jew and the Moor. Indeed, this dynamic is even more explicit in *Juan Latino*, in which Ana is courted by the Morisco Fernando before she marries Juan. Chapter 5 addresses in detail the complicated triangulation of whiteness, Blackness, and impure blood in the specific context of marriage and reproduction. For now, I simply wish to underline how the interpenetration of different racializing discourses can help us to understand the marriage at the end of *El valiente negro en Flandes* as reinforcing rather than complicating white supremacy. A discourse linking Blackness with enslavement enables the play to present Juan's various heroic acts as a form of nonthreatening service, while the characterization of "impure blood" rather than Blackness as the sine qua non of prohibited miscegenation enables his service to take the form of marriage to a white woman.

The following chapter turns to representations of Blackness in English theater, using the patterns laid out in this reading of the Spanish comedia to argue that the explicit connection between Blackness and enslavement on the early modern Spanish stage may help us to see a similar dynamic in English drama. I approach this comparison with some caution; the Spanish plays discussed above would not have been accessible to most early modern English readers or playgoers, as drama—unlike prose—was not frequently translated from Spanish to English.[46] Indeed, in earlier chapters I cautioned against taking an imagined Spanish model of racialized difference (in this case, purity of blood) and applying it to early modern English drama.

In this context, however, the Spanish comedia's sustained and explicit staging of Black characters as enslaved can help us to see a similar—but implicit—pairing of Blackness and enslavement in English drama. I do not argue that these Spanish plays directly informed early modern English drama, but rather that they reflect a growing discursive alignment of Blackness with enslavement more broadly, and that this broader context informs representations of Blackness within England. Historically, many early modern English encounters with Black people were mediated by the Afro-Iberian slave trade; thus it is logical that Spanish paradigms for understanding Blackness in relation to slavery would inform those found in England.[47] More specifically, this comparative framework reorients our approach to Black Moors in English plays that are set in or allude to Spain. Although Moors on the early modern English stage have often been linked to Spain in the context of Islamic difference, their connection to Spain also reflects the history of slavery.

CHAPTER 4

"I Have Done the State Some Service"

Moorishness and Slavery on the English Stage

In early modern Spanish drama, as the previous chapter demonstrates, the figure of the *negro* occupies a very different space than that of the *moro* or the *morisco*, engaging with slavery and defining itself *against* religious difference rather than as an expression of it. But what, if anything, does this dynamic tell us about representations of "Moors" on the early modern English stage? The term, after all, is notoriously vexed. It lies at the heart of a racially charged debate about *Othello* that has persisted at least since Coleridge's now-infamous assertion that the character must be conceived "not as a negro, but as a high and chivalrous Moorish chief."[1] We might arguably push the origins of this argument back even further, to Thomas Rymer's scathing 1693 indictment of the play as "fraught with improbabilities"—the most improbable among them that the Venetians would "set a Negro to be their general" and "trust a Moor to defend them against the Turk."[2]

Scholars today continue to grapple with this question, often using *Othello* as a point of entry into unpacking the relationship between anti-Islamic and anti-Black sentiments in early modern texts. At its most reductive, this becomes a debate between labeling Othello as either a North African Muslim or a sub-Saharan African. Conflicting readings of one key line in the play encapsulate the stakes of this discussion. When he recounts the story that won Desdemona's heart, Othello mentions having been "taken by the insolent foe / And sold to slavery."[3] For readers today, these lines, spoken by a character described as "Black" on multiple occasions, immediately evoke the specter of the Atlantic triangle and the widespread enslavement of sub-Saharan Africans. In recent years, however, many critics have warned against such associations on the grounds that they are anachronistic. They argue that we lose sight of *Othello*'s historical specificity if we read it in the context of racial categories that would only crystallize later in the century with the rise of a plantation economy.[4] Instead, scholars such as Jonathan Burton, Julia Reinhardt Lupton, and Daniel Vitkus have suggested that Othello's capture by the "insolent foe" should be read not in the context of the Atlantic slave trade but rather that of piracy and kidnapping in the Islamic Mediterranean. In this reading, the play becomes a "drama of conversion," in which Othello's "Moorishness" associates him with Islam as much as it does with Blackness.[5] Placing *Othello* in this Mediterranean context thus avoids naturalizing—enshrining as timeless and essential—vocabularies of race that are in fact the product of a particular moment in the development of a global economy.

In his introduction to the most recent Oxford edition of *Othello*, Michael Neill ably sums up the significance of this Mediterranean-focused approach to our understanding of the play's engagement with slavery:

> For modern audiences, Othello's story of enslavement will inevitably be colored by the horrors of that later history; but, as the work of Nabil Matar and Daniel Vitkus has demonstrated, "Moors" were, on balance, more likely to figure in the early seventeenth-century English imagination as enslavers than as slaves; and Othello's narrative of capture, enslavement, and "redemption thence" actually parallels the experience of many prisoners on both sides of a Muslim-Christian conflict that stretched back at least to the Crusades. As such it belongs not to the industrialized human marketplace of the Atlantic triangle, but to the same Mediterranean theatre of war as the Turkish invasion of Cyprus.[6]

Neill's argument is based on the logic of anachronism: "modern readers" find their reading of *Othello* "colored" (a telling word choice) by a "later history." The history of slavery is yet to be, and the framework that makes Othello and other early modern Moorish characters most legible is that of "a Muslim-Christian conflict that stretched back at least to the Crusades." This history of religious conflict is indeed central to Shakespeare's play, as numerous critical studies attest, but that does not mean it is the *only* history that should inform our understanding of *Othello*. My contention here is that the impulse to read Moors on the early modern English stage primarily in the context of Islamic difference betrays an anxious desire to disavow the circulation of anti-Black discourses in early modern England, and particularly to disavow the ways in which early modern English culture was already participating in a broader European discursive framework that linked Blackness to enslavement.

Exploring this question also exposes the intensity of resistance—among scholars, playgoers, and readers alike—to acknowledging the prevalence of anti-Black racism in early modern texts. Kim F. Hall documents this resistance in her essay "Othello and the Problem of Blackness," in which she describes an encounter with a customs agent at the airport on her way to give a talk on *Othello* in London. Once the agent has learned the topic of her talk, he asks, "Othello's a Moor, right? And a Moor is not really black, is he then?" Hall observes that "the question doubts the connection of this representation of a 'black' man to the peoples of the African Diaspora, people who have had to bear the economic and symbolic weight of historical regimes of enforced labor and contemporary discrimination. To say that Othello was not meant to be conceived of as 'black' is to liberate the reader from considering that history in reading, viewing, or performing the play and to liberate Shakespeare from possible charges of racism."[7] Indeed, Hall and numerous other critics have persuasively demonstrated the centrality of anti-Black discourses in *Othello*, and the extent to which a desire to explain away such discourses reveals a resistance to engaging with histories of racism.[8] In this chapter, I draw on a comparative framework to demonstrate the relationship the connections between *Othello* and other plays' discourses of Blackness and references to slavery.

As I do so, I am attempting a complicated balance. On the one hand, I am committed the holding on to the capaciousness and ambiguity of the term *Moor* in early modern England. The term can refer to North Africans specifically, to anyone from Africa, Muslims of any color or ancestry, or even occasionally dark-skinned peoples from the so-called New World or the East. In her book-length study of early of early modern Moorishness, Emily Bartels argues that "as a subject, 'the Moor' does not have a single or pure, culturally or racially bounded identity. Within early modern representations . . . the Moor is first and foremost a figure of uncodified and uncodifiable diversity."[9] It is important to hold on to this diversity and to register the range of significations of the Moor to early modern theatergoers. Indeed, racial signifiers are always laden with multiple meanings, at times mutually reinforcing and at times contradictory. Nonetheless, for all of the ambiguities inherent to early modern Moorishness, it is still possible to track patterns of usage across multiple plays, thereby registering which associations with the term are more and less prevalent. Doing so reveals, in simplest terms, that Black Moors in early modern English theater are associated frequently with enslavement and service and only infrequently with Islam.

There are, of course, many early modern English texts that address anxieties about the shifting and often-improvisatory religious allegiances that characterized the early modern Mediterranean, and especially of the power of the Ottoman Empire. Scholarship by Nabil Matar and others offers a crucial reminder that early modern England's relationship with the Islamic Mediterranean was not one of dominance but rather of anxious negotiation with the Ottoman Empire's superior might.[10] The issue I address here is not the indisputable importance of such scholarship, but rather one way that such scholarship has been put to use: references to Mediterranean piracy and Islamic preeminence have been used to elide or deemphasize the traces left on early modern English literature of an emergent traffic in Black bodies.

It is also true that anxieties about Blackness and about threatening religious difference often surface in the same plays, plays which are embedded in the early modern project of defining and reinforcing English—and more broadly European—whiteness. Often, this articulation of white identity has been understood to emerge within a binary system. The white Christian is differentiated from the "other," a character who is set apart by Blackness or religious difference or a combination of the two. In Spanish plays from this period, however, racial dynamics often take shape not as a binary opposition but rather are triangulated. The figure of the white Christian emerges in contrast with not one but two figures of difference: the Jew or Moor (whose difference does not manifest as color) and the Black (and often enslaved) Christian. The clear distinction between color and religious difference in the Spanish comedia provides a framework that may allow us to reconsider the assumption that Blackness must function as a sign of religious difference on the English stage. There are, as we shall see, some plays that represent Muslim characters as Black, and that Blackness as a sign of their inner perfidy, but in most cases Black characters are not explicitly linked with Islam. Conversely, most plays that explicitly engage with the fraught dynamics of conversion do not represent Muslim characters as Black; Anglo-Islamic encounters by and large are not played out against Black Moors but rather "Turks" and North African Moors who are not described as dark-skinned.[11]

To demonstrate that the Moor on the early modern stage' is more closely linked with service and slavery than with Islam, I have surveyed all of the English plays I could access with characters explicitly labeled as Moors, Black Moors, Ethiopians, or Negros written between 1590 and 1640. The chapter begins by drawing on this survey to discuss patterns that emerge across early modern English plays and masques with Black characters. I then turn to a close reading of two plays: *Lust's Dominion* (1599), attributed to Dekker, Day, and Houghton, and Shakespeare's *Othello* (1604). My goal is to intervene in present-day critical debates about the meaning of Moorishness on the early modern stage in two areas: first, to show that the term *Moor* is less closely tied to Islam than many critics have assumed; second, to demonstrate that the staging of Blackness is often paired with a sustained vocabulary of slavery, which is at times reframed as willing service. I am not suggesting that the figure of the Moor is completely dissociated from Islam; there are, indeed, multiple early modern plays that contain characters described as both Black and Muslim; these plays, however, are the exception rather than the rule. I wish, then, to query why we have so frequently read the exception *as* the rule, scanning texts for submerged and ambiguous references to Islam while explaining away explicit representations of slavery as anachronistic.

Race and Slavery in Early Modern England

Before I turn to the plays themselves, a thumbnail sketch of the history and historiography of racialized slavery within England exposes some assumptions that have shaped our literary analysis. It is true, as Neill asserts, that England's sustained involvement with the Atlantic triangle trade postdates *Othello*. It is also true that slavery was not explicitly codified under English law. Indeed, William Harrison's 1587 *Description of England* famously declared the absence of slavery on English soil: "For slaves and bondmen, we have none . . . if any come hither from other realms, so soone as they set foot on land they become so free of condition as their masters."[12] Early modern England, unlike Spain and Portugal, did not have a legal or financial apparatus that sanctioned, taxed, and recorded the traffic in enslaved people.

Some scholars have taken Harrison's jingoistic declamation at face value, operating under the assumption that early modern England was still innocent of the stain of racialized slavery. This assumption, however, demands a selective narrative of history. Infamously, Queen Elizabeth herself invested in John Hawkins's attempts to enter the slave trade (1562, 1564), and his attempts ceased only because his final voyage was an unmitigated disaster both financially and for Anglo-Spanish diplomacy. Beyond the crown's investment in slavery, archival research by Imtiaz Habib and Gustav Ungerer has demonstrated that there were a number of Afro-diasporic subjects living in early modern England. There are references to "Moors," "Blackamoors," "Ethiopians," and "negros" in court and household account books, parish records of baptisms and deaths, and court cases. In many cases, references to Black people appear in household records of those linked with Iberia and the Atlantic world: Portuguese conversos who came to England fleeing the Inquisition, English merchants who had worked abroad in Andalusia, and aristocrats (including Francis Drake) with ties to transatlantic imperial ventures.[13]

The precise legal status of these Afro-diasporic subjects within England is complex. This is because, as Ungerer has argued, slavery in early modern England was not so much illegal as it was largely uncodified. Slavery was not endorsed and administered under English law, but it was not clearly prohibited either. This dynamic produced what Habib has referred to as "an incremental if surreptitious influx of black people into England over the duration of [Elizabeth's] reign and beyond. Illicitly seized, secretly traded, the passage to or arrival in England uncertainly recorded if at all, and [their] status unrecognized by law."[14] In Spain and Portugal, the trade in enslaved people is documented in bills of sale, tax records, and wills. In England, by contrast, the absence of a clearly defined legal policy meant that the presence of slavery would have remained largely unrecorded.

The ambiguous status of slavery in early modern England can be seen in a petition lodged in Elizabeth I's Court of Requests. In 1587, the influential Portuguese-born merchant and physician Hector Nunes filed a complaint. He stated that an English sailor had recently sold him an enslaved person—an "Ethiopian" recently brought back from the Spanish colonies. To Nunes's surprise, however, the man he had purchased "utterly refuse[d] to tarry and serve," and Nunes discovered that he had no recourse under English law to compel his continued enslavement. Nunes asked the court to either force the man he had purchased to serve him, or to compel the slave's seller to refund his money.[15] Unfortunately, no record exists of the court's reply to his request. This petition tells us that at least one enslaved person was able to make a bid for freedom on the basis of English law (or lack thereof), although we do not know if it was successful. At the same time, however, it establishes the attempted sale of an enslaved person within England.

While the size and scope of racialized enslavement within early modern England is minuscule in comparison to the licit slavery practiced in other parts of Europe and in the Atlantic, it seems untenable to me to declare, as one public historian recently did, that "Tudor England really had 'too pure an air for slaves to breathe in.'"[16] It is difficult to imagine that the "Moors" and "Ethiopians" brought into England, whether purchased by English merchants in Spain or seized as spoils of war in privateering ventures, set foot on English soil and suddenly became free citizens, particularly given that many continued to serve in the households of those who had seized or purchased them abroad. Although some Black people in early modern England practiced independent trades, the trajectories of their lives were almost certainly shaped by racialized slavery, whether they themselves were kidnapped and brought into Europe or one or more of their parents were. In brief, the Afro-Iberian slave trade was the primary mechanism through which Africans entered early modern Europe and its colonies. In this way the institution of slavery very concretely undergirds English encounters with sub-Saharan Africans in this period.

Even if early modern England had somehow remained untouched by the practice of slavery (and to be perfectly clear, this is not a point I am conceding), a developing connection between Blackness and enslavement would still have informed the early modern English imaginary. After all, England does not exist in a vacuum, and enslaved Afro-diasporic peoples were a visible—and frequently described—presence in Spain, Portugal, and their colonies by the end of the fifteenth century, a full century before *Othello* was written. English travelers in Spain encountered Black people, many of them enslaved, as did English sailors in mercantile and imperial ventures.[17] Early modern English travel narratives describe the growing importance of enslaved Africans in the Atlantic world, and Spanish and Portuguese texts in English translation represent Blackness and slavery as intertwined, much as we saw in the Spanish dramas discussed in the previous chapter. Not all enslaved people described in travel narratives are Black, of course, and not all Black subjects described are represented as enslaved. Nonetheless, when we take this transnational context into account, it seems inevitable that Blackness and slavery would have been linked in the early modern English imaginary, even if that connection was less fixed than it became in the second half of the seventeenth century and later.

References to racialized slavery are not only to be found in travel narratives; they also appear in popular early modern English translations of Spanish picaresque novels. In Thomas Shelton's 1612 translation of *Don Quijote*, Sancho Panza fantasizes about marrying the princess of an imaginary

African country, Micomicon. Initially "grieved" at the prospect that his "vassals should all be black," he soon consoles himself with this thought: "Why should I care though my subjects be all black Moors? Is there any more to be done than to load them in a ship and bring them to Spain, where I may sell them and receive the price of them in ready money?"[18] An earlier text, David Rowland's 1586 translation of *Lazarillo de Tormes*, refers in passing to Lazarillo's enslaved Black stepfather, Zaide, referring to him as "black," a "black Morion," and a "bondsman or slave."[19] While Rowland translates the Spanish word *negro* as "black Morion," he translates the Spanish word *moro* not as "Morion" or "Moor" but rather as "Turk."[20] In doing so, he reflects the Spanish text's distinction between the *moro* as a figure of racialized religious difference, and the *negro* as a figure whose difference is marked by color. In both texts, the Spanish word *negro* is translated as "Black Moor" and linked with slavery.

James Mabbe's 1623 translation *The Rogue*, discussed in detail in Chapter 2, offers a particularly clear example of the racialization of slavery in early modern English translations of Spanish texts. In addition to several brief references to enslaved Black people, the novel mentions two different enslaved white women. In the Spanish source text, Guzmán describes one of these woman as "una gentil esclava blanca" [a graceful white slave]. Mabbe's translation is more expansive: "a dainty fine she-slave, not swart and tawny, as others commonly be, but fair and well-favoured."[21] Later, Guzmán describes an affair with another woman, "una esclava blanca, que yo mucho tiempo creí ser libre" [a white slave woman, whom I believed for a long time to be free]. Mabbe's translates this passage as: "a certaine fair white slave (none I wisse of these black moores, but a handsome well-favored Wench) . . . whom, for a long time, I took to be free-born."[22] Here, as in the translations cited above, the institution of slavery requires no further explanation. Mabbe does, however, take time to draw attention to the fact that the person enslaved is white, presenting this as an aberration from the norm.

Crucially, both these Spanish texts and their English translations casually reflect a worldview in which enslavement cannot be collapsed into the dynamic Neill describes as a "Muslim-Christian conflict that stretches back at least as far as the crusades." To the contrary, Sancho's dream of profit depends on the emergence of an "industrialized human market-place" that Neill describes as "yet to be."[23] As these examples suggest, early modern translators of Spanish texts into English assumed their readers' familiarity with the dynamics of racialized slavery.

Stage Moors and Islam

When scholars argue that racialized slavery did not yet inform early modern English representations of Black Moors, they often do so by reading the Moor as a figure of primarily religious—and specifically Islamic—difference. But how clearly was the figure of the Moor linked with Islam in early modern English drama? Here, I address this question by turning to a broad survey of English plays. The parameters I have set are concrete: Do these plays refer to Allah, Mohammed, the Koran, silver moons or crescents, Saracens, or other specifically Islamic references or symbols? I found that on the stage, characters designated as "Moors" are surprisingly infrequently accompanied with explicit references to Islam. Indeed, in a survey of thirty English plays with characters labeled as "Moors" or "Black Moors" (including white characters who disguise themselves as Moors), only six contain Moors who are explicitly described as Muslim: *The Battle of Alcazar*, *The Famous History of the Life and Death of Captain Thomas Stukely*, *All's Lost by Lust*, *The Fair Maid of the West Part I*, *The Fair Maid of the West Part II*, and *Hans Beer-Pot*.[24]

As a whole, this group of plays largely aligns with the model Matar proposes in relation to *Othello*: "The 'Turk' was the Muslim, the moral enemy at the frontiers of Mediterranean Christendom. Meanwhile, the term 'Moor' described an African with distinct racial and psychological features."[25] The absence of specific Islamic references in plays with Moorish characters is particularly notable when we compare them to "Turk plays," which do consistently and specifically refer to Islam.[26] The Prince of Morocco in Shakespeare's *Merchant of Venice* offers one example of the separation of the figure of the Moor from references to Islam. Despite the fact that religious conversion is one of the play's recurring themes, Morocco (who is, according to the stage directions, a "tawny Moor") is rejected by Portia on grounds of not religion but "complexion," and no mention is made of his religion at all.[27]

The tendency among scholars to conflate Moorishness with Islam can be attributed in part to the legacy of the black-faced devil of the medieval mystery play. As scholars have persuasively demonstrated, the motif of the Black villain directly descends from the black-faced devils of medieval mystery plays, which is then repurposed within a racialized framework.[28] In part because the polyvalence of the word *Moor*, the godlessness often associated with Black characters has become linked not just with devilishness but specifically with Islam. There is little evidence, however, that representations of Black characters as un-Christian or godless gestures specifically to anxieties about

Islamic beliefs or practices. Here, again, a comparison with early modern Turk plays is useful: although Turkish characters quite explicitly represent anxieties about Islam, Turkish characters are by and large not represented as Black. Thus the assumption that Blackness serves as a visual representation of specifically Islamic godlessness is not mirrored by early modern stage practices.

Importantly, several of the characters labeled "Moors" who are explicitly represented as Muslim are not represented as Black. Before continuing, I want to nuance the perhaps overly simplistic distinction I have asserted between "Black" and "not Black." It is entirely plausible, as Noémie Ndiaye has argued in relation to *The Bondsman*, that some stage characters not described as Black in the text of the play would have been played in blackface.[29] Similarly, as Jane Degenhardt has discussed, textual clues in the Turk play *The Renegado* may suggest that at least one of its Turkish characters was darkened cosmetically. This character, Mustapha, is ambiguously coded as dark-skinned (e.g., described as having a "wainscot" face and "tadpole-like" complexion) but not consistently described in terms of Blackness, as many stage Moors are. A more precise formulation of this distinction, then, is that between characters for whom Blackness is a repeated motif and those for whom it may have been part of stage practice, but not so central to their characterization as to be clearly preserved in the language of the play.[30]

The anonymous play *The Famous History of the Life and Death of Captain Thomas Stukely* (1605) and George Peele's *The Battle of Alcazar* (1594) both take their plots from an early modern history book, John Polemon's *The Second Part of the Book of Battles Fought in Our Age* (1587), and both plays recount the disastrous decision of Prince Sebastian of Portugal to side with the evil Moor Muly Hamet in a territorial battle in north Africa. The Moors in *Captain Thomas Stukeley* are described in terms of both geographic origin (North Africa) and religion (Islam) and are not described as Black. In *The Battle of Alcazar* only the wicked Muly Hamet is described as Black, whereas the complexions of the play's other African Muslim characters remain unremarked. In this, the plays follow their source, which describes only Muly Hamet as dark-skinned. The Moors in this play are clearly Muslim, in that there is a mention of banners with "silver moons" (1.1) but anxieties about conversion are not a central theme in this play as they are in Turk plays. Mohammed is not mentioned, and conversion to Christianity is only discussed in passing as a motivation for Christian incursions into Africa. Interestingly, although many of the characters represented on stage are North African Muslims, only the Black Muly Hamet is referred to in stage directions as "The Moor." This demonstrates how the word *Moor* can do two kinds of work even within the same play: referring in the play's dialogue to a group of people as a geographically bounded cultural and political entity not necessarily marked by phenotypic difference (the Moors who fight the Spaniards), and in stage directions to an individual character who is distinguished by his Blackness and was presumably played in blackface. The positioning of Muly Hamet in stage directions as *the* Moor also points to an important commonality among Black characters on the early modern stage: unlike Turks and non-Black Moors, Black Moors are more likely to appear as isolated individuals rather than as part of a larger collective.

Another play with a dark-skinned Muslim character, the little-studied *Hans Beer-Pot*, clearly separates the origins of this character's darkness (like Morocco, he is described as not Black but "tawny") and adherence to Islam. *Hans Beer-Pot* (1618) is a brief comic interlude set in the Low Countries.[31] Mostly a discussion of the merits and pitfalls of drunkenness, it contains one Moorish character with the intriguing name "Adnidaraes Quixot, a tawny Moor." His presence in the plot (such as it is) is largely extraneous; he simply shows up twice, each time singing a song before making an exit. He also, unlike many other early modern stage Moors, has a very specific pedigree:

I am a Moore borne in Numedia,
Parcht with the suns extreame and scorching heate;
My mothers name *Abdela Sydan* hight,
My Father was *Don Ian de Uechia*,
A noble Spaniard, braue Castilian:
I serude the King of swart Numidia . . .

Son of a Moorish woman and a Spanish lord, Adnidaraes Quixot informs the audience that he was a general in Numidia before coming to Europe to seek his father and his fortune. He is given lines in a nonsense language that is meant to imitate Arabic, and laments that fortune has caused him to lose his "store of Barbarie gold," and that he has gone from being in command of "many men" to serving his "Master's man." In his final line he promises that, if granted more gold, he will "run from hence to Spaine." Quixot is an exotic comic figure whose primary purpose seems to be to embody the Black Legend stereotype of Spanish-Moorish intermingling. He describes himself as both Black and Muslim, but the term he uses to describe his religion is not "Moor" but "Turk." He is a "Spaniard, Moore, half Turke, half Christian." "Moore" here is paired with "Spaniard" as a description of national and cultural origin, while the word "Turke" is used alongside "Christian" to describe religion.

Ultimately, I found only three plays that straightforwardly stage a character's Blackness as a sign of specifically Islamic difference. In *All's Lost by Lust* (1619), which recounts the fall of Spain to the Moors, Moors as a group are described as "barbarous and tawny," "swarty," "sooty," and "half-naked infidels." Although the play does not contain many references to Islam, when the evil "Mully Moomen, king of Africa" offers to marry the white noblewoman Jacinta, she refuses on the grounds that it would be a "second hell" for "a Christian's arms [to] embrace an infidel."[32] *All's Lost by Lust* represents the king as doubly threatening to the white, Christian Jacinta in that he is both Black and Muslim. The play exemplifies a dynamic often attributed to *Othello* in which Blackness can be read as both phenotype and metaphorical representation of Islamic difference. A version of this dynamic also appears in both parts of *The Fair Maid of the West*, in which the King of Fez is portrayed as both Black and Muslim and as a sexual threat to the beautiful white Bess, "the girl worth gold."[33] These plays do reflect a dynamic in which Blackness appears as an external sign of threatening Islamic difference. This is the dynamic that critics such as Lupton, Neill, and Vitkus evoke when arguing that *Othello* is tied more closely to religious difference than to anti-Blackness. However, these plays (which include, it is worth noting, a play and its sequel rather than three stand-alone works) are the exception rather than the rule.

There is one final play with both Moorish characters and a tenuous connection to Islam: John Fletcher's *The Island Princess* (1619–21). The play is set in the Moluccan Islands and presents a complex series of political maneuvers and romantic entanglements among Portuguese conquistadors, the royal family of the Island of Tidore (including the eponymous princess), and the governor of the neighboring island, Ternate. The play includes several unnamed minor characters labeled as "Moors" in the cast list and stage directions, and the governor of Ternate spends the last act of the play disguised as a "Moor priest." No internal evidence in the play indicates whether these "Moors" or any other characters in the play would have appeared in blackface; the governor's disguise as a "Moor priest" is uncovered by removing his false beard and wig, according to the stage directions, not by the revelation that he has darkened his skin.[34] The play's connections with Islam are equally vague, despite the fact that the princess's conversion to Christianity is a major plot point in the play. There are multiple references to pantheistic gods but none to Islam or the Koran.[35] Nonetheless, Clare McManus's recent Arden edition frames it as a Turk play that dramatizes the temptations and perils of conversion to Islam, "reversing the love affair between a Muslim man and a Christian woman familiar from another of Shakespeare's best-known plays, *Othello*."[36] Jonathan Gil Harris offers a detailed analysis of the ways that the edition stretches to reframe the inherently ambiguous play text to speak to the history of Anglo-Islamic relationships, noting that it finds "at best only oblique references."[37] *The Island Princess* is in many ways an anomaly; as Harris observes, it is "the only surviving pre-Restoration drama to be set in what was then known as 'India.'" Its Moors address neither Islam nor sub-Saharan African Blackness, although it is certainly possible that the designation of minor characters as Moors indicates that they were intended to be played in blackface. What is most relevant here is the ease with which the term *Moor* becomes a rationale for the play's editor to frame the play primarily in the context of Islam.

As I began this section by stating, my goal here is not to completely unlink the stage Moor from Islam: Muslim characters labeled as Moors appear in *The Battle of Alcazar* and *Captain Thomas Stukely*, although most of these characters are not Black, and Islam and Blackness are intertwined in both parts of *The Fair Maid of the West* as well as in *All's Lost by Lust*. Instead, looking at patterns across multiple plays allows us to see multiple categorizations of marginalized identities emerge even within uses of the same term. Moors explicitly represented as Muslim are more likely to be in positions of power and less likely to be represented as Black. Moors not explicitly aligned with Islam occupy a position that is more comparable to the Black characters on the Spanish stage discussed in Chapter 3, embedded in a rhetoric that attempts to articulate their service to white, Christian Europe.

Blackface, Service, and Slavery

While Blackness and Islam are not in fact closely linked on the early modern English stage, Blackness and service are. In this section, I draw on a larger survey of thirty-four plays with characters labeled not only as "Moors" or "Black Moors" but also as "Ethiopians" and "Negroes" to explore connections between representations of Blackness and of service or slavery.[38] These limited parameters have meant excluding a number of plays that speak to issues of race and color, most notably Shakespeare's *Antony and Cleopatra* and *The Tempest*. I have retained this tight focus to address as specifically as possible two particular intersections: of Blackness and Islam (under the rubric of Moorishness), and of Blackness and service or enslavement. Several other critics have surveyed Black characters on the early modern stage, notably Anthony Barthelemy in *Black Face, Maligned Race* and Virginia Mason Vaughan in *Performing Blackness on English Stages, 1500–1800*. The texts I discuss here are from a more limited time range, with none written after the closing of the theaters in 1642. More important, I have centered my analysis here on representations of slavery and service. Although both Barthelemy and Vaughan group the plays they discuss thematically, neither considers enslavement as a defining characteristic for Black characters in pre-Restoration drama.[39]

Of these plays with Black characters, twenty-one place those characters in positions of slavery or service. In six of these, the connection to slavery is explicit: Vangue in *The Wonder of Women, or Sophonisba* (printed 1606) appears in the list of characters as "an Ethiopian slave"; the white woman disguised as a Moor in Massinger's *Parliament of Love* (1624) is described in stage directions as "disguised as Moorish slave" and is given a fictitious back story in which she was "bought" from a "pirate of Marseilles" after being "surprised [e.g., kidnapped] in Barbary"; Jacometta/Jacomo in Richard Brome's *The Novella* (1632) is called a servant but is also described as having been "given" to the protagonist by her brother; in Brome's *The English Moor* (1640) the usurer Quicksand describes "borrowing" Moors from other merchants who trade in Barbary; a briefly seen Moor in *The Jew of Malta* appears as a slave for sale; and finally, the Moors of *The Memorable Masque of the Middle Temple and Lincoln's Inn* (1613) are "attir'd like Indian slaves." Five additional plays call for Black characters in nonspeaking parts to perform duties associated with enslavement; for example, the wicked Queen Elinor in Peele's *Edward I* (1593) enters in a litter "born by four negro Moors."[40]

An additional ten plays with Black characters represent them as servants or attendants. This is true of the Black female characters who appear briefly as the butt of the joke in "bed tricks"; of Zanche in *The White Devil* (1612), whose Blackness serves as an ironic commentary on her white mistress Vittoria's moral darkness; and of Zanthia in *The Knight of Malta*, whose Blackness and wickedness contrasts with the hyperwhiteness and virtue of her mistress, Orianna, and the "fair Turk" Lucinda (whose name, as the play points out, means "light"). These figures activate a series of references similar to those that Hall uncovers in court jewels from the late sixteenth century and portraits from the middle of the seventeenth century of white nobles with Black attendants, as Black servants are used to alternately reinforce and expose the fragility of the construction of whiteness.[41] In several of these plays, it is possible (though by no means certain) that early modern playgoers would have assumed that such characters were enslaved, though they are not explicitly referred to as such. In *The Knight of Malta*, for example, a character hopes to buy for his wife the enslaved white Turkish woman Lucinda "as a companion to thy faithful Moor," implying that Zanthia's position is aligned with (if not explicitly equivalent to) enslavement.[42] Similarly, Zanthia chastises her lover on two occasions for treating her "like a property" (1.1.168, 4.1.85). In *Lust's Dominion*, as we shall see, Eleazar frequently refers to the Moors who serve him as "slaves."

Those Black characters who are neither enslaved nor servants are almost invariably exoticized royalty (e.g., the King of Afric in *The Thracian Wonder*, the Prince of Morocco in *The Merchant of Venice*, the King of Ethiopia in *The Blind Beggar of Alexandria*, and the "daughters of Niger" in *The Masque of Blackness*). The only exceptions to this are two plays (*The White Devil* and *Sicily and Naples*) in which white noblemen disguise themselves as Black Moorish warriors to enact their revenge. Crucially, no stage Moors explicitly associated with Islam are represented as servants or as enslaved.

This association of Black Moors with service, and at times with slavery, allows us to reevaluate rhetoric employed by and about Moorish characters on the early modern stage. Consider, for example, Aaron the Moor in *Titus Andronicus*. Aaron is an oddly unfixed character. His relationship with the Goths (with whom he has entered Rome) is never specified in the text of the play itself, except that he is Tamora's lover. There is no textual evidence that suggests that Aaron is to be read explicitly as enslaved in this play, nor that the play intends to assign him to a concrete but unspoken social position. However, particularly in the context of early modern representations of Blackness outlined above, it is possible to see that the fact that he is a Black Moor means that he is already positioned in a field of associations with slavery and service. This position is further reinforced by the play's description of Aaron as a "swart Cimmerian," which Ndiaye persuasively links to the Spanish word *cimarrón*, a term designating runaway slaves in the Americas.[43]

Further, Aaron's language and the imagery he employs play with such associations. In his first speech, he proclaims his ambition, "Away with slavish weeds and servile thoughts!," and notes that he has held his lover, Tamora, "fettered in amorous chains."[44] Perhaps more notably, his descriptions of his son alternate between descriptions of the child as noble and as a racialized slave. He observes how "the black slave smiles upon his father" and hushes him: "peace, tawny slave, half me and half thy dam"; he describes his son as having been "enfranchised" from his mother's womb (4.2.122, 5.1.1.27, 4.2.127).

In simplest terms, I am suggesting that it is possible and indeed necessary to differentiate between different uses of the term *Moor* on the early modern stage. To return to Neill's terminology, a subset of Black characters are indeed aligned with "enslavers" and anxieties about Islamic might. Many more, however, clearly reflect early histories of enslaved Black Africans brought into Europe. The next two plays I turn to, *Lust's Dominion* and *Othello*, offer interesting limit cases. Both have Black central characters in positions of prominence. Both also, though, turn obsessively to metaphors of enslavement, binding, and chains as they delimit the parameters of these characters' inclusion in white, Christian Europe.

Spaniard, Moor, and "Saucy Slave": *Lust's Dominion*

On its surface, *Lust's Dominion* seems designed to address anxieties about the dangers posed by a racialized Islamic figure to European bloodlines and political stability. Its central villain, the Moor Eleazar, is a prince of Fez held captive in the Spanish royal court. Unlike the Moors in positions of service described above, Eleazar is given a very specific country of origin and linked to an Islamic royal family. The play's closing lines, echoing Spain's expulsion of its Moorish population in 1492, are "let all the Moors be banished from Spain."[45] It is particularly noteworthy, then, that the play contains no references to Islam or conversion but a number of references to slavery.

The play tells a complicated story revolving around a fictitious succession crisis in Spain.[46] The central villains are Eleazar, Prince of Fez, and the eponymous "lascivious queen," who is so infatuated with Eleazar that she will do anything—including proclaiming her own children illegitimate—to keep his love. When the King of Spain dies, the queen (his widow) and Eleazar set a series of stratagems into motion to put him on the throne. The queen's older son, who spends much of his time onstage trying to bed Eleazar's wife, is quickly dispatched. The younger son, Philip, proves trickier, and ultimately triumphs, assisted by his sister, Isabella. In the play's final lines, Philip expels the Moors from Spain, citing Eleazar and his servants' machinations as his reason.

Much of the play's tension revolves around Eleazar's ambivalent status—he is simultaneously a member of the court and a captive, a nobleman and a

Black slave and devil. However, he begins the play firmly embedded within the Spanish aristocracy and married to a white Christian noblewoman; in fact, his Blackness seems relatively unimportant at the play's opening. Eleazar's father-in-law, Alvaro, refers to Eleazar simply as his "son," and while the king warns his son Fernando to keep an eye on Eleazar, that warning is unrelated to his race. King Philip begins by praising Eleazar as "wise and warlike," then moves on to warn Fernando, "Ambition wings his spirit, keep him down / What wil [*sic*] not men attempt to win a crown."[47] The king presents neither Eleazar's military prowess nor his ambition as a racialized characteristic; instead, he is simply one of those "men" who will do anything to serve his own ambition.

As the play progresses, the significance of Eleazar's racial identity alters as two contradictory depictions of his ancestry and its influence on his personality emerge. The first revolves around his status as a prince of Barbary. Eleazar declares to his father-in-law, Alvaro: "father / Although my flesh be tawny, in my veines, / Runs blood as red, and royal as the best / And proud'st in *Spain*" (1.1.153–55). Two friars, Crab and Cole, refer to Eleazar as "a valiant gentleman," and a "Noble gentleman," and the queen describes him as "that Barbarian Prince" (3.3.69–70; 5.1.91). When Eleazar first makes a bid for the throne of Spain, he asks the courtiers to judge him "not by my sun-burnt cheek, but by my birth" (3.2.206–7). Eleazar, as a foreign prince, can marry a white Spanish noblewoman and even briefly occupy the Spanish throne. In this context, the most significant attribute he has inherited from his father is not his Blackness but his royal blood, and he lives in Spain as an honored prisoner of war.

The second depiction of Eleazar is equally determined by his ancestry, but that ancestry is no longer linked to a specific nation or noble—even royal—line. Instead, it is connected to his Blackness. Even in those moments when Eleazar asserts the value of his noble blood, he must do so against the color of his skin, asserting that although his flesh is tawny, his blood is royal, and asking to be judged not by his skin but by his birth. Philip, encountering Eleazar on the battlefield, derides him: "thou true stamp'd son of hell / Thy pedigree is written on thy face" (4.1.40–41). The only part of Eleazar's inheritance that matters here is his color, which marks him as demonic in origin. Just as Philip claims that Eleazar's skin color associates him with hell and evil, for some courtiers Eleazar's Blackness renders him "a slave of *barbary*, a dog" (1.1.152). For these courtiers, Eleazar's Blackness automatically renders his specific ancestry irrelevant, reducing him from a prince to the status of slave and dog. Two kinds of inherited identity uneasily coexist in this play: one in which bloodlines determine class status, and another in which Blackness has the power to consign a subject to devilishness and slavery.

By the end of the play, Eleazar's Blackness has definitively trumped his royal ancestry as his most significant inherited characteristic. In the last two lines of the play, Philip declares: "And for this Barbarous Moor, and his Black train, / let all the Moors be banished from Spain" (5.3.182–83). Philip extrapolates from Eleazar's plotting that the "Black train" of Moors as a collective entity is not to be trusted. In *Lust's Dominion* the characteristic that unites these Moors as a group—and that motivates their expulsion—is neither allegiance to a particular religion nor specifically the inheritance of Moorish "blood," but rather Blackness. Indeed, as I mention above, none of *Lust's Dominion's* Moors explicitly refer to Islam. Eleazar himself seems to be as much an atheist as anything else. Two friars, who draw back at first sight of him, explain, "Seeing your face, we thought of hell"; Eleazar responds laconically, "Hell is a dream" (2.2.124–25). Eleazar directs his only appeal to a higher power to "all our Indian gods," which evokes a vague notion of religious otherness rather than Islam specifically (4.2.85).[48] In *Lust's Dominion* Blackness becomes a sign of sinister difference. The lesson that the Spanish court has learned by the end of the play is that Moors—a group that the play unites by color—must be expelled from the nation to guarantee tranquility and lineal succession.

The way that Moorishness relates to anxieties about paternity emerges specifically in the scene in which the queen falsely claims that Philip is illegitimate. As the scene opens, Eleazar duplicitously suggests that the Philip's biological father make amends by marrying the queen: "If he be noble and a Spaniard born / Hee'l hide the apparant scarrs of their infamies / With the white hand of marriage; that and time, / Will eat the blemish off, say? shall it?" (5.1.61–64). The prerequisite for the father to make amends is not only that he be noble but also that he be born a Spaniard; in this context, it is not incidental that the "hand of marriage" is white. The conditions Eleazar sets rule out the possibility that he could be Philip's father. The cardinal responds to this by suggesting that Philip's true father might be a Moor: "Spaniard or Moor, the saucy slave shall die" (5.1.67). Eleazar describes a problem of Spanish succession from which he himself is excluded; the cardinal, on the other hand, reopens the possibility that a Moor could be the father of the Spanish prince.

Rather than continuing to separate himself from white Spaniards, Eleazar picks up on the cardinal's formulation, repeating it four more times over the course of the scene. This formulation both separates Spaniards from Moors and ropes Moors back into Spanish bloodlines, including a royal Spanish bloodline. First, it divides the candidates for the position of Philip's father into two separate categories: the father is either a Spaniard or a Moor. By setting up this opposition, the formulation establishes an absolute split between Spaniards and Moors. Nonetheless, by making it possible for a Moor to be the father of the Crown Prince of Spain, the assertion ties Moors into Spanish history and genealogies.

There is, of course, a third term in the repeated phrase "Spaniard or Moor, the saucy slave shall die," and the term *slave* here is particularly fraught coming from Eleazar's mouth. Eleazar, of course, is not literally enslaved in the play. But one of the ironies that the play uses to expose the villainy of Spaniards is that Eleazar's Blackness renders him slavish—both low-class and villainous, and inherently suited to enslavement because he is Black. When the cardinal attempts to banish him at the beginning of the play, he threatens to send Eleazar to "beg with Indian slaves" (1.2.158). His (white, Spanish, noble) father-in-law replies: "Why should my son be banished?" (1.2.159), demonstrating, again, the Moor's ambivalent position.

Eleazar's two henchmen, Zarack and Baltazar, are described in the list of characters not as slaves but as "two Moors attending Eleazar." Nonetheless, in the opening scene Eleazar immediately chastises them "hark you, slaves!" The word *slave* appears a startling forty-four times in *Lust's Dominion*. Nine of those times are iterations of the phrase "Spaniard or Moor, the saucy slave shall die." Five are general uses of *slave* as an insult (e.g., Philip derides his cowardly soldiers fleeing from battle as "slaves"). Three are references spoken by Eleazar referring to Spaniards as slaves. The remaining twenty-seven are used to describe Eleazar, Zarack, and Baltazar: fourteen of them are references to Zarack and Baltazar as slaves, and thirteen of them are insults leveled against Eleazar. In short, *Lust's Dominion* is permeated with references to Black characters as "slaves."

A stage prop on which the play's resolution turns also takes on particular significance in the context of slavery. Once he has the Spanish royal family under his control, Eleazar reminds Zarack and Baltazar: "And—ah! Now thus thou knows't I did invent, / A torturing Iron chain" (5.1.220–21), which Zarack helpfully clarifies is "for necks my Lord" (5.1.222). Eleazar sends his men to fetch it, and the next scene opens with the spectacle of the royal family of Spain in neck chains. The stage directions specify: "Enter Hortenzo, Queen Mother, Cardinall, and Phillip chain'd by the necks, Zarack, and Baltazar, busie about fastning Hortenzo." Hortenzo yet again draws attention to the nature of the chain in the scene's first line, calling Zarack and Baltazar "maps of night" and "element of Devills" and asking "why do you yoak my neck with iron chains?" (5.2.3–4). The royal family and cardinal of Spain remain onstage chained by the neck in a line throughout the scene, as Eleazar again emphasizes the spectacle in an elaborate extended metaphor comparing them to a tennis net:

> Methinks this stage shews like a Tennis Court;
> Do's not *Isabell*? I'le shew thee how;
> Suppose that Iron chain to be the line,
> The prison doors the hazard, and their heads
> Scarce peeping ore the line suppose the bals;
> Had I a racket now of burnish'd steel,
> How smoothly could I bandy every ball,
> Over this Globe of earth, win sett and all. (5.2.58–66)

Eleazar's description underlines not only the grotesqueness of the scene but also its function as a carnivalesque inversion. Imprisonment and execution are compared to a game of tennis; the royal family is chained in a line by the neck like slaves and guarded by Black Moors. This inversion is further emphasized by two references to the neck chains as chains of office. When Prince Philip insults Eleazar, the latter notes that he is "proud because he wears a chain" (5.2.68), and Baltazar quips as he as chaining Hortenzo, "Many do borrow chains, but you have this *gratis*, for nothing" (5.2.5).

These macabre comic inversions become even more pronounced as the play continues. Isabella convinces Zarack to free the imprisoned nobles and help kill Baltazar and Eleazar, claiming that she loves him. Instead, the nobles quickly kill both Zarack and Baltazar, and two of them (Prince Philip and the nobleman Hortenzo) disguise themselves as the Moors, blackening their faces "with the oil of hell" (5.2.171). When Eleazar returns, in a moment that defies all probability outside of revenge tragedy, he decides to put on a sort of play-within-a-play. Gesturing to various chains in his prison, he suggests that "Zarack" (actually Hortenzo in disguise) will impersonate Hortenzo, "Baltazar" (actually Philip in disguise) will impersonate Philip, and Eleazar himself, the cardinal. Eleazar, of course, draws attention to the metatheatricality of the moment: "Slaves, ha, ha, ha / You are but players, they must end the play / How like *Hortenzo* and *Philippo* ha, / Stand my two slaves, were they as black as you" (5.3.91–94). Eleazar then asks the faux Moors to fix a torture device (an "iron engine") on his own head and manacle his hands in his role as the "Cardinal." Once he is in chains, they reveal their true identities—and, of course, do not set him free but rather kill him. In the end, Philip takes up the crown of Spain, the noble Hortenzo marries Isabella, and the play ends with an act of expulsion: "And for this Barbarous *Moor*, and his black train, / Let all the Moors be banished from *Spain*."

To put it mildly, there is a lot going on in this final scene. And much of it is related not to slavery but to the Black Legend. As Eric Griffin has extensively documented, Protestant polemicists circulated a series of anti-Spanish propaganda tracts in early modern England.[49] As part of what has come to be called the Black Legend (of Spanish cruelty), these tracts (as I discussed in the first two chapters) vilified Spaniards as, among other things, the mongrelized descendants of Jews and Moors. Thus, for example, the anti-Spanish tract *The Copie of the Anti-Spaniard* (1590) asks: "What? Shal those *Marranos*, yea, those impious Atheistes raigne over us as Kings and Princes? Shall the Countrie of France become servile to the commandement of the Spaniard? . . . Of this demie Moore, demie Iew, yea demie Saracine?"[50] Another tract, *A Comparison of the English and Spanish Nation* (1589), refers to the Spanish as a "mongrell generation" and asserts that "even as waters which run out of sulphur Springs, have always a taste of brimstone, so men carrie alwaies imprinted in their manners, the vertuous or vitious qualitie of their ancestors."[51] Even nominally Christian Spaniards, according to these pamphlets, are the miscegenated offspring of Moors and Jews. Thus, part of what's at stake in the repeated declaration "Spaniard or Moor, the saucy slave shall die," in the queen's adultery with a Moor, and in the text's persistent harping on illegitimacy is an implied slur on Spaniards' mongrelized ancestry.

Indeed, anxieties about paternity—and particularly about the paternity of the queen's children, and thus the Spanish royal line—permeate the play. In the opening scene, the queen chastises Eleazar for his flagging affection, admonishing, "thou lovd'st me once"; he tersely responds, "that can thy bastards tell," suggesting that he may in fact be the father of some of Spain's royal family (1.1.66). And Eleazar later says of the queen, "all may doubt the fruits of such a Womb" (5.1.67). The play's ending makes a show of banishing the racially marked Moors and frames that process as a move from exogamy to consanguinity. The newly reformed queen laments that she wronged "he that was nearest to my blood, my son . . . To crown with honour an ambitious Moor" (5.3.125, 132). The queen frames her return to virtue as a shift from valuing a foreign Moor to honoring blood ties. Nonetheless, it is difficult not to read even the gesture of expelling the Moors at the end of the play as ironic—too little, too late. As Bartels has noted, the play ends with the Prince of Spain reclaiming the throne while still wearing blackface.[52]

The play's engagement with Blackness has most often been read in the context of Spain's history as a site of Jewish and Moorish difference. Blackness in this context becomes a visual sign of sin and religious difference; Islam becomes racialized; and anti-Blackness and the racialization of slavery disappears as an object of analysis. But the multiple models of difference circulating in early modern England do not align with this kind of either/or logic. Rather, the play projects multiple contradictory racializing discourses onto Spain. One of these discourses is certainly that found in anti-Spanish propaganda like the pieces cited above. Despite their pride in their "pure" descent, Spaniards are already mongrelized, infected with the "taint" of Jewish and Moorish blood. We can see an echo of this in Eleazar's vow: "Spain I will drown thee with thine own proud blood" (2.3.190). As we have seen, however, the discourses of reviled difference in this play are largely fixated on neither tainted blood nor religion but rather on color.

The anti-Black rhetoric that runs through *Lust's Dominion* is related to anxieties about religious difference, but it is not simply an extension of those anxieties. Rather, the racialization of Blackness as related to slavery is both criticized and reinforced in this play. It is Spain and not England where a Black Moor can be sent to beg in the streets with "Indian slaves." One of the things that the play criticizes is a presumed Spanish tyranny that profits from slavery. But at the same time, the notion that Black people are both slaves (as a social/economic position) and slavish (evil, not to be trusted, incapable of honor) runs through the language and imagery of the play.

Othello and Slavery

The chapter ends with a reading of the urtext for discussions of Moorishness in early modern English drama, which is, of course, Shakespeare's *Othello*. As in my discussion of *Lust's Dominion*, my focus on Blackness and service is not framed as an exclusion of considering the play's status as a "drama of conversion." I argue that reading Othello as a Mediterranean "Moor" need not contradict readings of him as a sub-Saharan African who arrives in Venice via slavery. I do, though, wish to interrogate the ways that representations of Moorishness as related to Islam have been framed as a less anachronistic alternative to considering the play's focus on Blackness and slavery. Othello's status as a Black African in Venice and as formerly enslaved is crucial to understanding the rhetoric of service that permeates the play.

"*Othello* is a drama of conversion." So begins Vitkus's much-cited article on the play.[53] His study, and a number of others, rely on the assertion that Othello is meant to be understood to have converted to Christianity from Islam. Dennis Britton astutely observes that "criticism . . . has often overlooked or at least discounted Othello's Christian identity."[54] Even Britton, however, ultimately focuses on Iago's attempts to "re-turn Othello to what is presumably his prior Muslim identity" and draws on a historical archive of "infidel conversion" to inform his reading.[55] Britton's careful language here, however, is suggestive: at no point does the play itself explicitly identify Othello as having converted from Islam—or indeed as a convert at all. Othello describes himself as a Christian, asking his troops, "have *we* turned Turks? And to *ourselves* do that / Which heaven hath forbid the Ottomites? / For Christian shame, put by this barbarous brawl" (2.3.132–35; italics mine). No other character refers to Othello's religion at all, except for Iago's claim that Othello's love for Desdemona is so strong that he would renounce his baptism for her sake. Indeed, it is significant, though it has remained unacknowledged, that none of the slurs against Othello voiced by Iago, Roderigo, or any other character refers to religion. Instead, they focus on his Blackness, his age, and his status as a "stranger"; he is never referred to as an "infidel," as is Shakespeare's other famous convert, Jessica.

Nonetheless, it is true that the rhetoric of adultery as conversion that runs through the play suggests anxiety about the stability of Othello's status as a Venetian Christian. The play comes closest to implying that Othello embodies threatening Islamic difference in his suicide, when he compares stabbing himself to killing a "turbaned Turk" and "circumcised dog" who "beat a Venetian and traduced the state" (5.2.369–72). These lines have been read as indicating a kinship between Othello himself and the "turbaned Turk" he once killed in defense of Venice. But the lines more clearly represent Othello as an outsider and a threat to Venice, like this Turk; it does not necessarily follow that the *kind* of threat he embodies is the same as that of the Turk.[56] It is instructive in this context to compare Othello's death to that of Antiobo of Lope de Vega's *El negro del mejor amo*, discussed in Chapter 3. Antiobo dies protecting his monastery from invasion by Turkish forces, much as Othello attempts to protect Venice. One of the troubling questions the play raises is whether Othello sees himself as a threat because he cannot erase his fundamental Islamic difference, or whether he comes to understand that his Blackness constitutes a threat in and of itself.

Othello's connection to religious difference in general and Islam in particular, then, must largely rest on the fact that he is called a "Moor," and to a lesser extent on what Griffin has termed the play's "Spanish spirits." Griffin's reading of the play argues that the name *Iago* evokes the patron Saint of Spain, Santiago Matamoros or Saint James the Moor-slayer, while the villain Roderigo's name evokes Spain's great hero: "Rodrigo, the Christian name of 'Ruy' Díaz de Bivar, El Cid Campeador."[57] In Griffin's reading, Othello becomes a converted Moor or Morisco who is destroyed by the Machiavellian Christian Spaniard Iago; thus, Griffin suggests that the play obliquely criticizes Spanish racism against those of Moorish descent. But as we saw in *Lust's Dominion*, in drawing on Spain the play evokes the enslavement of Black Africans as well as questions of purity of blood. Othello's connections to Islam, after all, are quite tenuous, while the play explicitly informs us that he is Black and has been enslaved.

Taking the broader rhetorical framework that links Blackness with slavery in early modern English drama into account also shifts how we read Othello's description of his past: "Of being taken by the insolent foe / And sold to slavery, of my redemption thence / And portance in my traveler's history" (1.3.136–38). In recent years these lines have often been read as evidence of Othello's place in the complex culture of Barbary piracy, a site of shifting religious and national allegiances as pirates and captives alike converted from Islam to Christianity depending on the demands of their personal circumstances and the possibility of social and economic advancement.[58] However, the Mediterranean world of Venice is a site of slavery as well as piracy in this period, as Shakespeare mentions in his other Venetian play, *The Merchant of Venice*.[59] While Othello is certainly not enslaved in Venice, it is important to recognize that it is through the slave trade that he has arrived in Europe.

This observation can inform our reading of the play's pervasive—and much discussed—allusions to service, particularly when we keep in mind the extensive link between Blackness and service in early modern English drama outlined above. The play is bookended by Othello's allusions to the work he has done for the state. Othello begins the play by highlighting his usefulness: "My services, which I have done the signiory, / Shall out-tongue his complaints" (1.2.18–19). The duke first addresses Othello: "Valiant Othello, we must straight employ you" (1.3.48). And finally, Othello's suicide speech begins with the reminder, "I have done the state some service, and they know't" (5.2.344). Indeed, Othello's primary relationship with Venice is one of service; one of the play's enduring preoccupations is what the rewards of such service are or should be. (This is also, of course, in a different register, Iago's preoccupation, particularly about Cassio's promotion over him.) Othello's successes are articulated in the context of the service he performs as an outsider for a European community.

In *Othello*, descriptions of service often yoke together older discourses of chivalry and patronage with newer discourses of chattel slavery. So, for example, when Iago declares of Othello's feelings for Desdemona: "His soul is so enfettered to her love / That she may make, unmake, do what she list," he draws on the language of chivalry; nonetheless, he also evokes an emergent discourse that links Blackness with slavery in describing Othello's soul as "enfettered" (2.3.333–34). In his essay "Othello and Venice: Discrimination and Projection," Alessandro Serpieri observes of the play's lexicon that "*bondage, bondslave* and, above all, *bound* significantly recur in crucial passages."[60] As in *Lust's Dominion*, where Black characters are repeatedly labeled slaves and an elaborate chain visually dominates the final act, Blackness in Shakespeare's play is articulated alongside a pervasive rhetoric of bindings and fetters. Such ironic doubling of metaphorical and actual slavery is also, as we have seen, a common motif in representations of Black characters in the Spanish comedia, which does explicitly and frequently stage Black characters as enslaved.

Nonetheless, as I discuss above, reading *Othello* in the context of slavery has often been understood to be a fundamentally anachronistic project, an imposition of later histories on an early modern text. Instead, it has been suggested that we should interpret the play's repeated references to service, mastery, and binding in the context of medieval discourses of vassalage and lordship rather than the later institution of race-based slavery. For example, Neill's essay "'His Master's Ass': Slavery, Service, and Subordination in *Othello*" outlines the way that medieval discourses of service inform Othello and Iago's relationship: "In fact, slavery bore little or no relation to discourses of 'racial' difference in early modern thought; rather, it was part of a much older construction of human difference in which the distinctions that mattered were not those between different 'colors' or 'races,' but those between master and servant, or between bond and free."[61] It is important to register that this medieval discourse of service operates powerfully in the play. Equally important, however, is to recognize that part of the tension that drives *Othello* results from the conflict between that ideology and an emergent discourse that links Blackness with slavery (and both Blackness and slavery with Spain).

Indeed, there is no reason that *Othello* cannot be understood as drawing on both older discourses of service and an emergent discourse of slavery. Comparing uses of the word *slave* in *Othello* to those found the rest of Shakespeare's canon illustrates this particular tension. The words *slave, slaves, slavish,* and *slavery* appear a total of 178 times in Shakespeare's plays and poems.[62] Most uses of these words do not refer to enforced labor; rather, they most often appear as an insult implying baseness, servility, and villainy.[63] In *Othello*, these variations on the word *slave* appear eleven times. Only two of Shakespeare's other plays use the word more frequently: *King Lear* (fifteen instances) and *Timon of Athens* (fourteen instances). Both of these plays are preoccupied with the nature of service and mastery in the context of the "older construction of human difference" described by Neill (as well as, in *Timon*'s case, referring to slaves in Roman households). *Slave* and its variants appear more often in *Othello*, however, than they do in *The Tempest* and *The Comedy of Errors*, both of which feature enslaved characters. And when the word is used in *Othello*, it takes on different connotations than it does in either *King Lear* or *Timon of Athens*.

In the final scene of *Othello* alone, the word *slave* appears four times. Two of those uses can be read as referring to Othello himself. Othello condemns himself as a "cursèd, cursèd slave," which is echoed by Lodovico's admonition, "O thou Othello, that was once so good, / Fallen into the practice of a cursèd slave" (5.2. 282, 296–97).[64] If we read these lines in the context of an emergent discourse that links dark skin to slavery, they seem to evoke the biblical curse of Ham, which condemned all of Ham's descendants to slavery. In some versions of the story, the descendants of Ham populate Africa; this frequently appears as a justification for the enslavement of Black people well into the nineteenth century.[65] The fact that the word *slave* is prefaced by *cursed* supports such a reading, especially because no other uses of the word *slave* in Shakespeare are prefaced by either *damned* or *cursed*.

However, it is equally possible to read these lines in the final scene of *Othello* as condemnations of Iago. Lodovico's assertion that Othello has "fallen into the practice of a cursed slave" may refer to the fact that he has been hoodwinked by Iago's trickery rather than suggest that Othello himself has reverted to the behavior typical of one who suffers under the curse of Ham.

Indeed, in the play's final moments, just before Othello's suicide, Lodovico explicitly calls Iago a slave as he strips Othello of all "[his] power and [his] command," designates Cassio ruler in Cypress, and then turns to Iago: "For this slave, / If there be any cunning cruelty / That can torment him much and hold him long / It shall be his" (5.2.337–40). To call Iago a slave is to represent his behavior as slavish; that is to say, his machinations expose him as villainous both in the sense that he is of a lower class—a villein or villain—and in the sense that he is evil. (It is also significant, in this context, that in the medieval period serfs, peasants, and villeins were often described as the offspring of Ham, cursed with servitude.)[66]

Rather than privileging one of these readings over the other, we can register that *Othello* dramatizes the conflict between these divergent notions of slavery. The frequent repetition of the word *slave* in the final scene both evokes the enslavement of Black Africans and, by being applied to Iago rather than to Othello, serves as one of the play's many ironic reversals: it is not the Black Moor "sold into slavery" in his youth but the white ensign with a Spanish name who is termed a slave in the play's final scene. Here, too, reading *Othello* in the context of a larger survey of representations of Blackness on the early modern English and Spanish stage is useful. As we have seen, these plays frequently turn to the vocabulary of slavery and service even when Black characters are not explicitly enslaved, because associations between Blackness and slavery are already embedded in the early modern European imaginary. This dynamic also applies to the frequent uses of the word slave in *Othello*. Even when the term is applied to Iago, it still reflects on Othello's condition as a Black man who serves the state of Venice.

We might also consider Othello's relationship with Desdemona in the context of service and enslavement. Othello, like Juan de Mérida in *El valiente negro en Flandes*, frames his relationship not in terms of his own desire but in terms of responding to Desdemona's wishes. He begins to court her only in response to her prompting; she accompanies him to Cyprus not at his request but hers. Iago's description of Othello's soul as "so enfettered to her love" that "her appetite shall play the god /with his weak function" (2.3.266–67) represents Desdemona as the desiring subject and Othello as a bound and passive object. This pattern is similar to the dynamic between Aaron and Tamora in *Titus Andronicus*, and between Eleazar and the queen in *Lust's Dominion*, all of which position the Moor as responding to the desires of a white female character rather than expressing his own.[67] The anxiety that subtends Othello and Desdemona's relationship is not only about miscegenation; it is also about the implications of a white woman being placed in a position of sexual mastery that itself relies on a discourse linking Blackness with enslavement.

Much has been made of the devastating line that sums up *Othello*'s end: "This object poisons sight. / Let it be hid" (5.2.368–70). Equally important, though, are the lines that follow: Gratiano, keep the house / And seize upon the fortunes of the Moor, / For they succeed on you" (5.2.370–72). In the comedia, as we have seen, the accomplishments of Black characters are inevitably framed as enriching others: Juan Latino's genius burnishes the reputation of his enslaver; Juan de Mérida's military might serves the Spanish crown; and Black saints represent themselves as the humblest slaves of the "greatest master," the Christian God. The ending of *Othello* subtly accomplishes a similar feat. Othello himself is hidden from sight, as his property is seized to be incorporated into a white Christian community.

Conclusion

In this and the previous chapter, I have attempted to trace the circulation of discourses that naturalize a connection between Blackness and enslavement in early modern English and Spanish drama. In doing so, I do not wish to imply that such discourses were totalizing or all-encompassing. As we have seen, Black characters appear as generals, kings, and princes on the early modern stage in both England and Spain. As the example of the Spanish comedia shows, however, representing individual Black characters in lofty social positions is not incompatible with representing Blackness and slavery as intertwined. Indeed, in *Juan Latino*, *El valiente negro en Flandes*, and numerous other Spanish plays, the heroic Black protagonist's enslavement is reframed as willing service, thereby serving as an implicit justification for slavery. The sustained, explicit discussion of slavery in relation to Blackness found in the Spanish comedia is, of course, not present in early modern English drama. But if we keep the Spanish framework in mind, certain resonances emerge across plays such as *Juan Latino* and *El valiente negro en Flandes* and *Othello* and *Lust's Dominion*: recurring imagery of chains and binding, sustained meditations on "service," and a pattern of individual Black characters isolated from their place of origin represented as attempting to integrate (whether successfully or not) with a white commonwealth.

The resonances I identify here between English and Spanish plays are not particularly surprising. Although the status of slavery was not codified in early modern England, we know that most Black people who lived there were in positions of service and had arrived via the slave trade. We also know that travel texts and English translations of Spanish literature describe enslaved Black Africans, often labeling them "Moors" or "Black Moors." Why would this historical context not be reflected on the stage? What *is* surprising—or perhaps not surprising at all, but rather demands further scrutiny—is how the field of early modern English studies has resisted engaging with this historical context.

CHAPTER 5

Staging the "Unrepresentable"

Blackness, Blood, and Marriage in England and Spain

Lope de Vega's *Servir a señor discreto* [To serve a wise lord] (1604–18) ends, as most early modern comedies do, with multiple marriages.[1] The central noble couple, the wealthy heiress Leonor and her poor but noble suitor Don Pedro, successfully thwart her father's plan to marry her to a wealthy older man, and her father gives his blessing for their marriage. Leonor's attendant, Elvira, voices her desire to marry Pedro's servingman, Girón, who happily acquiesces, and on that note the play ends. The play's ending, as I have just outlined it, is completely conventional, but *Servir a señor discreto* departs from convention in one critical way: Elvira, the heroine's attendant, is mixed-race and enslaved.

Although the play's terminology indicates that Elvira is of Black and white ancestry (she is labeled a *mulata*), she is consistently described as Black throughout the play. Indeed, the play draws a great deal of attention to her Blackness in its final lines. When her beloved, Girón, is asked if he will agree to marry her, he cheerfully proclaims: "Que me entrego / a un mar de tinta en sus brazos" [I deliver myself up to an ocean of ink in her arms] (III.2917). In fact, their marriage is the culmination of a prophecy delivered by a mysterious soothsayer midway through the play, who tells Girón: "Harás de tu sangre ajedrez" [you will make your blood into a chess set] (l. 1702). Girón underlines this connection at the play's end: "el astrólogo me dijo / verdad pura, que si tengo / hijos, ajedrez serán / pues serán blancos y negros." [The astrologer told me the pure truth: if I have children, they will be a chess set, since they will be black and white] (ll. 2919–22). His quip echoes an anecdote preserved in the 1574 joke compendium *Floresta española*, in which Seville (which is also the setting of the play) is described as resembling a chess set with black and white pieces, because "there are so many slaves in that city" [por los muchos esclavos que hay en aquella ciudad].[2]

Girón's breezy acceptance of future mixed-race children at the end of a comedy could not be more different from the only early modern English comedy (at least the only one that I am aware of) that ends with a marriage between a white man and a Black woman. At the end of *The Knight of Malta* (1618), the villain Mountferrat is punished by being forced to marry the Black woman Zanthia, with whom he has had a sexual relationship. He and Zanthia are banished and told, "Go . . . and engender young devillings" (5.2. 280).[3] As numerous critics have discussed, early modern English drama approaches interracial sexual relationships with horror and fascination, most famously in *Othello*, but also in plays such as *Titus Andronicus* and *Lust's Dominion*, where the villainy of a white female character is reinforced by her sexual alliance with a Black man.[4] Even more striking, as Lynda Boose has argued, is the fact that representations of sexual relationships between white men and Black women are largely absent from early modern English drama. In marked contrast to representations of interreligious marriages, which celebrate what Ania Loomba terms the "delicious traffick" of fair (and wealthy) Jewish and Muslim women who convert to Christianity and marry (and enrich) white men, the assimilation through marriage of Black women on the early modern English stage remains, in Boose's language, "unrepresentable."[5]

For Boose, the reason for this unrepresentability lies in the Black woman's "signifying capacity as a mother [which] threatens nothing less than the wholesale negotiation of white patriarchal authority."[6] In other words, the fact that a Black woman will have a Black child rather than acting as a conduit for the reproduction of a white father's identity and lineage is so alarming as to be unrepresentable in the early modern English imaginary.[7] Why, though, does this possibility become a source of anxiety so deep it cannot be staged in England, while it serves as a source of comedy—a comedy born from anxiety but far from an unspeakable taboo—in Spain?

This chapter explores some answers to this question by bringing together analyses of representations of Blackness and of purity of blood within the fraught space of gender and reproduction. As in Chapter 4, I argue that we must read Blackness and purity of blood as contrasting rather than overlapping categories, both of which are triangulated against whiteness. The first part of this chapter provides an overview of representations of Black female characters in the Spanish comedia, before turning to a closer reading of two plays by Lope de Vega: *Amar, servir y esperar* and *Servir a señor discreto*. I conclude by placing these Spanish plays in dialogue with an English play that addresses both religious conversion and Blackness: Shakespeare's *The Merchant of Venice*. In the Spanish plays, as we shall see, the marriage of an enslaved mixed-race woman to a white Christian Spaniard is enabled by implicit comparison to a prohibited alliance: that between white Christians and those of impure blood. The English plays stage a similar trajectory, but with the categories reversed: the non-Christian woman marries a Christian man, and her marriage is justified by references to a prohibited alliance between a Black female and white male character. Ultimately, all these alliances—those that test but do not exceed the boundaries of licit exogamy, and those that cross over into prohibited miscegenation—serve as sites onto which anxieties about the central white female protagonists' social and economic power can be projected.

Staging Black Female Characters in Early Modern Spain

Before turning to a close reading of *Servir a señor discreto*, it is important to situate the representation of Elvira in the larger framework of Black and mixed-race female characters in early modern Spanish drama.[8] Black women are most often portrayed as objects of mockery in the comedia. They speak in *habla de negros* (Black speech) and are frequently satirized for attempting to move beyond their station, often by courting a male love object deemed inappropriate for them by the logic of the play they inhabit. The "joke" that underlies such representations is that Black women are always already barred from participating in discourses of courtly love and racialized fairness, rendering their attempts to do so categorically futile.[9]

The enslaved woman Eulalla in Lope de Rueda's *Eufemia* (1542) offers a particularly complex example of this figure. She appears in one scene, in which she is courted by the white Spanish *lacayo* (lackey or valet) Polo. The scene is presented as a parody of courtly love. As the noblewoman often does in the comedia, Eulalla appears at the balcony, to the apparent delight of her devoted swain. She sings a song from the chivalric tradition. He courts her; she demurs, saying he only wants to steal her virtue; he finally convinces her to run away with him, and the lovers say their fond farewells.

In this case, however, the chivalric song is sung in *habla de negros* (to intended comedic effect), and Eulalla's desires for the trappings of nobility (a parrot she can teach to speak and a monkey, both of which she requests as gifts) are represented as ludicrously inaccessible. Most cruelly, Polo reveals in an aside that his entire courtship is a trick:

> ¡Pese a tal con la galga! Yo la pienso vender en el primer lugar diciendo que es mi esclava, y ella póneseme en señoríos. Espántome cómo no me pidió dosel a todo en que poner las espaldas. No tengo un real, que piensa la persona sacárselo de las costillas, y demándame papagayo y mona.

> [Damn that dog! I plan to sell her at the first opportunity, saying that she is my slave, and meanwhile she plays at lord-and-lady. I'm shocked she doesn't ask for a fancy robe to wear, too. I haven't a cent; this person thinks she can get blood from a stone (literally: pull money from my ribs), and she's asking me for a parrot and a monkey.][10]

Later, when Eulalla asks Polo for a skin-whitening cream, he tells her he is happy with her color as it is ("con esa color me contento yo") then goes on to inform the audience that she would not be worth anything if she was white—presumably because he would then be unable to sell her into slavery. Eulalla presents herself as worthy of courtship and gifts in her own right, but the *entremés* shows up this desire as a ludicrous fantasy.

Nicholas R. Jones offers a very different reading of this scene and of the staging of Black women in the comedia in general. Jones pushes back against reading characters like Eulalla merely as objects of scorn, suggesting that close readings of this and other plays that contain *habla de negro* are not only examples of racist parody but also contain traces of Afro-diasporic voices. In Jones's reading, Eulalla becomes a "diva," participating in an act of radical self-fashioning in coloring her hair and skin and boldly asserting her own desirability.[11] Jones brings a valuable new perspective to early modern Black studies, demanding that we not dismiss characters such as Eulalla as mere racist stereotypes. This intervention is particularly important in critical studies of Iberian literature, in which representations of Blackness remain largely understudied.

Jones's intervention, however, demands a tricky balancing act. It allows us to see Eulalla's confident estimation of her own worth and draws attention to moments of pathos in her scene—her desire, for example, to have a parrot so that she can teach it to speak as she does. But it is also critical to recognize the larger context in which these moments operate. The scene turns around the joke that Eulalla's assertions of her own worth are not responded to in kind. Although she does not realize it, she is not being treated as a potential wife, but as a piece of property to be stolen and then resold. The play itself was written by a white man and performed by white actors in blackface, and much of its comedy is at the expense of Eulalla. Polo is the trickster, and she is the butt of the joke. Thus we must be prepared both to take Eulalla's assertions of her worth at face value (as Jones does, noting, for example, the specific royal families she references in her claim to illustrious ancestry rather than assuming such claims are empty boasts) and also to recognize that such readings are pushing against the most apparent aims of the text itself: to present the enslaved Black woman as a parodic inversion of white femininity.

Indeed, Eulalla and other Black female characters in the comedia are consistently used to reinforce, through contrast, discourses of whiteness and particularly white femininity. This dynamic takes an unexpected form in several Black saint plays, where Black female characters are used—counterintuitively—to highlight a Black male saint's inner whiteness.[12] For example, an enslaved Black female character takes on a prominent secondary role in two separate plays about the Black saint San Benito de Palermo: Lope de Vega's *El santo negro Rosambuco* [The sainted Black man Rosambuco] (1599–1603) and Antonio Mira de Amescua's *El negro del mejor amo* [The Black man/ slave of the greatest master] (1643).[13] In both cases the heroic protagonist begins the play as a Muslim warrior named Rosambuco who is captured in battle and brought to Spanish Italy (1599–1603), where he is enslaved. In both plays, his enslavers recognize his innate nobility and military prowess before he converts; they are even more impressed by him when he receives a vision from God and becomes a Christian, and most impressed of all when he begins performing miracles. In both plays he is made chief abbot of the local monastery, over his protestations that as a humble Black man he is not worthy of such honors, and he ultimately sacrifices his life for the good of the white, Christian commonwealth.

Both plays also stage Rosambuco's (later Benito's) rejection of romantic overtures from an enslaved Black woman. In *El santo negro Rosambuco*, when the ironically named Lucrecia (Lucrece) first meets Rosambuco, she immediately propositions him: "si querer ser mi galán, / pue que Lucrecia li andora" [if you want to be my suitor, then Lucrecia adores you]. Rosambuco's response is succinct and targeted: "que me atormenta el oirte" [it torments me to listen to you].[14] His response immediately sets up a distinction between himself and Lucrecia: because he is a speaker of standard Castilian, her *habla de negros* dialect torments him. His use of standard Castilian thus separates him from the play's other Black character, reinforcing the notion that his Blackness (but not, crucially, Lucrecia's) is merely external, concealing a white soul.

In the other play about San Benito de Palermo, Mira de Amescua's *El negro del mejor amo*, the enslaved Black woman's status as foil to the Black saint is even more explicit. In their first onstage encounter, Rosambuco asks the enslaved woman, in this play named Catalina: "que es lo que la galga quiere a Rosambuco?" [What does this dog (literally greyhound) want from Rosambuco?][15] Catalina responds angrily that although she has been dying to see him ("moliendome yo por velle"), all he offers her is cruelty (1.468). She continues, pointing to their shared Blackness: "Zi zamo galga la negla, / galgo zamo su merced" [If the Black woman is a dog, then you are a dog my lord] (1.470–71). Rosambuco, who at this point has not yet converted to Christianity, responds: "que por Alá, que a entender / que como tú me pareces, / parezco yo a los demás / me diera doscientas muertas." [By Allah, knowing that I appear to everyone else as you appear to me (i.e., Black) makes me die two hundred deaths] (1.478–81). The exchange again points to the well-worn trope that Rosambuco, like other heroic Black male characters, is really white on the inside. His Blackness shames him as Catalina's does not. As in Lope de Vega's play, the standard Castilian spoken by Rosambuco is juxtaposed with the *habla de negros* spoken by Catalina, and his lack of interest in sex is contrasted with her active pursuit of her object of desire.

Catalina's presence as a foil to Rosambuco consistently reinforces the uncomfortable juxtaposition of his outer Blackness and imagined inner whiteness. Once he has converted to Christianity and becomes a monk, Catalina asks him not to forget her, since they are both Black ("ya que somos entrambas pretas") (3.2462–63). Rosambuco's response (now as Benito) demonstrates the extent to which his conversion hinges on internalizing white supremacy: "Hagamos, hermana mia, / que las almas no lo sean / ya que los cuerpos lo son." [Let's make sure, my sister, that our souls are not what our bodies are (i.e., Black)] (3.2464–66). Indeed, his final words in the play reinforce his desire for whiteness. As he lies on his deathbed, he commends his soul to God: "encomiendo en vuestros manos, / mi espíritu, recibidle, / volviendo a un negro tan blanco" [I commend my spirit to your hands; receive it, thus turning a Black man white] (3.3261–64).

In these saint plays, Black female characters embody a series of gendered stereotypes that will be familiar to scholars of early modern English critical race studies: they are represented as lustful and bodily, compared with non-human animals, and their bodies are objects of scorn.[16] As in English drama, their presence serves to reflect on an aspect of whiteness. Here, though, they are not compared to the white woman's tested chastity but rather to the male Black saint who is "really white" on the inside—both within the world created by the play itself, and by virtue of the fact that the actor playing the saint would have been a white man in blackface. Gender and race are inextricably linked here, as they are in the English context, but to very different ends.

The Limits of Inclusion: Mixed-Race
Marriage in Lope de Vega

Elvira and other characters labeled as mixed-race in the Spanish comedia occupy a different social position than those labeled as Black (*negra*). As mentioned above, these characters are more integrated into upper-class social milieus and speak in standard Castilian rather than *habla de negros*. There is, then, a complexity inherent in discussing such characters within the larger framework of what Boose terms the "unrepresentable Black woman," given that they are already placed in a liminal position. It is certainly true that these characters' intermarriage with white Spaniards relies on their position as mixed-race. It is also true, however, that their Blackness is an important motif in the plays that feature them. The parallels I draw in this and the following section between mixed-race female characters in Spanish theater and "Black Moors" in English theater are not meant to rely on equivalence, but rather on a shared preoccupation with color in relation to identity.

The characterization of Elvira and other mixed-race female characters is caught between that of the heroic or saintly Black male protagonist and the stock caricature of the enslaved Black woman. Like Black male heroes and saints, these mixed-race female characters speak aristocratic Castilian Spanish and assimilate into a white Spanish social order. Unlike Black male heroes, however, they are not explicitly represented as singular or exceptional. Instead, they occupy a stock role familiar to readers of Renaissance drama: the witty serving woman who advises and amuses her noble mistress and in the end marries the white attendant who accompanies her mistress's spouse. Nonetheless, their status as not servants but rather enslaved is emphasized in both jokes and threats; no mention is made of what bearing, if any, these characters' enslavement has on their marriage to their new master's right-hand man.

In Lope de Vega's *Amar, servir y esperar* [To love, serve, and hope/wait] (ca. 1624) the love story between the central female protagonist, Dorotea, and the nobleman Feliciano is doubled with the courtship of Dorotea's enslaved waiting woman, Esperanza, by the protagonist's servant, Andrés. Esperanza is a relatively minor character, but her presence is given greater prominence by virtue of her name, which is the noun form of the last word in the play's title: *esperar*. As the play's central romantic pair overcomes obstacles to be together, variations on the phrase "amar, servir y esperar" appear over and over. To give just one example, Feliciano, the play's noble protagonist, tells his beloved, "Yo quiero amarte y servirte / si yo esperanza tuviere" [I want to love and serve you if only I had hope].[17] Esperanza's name becomes a sort of catchphrase or repeated refrain, and the play even makes this connection explicit. When Esperanza brings bad news from her mistress to the protagonist, Feliciano, he remarks of her: "Oh como parece mia / en ser negra y Esperanza" [how much she resembles my situation, in being black and Esperanza/in being as black as my hope] (59). Because of the centrality of her name, Esperanza takes on a symbolic resonance in the play that exceeds the time she spends on stage. This is exacerbated by the way that her romance with the servant Andrés is presented as a comedic double of the love affair between the main lovers, to the extent that both master and man rely on the same trick—pretending to fall into a dead faint because of the extremity of their love—to trick their respective beloveds into expressing their true feelings.

The doubling of an idealized noble couple's romance with a bawdier, more contentious counterpart between servants is, of course, standard in early modern drama. What is perhaps surprising about the way this doubling works in this play is that neither Esperanza's Blackness nor the fact that she is enslaved presents an obstacle to her romance. Before she first appears onstage, Esperanza is described as follows:

una esclava mulatilla,
de semblante socarrón, que ya sabes que estos son
los lunares de Sevilla; sin envidiar el marfil
la tez de ébano lustrosa,
mas limpia y olorosa
que flor de almendro en Abril. (38)

[A little *mulata* slave girl with a sarcastic countenance—you already know that these are the beauty marks on the face of Seville. Skin of lustrous ebony, without envy of marble, more clean/pure and sweet smelling than the almond flower in April.]

These lines, spoken by the waiting man who will eventually marry Esperanza, continue in an extended blazon anatomizing her beauty. Thus she is initially presented as an object of desire. Her Blackness is aestheticized without irony or excuse. The blazon also explicitly describes her as "limpia" (pure, literally clean), a subtle reminder of the discourse that insists that Black Africans have more claim to purity of blood, or *limpieza de sangre*, than those of Jewish or Moorish descent.[18]

Indeed, although there are no Jewish or Muslim (or converso or Morisco) characters in the play, the text does frequently invoke the importance of purity of blood. Feliciano, the noble male protagonist, has his worth confirmed by the fact that he has received admission to a knightly order that demands purity of descent. (In fact, his beloved's father is the one responsible for inducting him into the order.) And the servant/lackey Andrés is at one point so frustrated by his master that he notes that if he had been consulted about Feliciano's descent, he would have labeled him a Jew and had his cross (sign of membership in his knightly order) stripped from him. In this play, as in the plays with Black male protagonists discussed in Chapter 3, Blackness becomes an acceptable form of exogamy by implicit comparison to the prohibited invisible difference of impurity of blood.

This dynamic is even more pronounced in *Servir a señor discreto* [To serve a wise lord].[19] The enslaved waiting woman Elvira—and particularly her Blackness—come to take up more space and significance in the play than her role in the plot of the play suggests they ought to. Her unexpected prominence can be attributed to the way the play displaces tensions about nobility, wealth, regionalism, and cosmopolitanism from its central romantic pair, projecting them onto Elvira.

Servir a señor discreto is a typical Lope city comedy, stuffed to the brim with superfluous double-crossings and shenanigans, highly conscious of class identity and mobility, immersed in the details of city life, and focused on the erotics and economics of marriage alike. The main plot involves a young man, Pedro, a lower-ranking noble, who travels from Madrid to Seville. In Seville he falls in love with Leonor, the daughter of a wealthy *indiano* (a Spaniard who made his fortune in the so-called New World).[20] Pedro pretends to

be wealthier and more titled than he is to win over his lady-love, and at first
this works. But the two keep their romance secret because Leonor's father
wishes his daughter to marry another man, an older and very wealthy *indiano* who has just returned to Spain. Then Pedro runs into difficulties: he has
spent all his money keeping up the pretense of being wealthy and doesn't
want to admit the truth to his beloved, Leonor. Instead, he pretends that he
must return to Madrid to receive membership in a knightly order—a sign
of his Old Christian nobility—and basically disappears out of shame. While
in Madrid, he meets and becomes the secretary of the eponymous *señor discreto*—the conde de Palma. The count is immediately taken with Pedro and
allows him to take over his own household so that Pedro can woo Leonor as
though he were in fact wealthy and titled.

Interestingly, the young lovers' trials turn out to be entirely self-created.
Once Leonor's father finds out that she has fallen in love with a man not of his
choosing, he assures her that he just wants her to be happy and helps her to
reunite with Pedro (whom he and Leonor still believe to be rich and noble).
Even more surprising, once the truth of Pedro's poverty comes out, Leonor's
father declares that he loves his son-in-law "even more" for his humility:
"agora quiero a mi yerno / mucho mas que le queria / que rico fuera soberbio /
y pobre ha de ser humilde" [Now I love my son-in-law much more than I
loved him before, since rich he would have been haughty, and poor he must be
humble] (ll. 2904–5). The count of Palma, who acts as a deus ex machina, even
manages to secure a knightly habit for Pedro by calling in some favors, thereby
ensuring Pedro's reputation for pure lineage and making good on at least one
of his false promises.

This central romance plot is doubled by a love affair between servants.
Pedro's manservant, Girón, falls in love with Leonor's enslaved lady-in-
waiting, Elvira. Elvira's Blackness is a central feature of the rhetoric of their
courtship. This secondary courtship also serves as a site onto which anxieties about the primary couple's relationship are displaced: anxieties about
Leonor's wealth and power in comparison to Pedro's, and about the ways
that wealth extracted from Spain's colonies disrupts local economies and
hierarchies in early modern Spain.

Elvira occupies an ambiguous social position within the world of the play.
She is enslaved, and repeatedly referred to as such, but she also serves as the
lady-in-waiting and trusted advisor to her mistress. She also hints in passing
that she is the illegitimate child of a nobleman, refusing to be paid for deliv-
ering a message "por el siglo del hidalgo / que me engendró" [for the honor of

the nobleman who begat me] (I.887–88). Most importantly, Elvira's marriage to Girón at the end of the play is not presented as particularly scandalous or transgressive. As I began the chapter by discussing, although Girón makes a number of jokes at the expense of her color and ancestry, when she asks the count if the two may be wed, he cheerfully promises: "Que me entrego / a un mar de tinta en sus brazos" [I deliver myself up to an ocean of ink in her arms] (III.2917).

At first, then, the play's presentation of Elvira might seem like a telling counterpoint to the paucity of unions between Black women and white men on the early modern English stage. The play presents us with a prominent female character whose Black beauty is the subject of praise, and who integrates herself into white Spanish social networks. Her marriage and potential interracial children are described as a curiosity but not as taboo; Girón does not seem troubled that his descendants will become "ajedrez," or a chess board. It would be possible, then—if we take this play as emblematic of broader cultural currents in early modern Spain—to suggest that the union of Black (or at least mixed-race) women with white men is not "unrepresentable" in early modern Spain as it is in England.

Perhaps we could even turn this celebratory reading toward questions of female agency and autonomy and note that Pedro and Girón both marry women who are wealthier than they are. Elvira asks the count for permission to marry Girón, not the other way around, and Pedro's new father-in-law expresses his pleasure at Pedro's lack of pride, which we might read as a sign that he will be more biddable than a more exalted son-in-law. The play thus celebrates both a cross-class and an interracial alliance, displaying relatively few anxieties about how such marriages disrupt caste systems and patriarchal descent.

Unsurprisingly, however, on closer inspection the play's engagement with questions of Blackness and female agency alike do not seem nearly so sunny. While Elvira does occupy a privileged position as lady-in-waiting, the play also repeatedly draws our attention to her vulnerable enslaved status. So, for example, when Leonor's father wishes to get information from Elvira about his daughter's love life, he extracts information from her by threatening torture, telling her he will burn her with hot grease (the Spanish term is *pringar*)—a particularly cruel punishment reserved for the enslaved (l. 1741). And while Girón happily agrees to marry Elvira, and at times lauds her Black beauty, he also draws on a mocking, dehumanizing rhetoric in his courtship. He belittles her on more than one occasion by animalizing her. In one scene, when the two pairs of lovers say their fond farewells, the protagonist Pedro remarks of his noble white beloved: "los ojos se me van tras aquel angel" [my eyes are drawn to that angel]. In a debased parody of his romantic rhetoric, Girón echoes in praise of his beloved, Elvira: "Y a mi tras el hollin de aquella perra . . . perla quise decir" [And mine to the soot of that bitch . . . pearl, I meant to say] (ll. 1412–13). The play exploits the phonetic similarity between *perla* (pearl) and *perra* (bitch) on multiple occasions, at once ironizing the notion that Elvira's Blackness could be beautiful (by comparing her to the whiteness of a pearl) and reducing her to the status of an animal, and more cruelly a bitch. And this is just one of a series of examples in which the play offers dehumanizing jokes at the expense of Elvira's color or ancestry. The play does highlight a prominent Black female character and praises her beauty and wit, but makes a point of mocking her and drawing our attention to her enslaved status as it does so. It carves out a surprisingly prominent place for her in the play, but the jokes that circulate around her suggest that that place is fraught with tension.

It may be that Elvira's character offers a contained site onto which the play's broader anxieties about female agency, social mobility, burgeoning cosmopolitanism, and New World wealth can be displaced. More specifically, Pedro marries into extreme wealth when he marries Leonor. He clarifies in the play's first scene that he is "de mediana calidad" [middle-ranking gentry], an "hidalgo" but not a "caballero" (I67, 70–71).[21] Leonor is titled and perhaps of more noble rank than he (the play does not specify), but she is extravagantly wealthy as a result of her *indiano* father's participation in Spain's imperial ventures. Elvira, too, as the play notes on multiple occasions, has come to Spain not directly from Africa but from Spain's colonies in the Americas via the early transatlantic slave trade. The first mention of Elvira is as "una cierta esclavilla / mulata y no de Sevilla / porque ser indiana es fama [a certain little slave girl, *mulata* and not from Seville, since rumor has it she is *indiana*] (l. 235–36). At the end of the play, when Elvira is asked to perform a traditional "baile de negros" [black dance] she cautions: "advierte que es guineo / enjerto en indio" [be warned that this is Guinean grafted with *indio*] (Ill. 2776–77). Elvira is thus linked with her mistress's New World wealth. Her "grafted" dance, like her embodied presence as a mixed-race woman, also becomes a sign of the ways that colonial enterprises are intertwined with the specter of adulterous mixtures of cultures and bloodlines.

By projecting anxieties about adulterous mixtures onto Elvira rather than Leonor, the play preserves the fantasy of purity in the marriage of the central romantic couple. Elvira's status as an acceptable partner for marriage—at least for a serving man—is further reinforced by the ways she is identified as *limpia* or pure-blooded. As we have seen, in early modern Spain Blackness is at times presented as evidence of the absence of "impure" (e.g., Jewish or Moorish) blood. The mixed-race Elvira, like the Black male protagonists discussed in the previous chapter, offers a less threatening alternative to the hidden (and presumably perfidious) difference of the converso or the Morisco.[22] Thus the "verdad pura," or pure truth, of the astrologer's prediction to Girón, that his blood would be made into "ajedrez," or chess set, offers a less threatening alternative to marriage with a white woman of impure blood. This does not, however, constitute an unproblematic acceptance of Blackness in the play. Rather, Elvira's inclusion in a Spanish national community is enabled by repeated assertions of her difference, whether in the form of jokes about her Blackness or references to the fact that she is enslaved.

The play also uses Elvira to scrutinize the unequal economic status of the lovers. When Pedro leaves Seville to return to Madrid, he has no money even to fund his return voyage. Although Pedro is too proud to admit this to his beloved, Leonor, his lackey, Girón, has no such compunctions about turning to Elvira. Rather obliquely, Girón asks Elvira for something to remember her by. Thinking he wants a love token, she offers him a lock of her hair. When he refuses this Elvira offers him her soul: "que lleves mi alma quiero." Girón's reply is more prosaic: "Mejor tu cuerpo quisiera / que, en efeto, le vendiera,/ y me valiera dinero." [I would rather have your body—so that, in short, I could sell and it and make money] (ll. 1334–36). Overall, the scene emphasizes Girón's (and Pedro's) lack of economic power in comparison to their respective ladies. Girón's brutal joke about selling Elvira attempts to invert the balance of power between them. Despite his position as a supplicant, Girón's suggestion asserts his authority over Elvira by reminding her that she is a slave and so can be reduced to a commodity, and echoes the central conceit of Polo and Eulalla's faux courtship in Lope de Rueda's *Eufemia*, discussed above. Although Elvira is initially furious with him—not so much for asking for money as for the manner in which he has done so—she nonetheless ultimately gives him a hundred escudos [ll. 1384–85]. In doing so, she quietly undermines his insult and reestablishes her economic power over him. Ironically, despite the fact that she is enslaved she retains the ability to ease his way financially—or refuse to do so.

Although the noble Pedro is ashamed to admit it, he is as poor as Girón. The dynamic between lord and lackey at times resembles that between

Lazarillo de Tormes and the hapless and hungry knight he goes to serve and ends up supporting. What Pedro offers in his marriage to Leonor is gentlemanly behavior and—more important—his pure Old Christian nobility. The play makes this point on multiple occasions, most explicitly in the opening scene when Girón reassures Pedro that he is still a gentleman—a hidalgo—despite his lack of wealth: "y sabes que la nobleza / está en la limpia hidalguía / que lo que es caballería / mas consiste en la riqueza." [And you know that true nobility lies in pure-blooded gentlemanliness—and that which we call knighthood is more about wealth] (l. 73–76). Throughout the play, Pedro is associated with a native and pure-blooded Spanish nobility, one that is free of suspicion from Jewish and Moorish ancestry (since membership to a knightly order required proofs of purity of blood) as well as from the specter of miscegenation that at times attends representations of colonial wealth. The possibility that such purity might be corrupted by marriage to the wealthy *indiana* Leonor, or that Pedro's authority might be compromised by his wife's greater economic power, are displaced from Pedro and Leonor onto the couple that more obviously disrupts existing social categories: Girón and Elvira.

Just as the connection between Esperanza's name and the title of *Amar, servir e esperar* gives her presence greater symbolic resonance throughout the play, Elvira is connected to her play's title by her delivery of the play's closing lines. The protagonist, Pedro, begins the typical ending: "Esta comedia, senado / hecho por daros contento, / se llama . . ." [This play, honored audience, made to give you pleasure, is called . . .]. At this moment, curiously, Elvira jumps in, exclaiming: "¡Yo lo diré!: servir a señor discreto" [I will say it!: to serve a clever/wise lord!] (lII. 2925–26). On the one hand, this moment offers a startling glimpse of a Black female character usurping the white male protagonist's place of prominence, centering herself at his expense. On the other, having Elvira speak these lines serves as a reminder of the difference between Elvira's social position and Pedro's. Most explicitly, the title refers to Pedro's service to the conde de Palma, who has engineered his protégé's marriage. From Elvira, however, the words take on a different resonance. The moment becomes, as we have seen in so many other examples in previous chapters, an expression of the disturbing fantasy of slavery as willing service. As we have seen in many other Spanish plays, the price of Elvira's inclusion in white Spanish Christendom is that she celebrate enslavement as mutually beneficial "service" in the play's final line.

The Limits of Inclusion in *The Merchant of Venice*

How, if at all, can this reading of Black female characters in the Spanish comedia, in particular Elvira's position in *Servir a señor discreto*, illuminate our
understanding of intersections of race and gender in early modern English
drama? After all, no Black or mixed-race female character in early modern
English drama ends a play in a position comparable to Elvira's. Interracial
sexual relationships are a recurring motif in early modern English drama, as
Celia Daileader, Arthur Little, Ania Loomba, and others have demonstrated,
but they are almost always staged as occurring between a Black man and a
white woman.[23] If we center the staging of white femininity, however, and
particularly the economic agency of white female characters, certain parallels begin to emerge between English and Spanish plays. Counterintuitively,
perhaps, *Servir a señor discreto* and Elvira's place within it may be most useful
for better understanding not Blackness but rather one aspect of whiteness:
specifically, the ways in which white female characters manipulate anxieties
about miscegenation to retain social and economic agency.

Like *Servir a señor discreto*, Shakespeare's *Merchant of Venice* dramatizes
the marriage of an extraordinarily wealthy white woman to a white man of
modest means and "gentle" but not illustrious ancestry. In both plays, this
union is staged alongside a marriage between two secondary characters that
tests—but ultimately does not transgress—the boundaries of acceptable
exogamy. Further, both plays allude to (without staging) sexual alliances that
cross into prohibited miscegenation. In the Spanish case, as we have seen, the
prohibited alliance is between those who are pure-blooded, or *limpio*, and
those of impure (Jewish or Muslim) descent. *The Merchant of Venice*, by contrast, dramatizes the assimilation of the "fair" stranger alongside references
to prohibited miscegenation between a white man and a Black woman.

The reference to prohibited miscegenation in *The Merchant of Venice*
occurs in a now-notorious brief conversation extraneous to the play's plot,
in which the clown Launcelot Gobbo interrogates the possibility of the "fair
infidel" Jessica's assimilation into Christendom. Jessica informs her new husband: "Launcelot and I are out—he tells me flatly there's no mercy for me in
heaven, because I am a Jew's daughter: and he says that you are no good member of the commonwealth, for converting Jews to Christians, you raise the
price of pork."[24] Lorenzo's response is not to deny Launcelot's claim but rather
to deflect it: "I shall answer that better to the commonwealth than you can
the getting up of the negro's belly: the Moor is with child by you, Launcelot!"

This figure is at the center of Kim F. Hall's 1992 essay "Guess Who's Coming to Dinner? Colonization and Miscegenation in *The Merchant of Venice*." As Hall has demonstrated, the Moor serves as "a silent symbol for the economic and racial politics of *The Merchant of Venice*," a play that exposes the ways that the fantasy of a hermetically sealed white Belmont relies on the influx of wealth from Europe's early imperial ventures.[25] Within Hall's framework, the Moor disrupts the play's "eradication or assimilation of difference" by introducing a mixed-race child into Venice whose Blackness, unlike Jessica's Jewishness, "may not be 'converted' or absorbed within the endogamous, exclusionary values of Belmont."[26] Thus the figure of the Moor represents a number of the tensions that animate the play, among them the anxious pursuit of a fantasy of impossible purity that is always already compromised by transnational commerce.

At first glance, these English and Spanish plays offer diametrically opposed representations of race. In Lope's plays, Black-white marriage is staged and Christian-Jewish sexual alliance disavowed; the English plays stage precisely the opposite formation. If, however, we shift our focus to the intersection of race and gender for both plays' white female protagonists, a structural similarity emerges. Each play shows a central endogamous marriage flanked by two different forms of exogamy, one acceptable and one prohibited (although it is important to note in this context that the prohibited alliance I am reading into the Spanish plays is never explicitly staged or even addressed). In the English play, Blackness is prohibited; in the Spanish, impure blood is. In this reading, the English and the Spanish plays represent exogamy in similar ways, with the ultimate goal of demarcating the boundaries of inclusion in a national identity.

In short, both plays triangulate religious difference and color against white femininity to implicitly valorize their white female protagonist's assertion of agency. Indeed, *Servir a señor discreto* shares many of the concerns that Hall identifies as central to *The Merchant of Venice*: not only the limits of acceptable exogamy, but also the desire to assimilate the wealth of global markets (and in the case of Lope's play imperial plunder) while retaining a fantasy of purity within a European community. In both plays, such concerns are most clearly viewed through the lens of gender and marriage: the presence of the foreign—of prohibited miscegenation—suddenly raises the value of the male protagonist's whiteness and Christianity, enabling him to marry above his station by virtue of his status as a European gentleman. In *Merchant*, as we have seen more explicitly in many Spanish plays, cross-class alliances are enabled by evoking fear of the foreign, thereby granting relatively higher value to whiteness and "purity." Bassanio's value on the marriage market as a Venetian gentleman whose only wealth "runs through his veins," like Pedro's as an Old Christian, relies on the presence of the foreign (or perhaps the fantasy that the native is scarce) to legitimate these marriages.

Bassanio's and Pedro's upwardly mobile marriages enact, at a remove, the tired colonial trope of the "fair infidel" willingly exchanging unimaginable wealth for access to Christianity and subjection to a distant monarch—a trope that itself reenacts the structure of the traffic in women.[27] In both *The Merchant of Venice* and *Servir a señor discreto*, however, this model is distributed across multiple positions and characters. Plays such as *The Renegado* and *The Island Princess* stage a marriage of a white Christian to a white non-Christian princess, relying on the premise that the male characters' status as European Christians is of comparable value to the "fair infidel's" wealth and station. In *The Merchant of Venice* and *Servir a señor discreto*, by contrast, the foreign wealth is rerouted through a white Christian woman in the central couple, while marriage to a "woman from elsewhere" takes place in the match between secondary characters. Elvira and Jessica each serve as the "woman from elsewhere" in their respective secondary marriages, absorbing the anxiety produced by an influx of foreign wealth. The primary holder of that wealth, however, is the central white female protagonist: Leonor in *Servir a señor discreto*, and Portia in *The Merchant of Venice*. The exchange of beauty and wealth for Christianity is interrupted; the white female character does not need to pay a price for inclusion and so is able to retain control of her wealth even after marriage.

Thus this displacement creates a space for greater autonomy for the central white female protagonist. If we read Elvira as a double for Leonor in *Servir a señor discreto*, we can see how anxieties about a white woman's economic power and independence are displaced onto a woman of color. Both Leonor and Elvira disobey Leonor's father; only Elvira, however, is threatened with torture. Both Leonor and Elvira have more access to wealth than their respective love objects, but only Elvira's suitor can attempt to put her in her place by suggesting he sell her for ready money.

Jessica does not, as Elvira does in *Servir a señor discreto*, occupy the more conventional secondary place of lady-in-waiting. The play does, however, repeatedly emphasize connections between her trajectory and Portia's. Both are women of fortune whose husbands marry them for their money; the play's first reference to Portia is as "a lady richly left" (1.1.164), and Jessica's first gesture when Lorenzo comes to steal her away is to throw him a casket of money (2.6.34). Both women disguise themselves as men. When Portia promises herself to Bassanio, she tells him, "Myself and what is mine to you and yours / is now *converted*," a word choice that echoes Jessica's desire to become a Christian by her own marriage to Lorenzo (3.2.169–70). Most explicitly, when Portia leaves Belmont to rescue Antonio, she literally puts Jessica in her own place, informing Lorenzo that her servants "will acknowledge [him] and Jessica / In place of Lord Bassanio and [herself]" (3.4.39–40). Jessica's open defiance of her father's will offers a space onto which anxieties about Portia's more subtle circumventing of authority can be projected, much like anxieties about Leonor's economic power are displaced onto Elvira in *Servir a señor discreto*.[28] And as Portia compensates for her own failure to submit to patriarchal authority by aligning herself with it, securing Shylock's seized wealth for Christian Venice by ensuring that wealth passes to "his son Lorenzo" (4.1.401), Jessica dwindles into silence by the play's end.

Conclusion

In the plays discussed above, transgressions against white patriarchal norms are enabled by displacing anxieties about white female characters who transgress gender boundaries onto racialized characters marked by either impure blood or Blackness. More specifically, female protagonists are represented as leveraging their whiteness to achieve economic power, control, and agency. This pattern is not unique to *The Merchant of Venice* and *Servir a señor discreto*. In English drama, the archetypal example is Bess of *The Fair Maid of the West*, whose much-lauded "fairness" propels her into an upwardly mobile marriage—but only on the condition that its value be enhanced by sustained proximity to threatening nonwhite difference.[29] Inés's marriage in *La villana de Getafe*, discussed in the first chapter, is similarly predicated on her status as *limpia*, or pure-blooded. The ways that whiteness can substitute for nobility for lower-ranking female characters in early modern drama is relatively easy to assimilate into our understanding of patrilineal descent and kinship structures. What is less intuitive, perhaps, is the dynamic in which wealthy and titled white female characters leverage the notion of the "native" to retain power by marrying suitors who are less wealthy and titled than they are—and the extent to which their position relies on projecting anxieties about such alliances onto a female character who is clearly coded as an outsider.

If we focus on similarities across the English and Spanish plays, a shared pattern emerges: a white female protagonist appears at the top of a hierarchy of identity categories. Equally important, though, is the difference: in the Spanish example, the prohibited alliance that is only peripherally engaged with involves impure blood, while in the English example the prohibited alliance briefly alluded to is with a Black woman. These dynamics offer an example of the strategic deployment of different kinds of racialized rhetoric in defense of the "native" subject.

Differentiating Blackness from religious difference in early modern English and Spanish drama reveals the complexity and historical specificity of racial formations. It also underlines the extent to which early modern English discourses of identity were already being articulated within a Black/white binary by the turn of the seventeenth century. *The Merchant of Venice* is one among many English plays in which whiteness is valorized by the marginalization or expulsion of a Black character. Comparing this dynamic to that found in Spain—where Blackness is linked to enslavement and marginalized, but not represented as a threat to be expelled—highlights the extent to which whiteness serves as a crucial marker of inclusion in early modern English drama. If the primary condition for inclusion in Spanish drama is purity of blood (however ironized and complex the presentation of it), the primary condition for inclusion in early modern English texts may be whiteness.

Considering English whiteness (as both color and imagined moral purity) alongside Spanish representations of race can help us see how a pattern of anxious displacement has shaped our reading of early modern English literature up to the present day. In some studies of race in early modern texts, the idea of Spain occupies a place similar to Jessica's in *The Merchant of Venice*: a troubling but acceptable form of difference that can be imagined as part of England's literary history, one that tests the boundaries of our understanding of race without crossing into prohibited territory. The idea of Spain as a site of "impure blood" that then informs discourses of race in early modern England has proved, like Jessica in *Merchant*, to be comfortably assimilable into scholarship. This idea of Spain has also enabled us to mitigate early modern England's racism by locating its origins elsewhere, much as anxieties about Portia's subtle manipulation of patriarchal authority are displaced onto Jessica's direct defiance of her father. Meanwhile, the centrality of racialized slavery to early modern discourses of race remains overlooked, much as the "Moor" impregnated by Launcelot is relegated the margins of the play.

Indeed, this figure was similarly confined to the margins of scholarship until Hall's vital essay demanded that we reckon with her.

To extend this analogy still further, if we align the idea of Spain with Jessica, we might align a certain fantasy of "pre-racial" early modern England with Portia. Perhaps English whiteness is above all a fiction of innocence predicated on denial. This England, much like Shakespeare's Portia, profits from the influence of imperial plunder and an emergent slave trade even while denying and displacing it.

Conclusion

Beyond English Whiteness / Another Idea of Spain

Throughout this book, I have traced a scholarly tendency toward displacement or disavowal of representations of anti-Black racism in early modern texts, and particularly in Shakespeare's plays. I have done so largely by exposing the relationship between the "idea of Spain" (i.e., Spain as a site of older racial regimes of pure and impure blood) and representations of race in Spanish texts themselves, which demonstrate the centrality of the Afro-Iberian slave trade to representations of Blackness. In this context, my argument is as much about how scholars have talked about race in the early modern period as it is about early modern texts themselves. The idea of Spain I describe serves two functions: it obscures representations of racialized slavery within early modern English texts, and it locates the source of racialized religious difference elsewhere, in Spain rather than in England. In taking this dynamic into account, this book asks us to reconsider not only our understanding of early modern discourses of race, but also the history of early modern literary studies in the United States and England in the twentieth and twenty-first centuries.

More broadly, I hope I have shown how a fantasy of whiteness undergirds not only English national identity in the sixteenth and seventeenth centuries but also scholarly approaches to early modern English literature.[1] This whiteness is imagined not only in terms of phenotype but also of innocence. As I argue in Chapter 4, Blackness and enslavement are indeed linked in the early modern English imaginary, but this racialized slavery is most often staged as occurring elsewhere. If we look only to early modern English texts to understand the early years of England's involvement in racialized slavery, we will find denial, displacement, and disavowal—not because a regime of enslavement predicated on anti-Blackness had not yet reached England, but because English ethnic nationalism in the period is predicated on the denial not only of racial difference but also of racism. As I argued in the introduction, early modern English propaganda texts represent Spaniards as simultaneously more racialized and more racist than their English counterparts; this dynamic demands that early modern English involvement in racialized slavery be denied from its beginnings. Bringing English texts into dialogue with Spanish, as I have done here, forces us to see English whiteness-as-innocence as an anxiously defended fantasy rather than a historical reality.

We can perhaps most clearly see the stakes of anxiously defended whiteness by reading—to paraphrase Kim F. Hall—what "isn't there." In Chapter 4, I briefly mentioned Aaron the Moor's use of the word *slave* in *Titus Andronicus*. He uses the word three times, and all three describe his infant son: "look how the black slave smiles upon his father"; "come on, you thick-lipp'd slave, I'll bear you hence"; and "peace, tawny slave, half me and half thy dam" (4.2.122, 5.1.1.27, 4.2.127). In all three instances the word is paired with racializing imagery. Among the 178 uses of *slave* and its variants in Shakespeare, these are the only three instances where the term is paired with unambiguously racializing language.

When my students read *Titus Andronicus*, often encountering the play for the first time, these passages inevitably raise questions: Why does Aaron repeatedly refer to his son, the child of an empress, as a slave? These lines can offer a useful point of entry into a discussion of the metaphorics of slavery and anti-Blackness in early modern texts. But if a student turns to the footnotes of the Arden edition of *Titus Andronicus*, they would find scant assistance. There are no notes at all on the first two lines, and on the third, one brief note on the word *tawny*, which reads "black, not yellowish brown as now."[2] The Oxford edition, similarly, has no notes on Aaron's first two uses of the word *slave*. On the third, it also glosses *tawny* as "black," then glosses *slave* as "said playfully, as is villain below."[3] What these notes fail to mention is that nowhere else in all of Shakespeare is the word *slave* used "playfully," as a term of endearment, or to refer to a child. The notes' insistence that the baby is not really "tawny" but "black" reveal a subtle undercurrent of anxiety about racial mixing, diverting the reader from Aaron's characterization of the child as "half me, and half thy dam." Perhaps more important, by improbably glossing *slave* as a term of endearment, the Oxford edition's notes quietly reaffirm the notion that racialized slavery does not inform Shakespeare's worldview. The Arden edition, meanwhile, implicitly normalizes Aaron's description of his son as a "black slave" by failing to register it as noteworthy at all.

The absence of information in these footnotes is indicative of a much broader tendency in early modern English literary studies: to avoid engaging with the history of racialized slavery, often by using the idea of Spain to argue that Blackness functions primarily as a metaphor for religious difference. This is not, however, the only "idea of Spain" that circulated in twentieth-century academia. In 1938, Velaurez B. Spratlin published the first (and still the only) English translation of Ximénez de Enciso's *Juan Latino*, a play I discuss in detail in Chapter 3. Spratlin, a professor at Howard University, was the first Black American to receive a Ph.D. in Spanish in the United States. The translation is part of a larger monograph, *Juan Latino: Slave and Humanist*, which highlights the accomplishments of the historical Juan Latino, a formerly enslaved Black man who became a celebrated poet, Latinist, and professor.

Juan Latino: Slave and Humanist has not been reprinted since its first edition in 1938. The text is widely accessible online (it has been digitized and is in the public domain), but few hard copies are still in circulation. Several years ago, I stumbled across a first edition on a second-hand booksellers' site and quickly ordered it. When the book arrived, I discovered it was inscribed several times over. The first inscription is from the author and reads: "To Mollie and Fred, with best wishes, from Velaurez. October 16, 1938." The second reads: "To Dr. Marion Elizabeth Carter, my former pupil and a distinguished Dunbar graduate, with kind remembrances, Mary Gibson Hundley. May 20, 1970." Mary Gibson Hundley (1897–1986) was an educator and civil rights activist who graduated from Radcliffe in 1918 and then taught English, French, and Latin at Dunbar High School and Howard University. She is also, I suspect, the "Mollie" to whom Velaurez B. Spratlin inscribed the copy of his book, as her second husband, whom she married in 1938, was named Fred. Her pupil Marion Elizabeth Carter (1915–2008) earned a Ph.D. in Romance languages from Catholic University of America and in linguistics from Georgetown University. According to Marion Carter's obituary, she was also the first person to teach Spanish on national television.[4] She is also a descendant of Elizabeth Hemmings, Sally Hemmings's mother. Audio files that feature her recounting family stories can be heard on the Thomas Jefferson Foundation website.[5]

Taken together, these inscriptions trace a genealogy of Black intellectuals in the twentieth century whose interest in Afro-diasporic history and cultural production led them to early modern Spanish. They are not alone in this; indeed, a different kind of idea of Spain emerges out of Black American intellectual communities in the 1920s–1940s, one that has been largely overlooked by a predominantly white academy. In the first half of the twentieth century, references to early modern Spain's Afro-diasporic population—and particularly to Juan Latino—peppered African American journals. Juan Latino is mentioned in publications such as the *Journal of Negro History* and the *Journal of Race Development* and is the subject of an essay by Arthur (Arturo) Schomburg, who traveled to Spain to uncover more information about him.[6] A fictionalized account of his early life appears in a 1946 book designed to meet "the need for extending the study of the Negro in junior and senior high schools," *Distinguished Negroes Abroad.*[7]

This engagement with Spain extended beyond Juan Latino as a singular model of Afro-diasporic intellectual history. W. Napoleon Rivers's 1934 article "Why Negroes Should Study Romance Languages and Literature" succinctly makes a case for moving beyond the English canon:

> Briefly, the Negro should study the Romance languages and literatures in order to (1) increase his knowledge of the history and literature of his race; (2) to combat falsehood with truth, by searching the sources in these languages and bringing to light important facts which have been obscured, falsified, or omitted, and to rehabilitate distinguished personages of African descent who have contributed richly to world culture but have been detracted or omitted in books printed in the English language; (3) to compete more effectively for additional economic opportunities at home and abroad; and (4) to open up for himself a newer and larger world of ideas.[8]

Rivers points not only to Spain but also to France, Italy, and Portugal, arguing that this transnational perspective will counteract a whitewashed historical narrative centered on England and the United States. For Rivers and other Black Hispanists in the first half of the twentieth century, early modern Spanish representations of Blackness offered importance evidence of the Black presence in early modern Europe, particularly Spain, and can be used to highlight the accomplishments of Black soldiers and scholars. Indeed, Rivers invokes not only Juan Latino but also Juan de Mérida, the fictional protagonist of Andrés de Claramonte's play *El valiente negro en Flandes* [The valiant Black man in Flanders], discussed in Chapter 3.

This turn to early modern Spanish representations of Afro-diasporic history was not only concerned with highlighting the accomplishments of exemplary figures. It was also part of a larger political project to establish solidarity between the fight against fascism in Spain and that against white supremacy

in the United States in the 1930s. As Robert F. Reid Pharr has argued: "many
African Americans, particularly those of the intellectual class, saw the Spanish civil war as nothing less than the continuation of particularly virulent
forms of anti-African, anti-black aggression by governments in both Europe
and the United States. . . . [They] made no bones about the essential connection between capitalism and white supremacy in the United States, colonialism on the African continent, and the Fascist rebellion in Spain."[9] Solidarity
with Spain became linked with resistance to anti-Black racism. Indeed, both
Paul Robeson and Langston Hughes traveled to Spain and wrote about their
sympathy with the Republican cause. The surge in interest in figures such as
Juan Latino in the 1930s can thus be read as part of a larger discourse of cos-
mopolitan Afro-diasporic history, in conjunction with a movement for transnational solidarity in the fight against fascism. In this context, early modern
Spanish plays with Black protagonists were examined and cited. Since then,
they have largely disappeared from public view.

There is, however, one important exception. In his foundational work
Black Skin, White Masks, Frantz Fanon turns to the Spanish comedia, offering
a reading of several passages from *El valiente negro en Flandes*. Fanon may
not have read the play in its entirety; he cites as his source Oliver Brachfeld's
1945 *Inferiority Feelings*, which excerpts several of the protagonist's speeches
in the original Spanish. Fanon translates these excerpts into French and, like
Rivers, Spratlin, and others, uses them as a form of evidence. For Fanon,
however, the play is of interest not in its representation of a heroic Black figure, but rather in how it demonstrates the long history of white supremacist
ideologies. Fanon explains: "Here we see that the black man's inferiority does
not date from this century, since Claramunte [*sic*] was a contemporary of
Lope de Vega. . . . As we can see, we should understand Juan de Mérida from
the perspective of overcompensation. It is because the black man belongs to
an 'inferior' race that he tries to resemble the superior race."[10] Fanon reads
these passages as evidence of a racializing ideology that requires a heroic
Black protagonist to aspire to whiteness.

It is telling—if not particularly surprising—that none of these analyses of
representations of Blackness and early modern Afro-diasporic history have
informed Shakespeare studies. As William Childers has noted, even scholars
who draw on Fanon in readings of Shakespeare and race have overlooked his
discussion of *El valiente negro en Flandes*, instead evoking Spain only in the
context of the Black Legend and purity of blood.[11] We have similarly failed to
attend to Rivers's suggestion that turning to non-English texts would "combat

falsehood with truth, by searching the sources in these languages and bringing to light important facts which have been obscured, falsified, or omitted."
Rivers's argument, of course, comes from a different and more urgent place
than mine, that of a Black man writing to Black students and scholars in the
1930s. But his injunction to look outside the English canon to better understand histories of race and racism remains relevant.

Indeed, it is particularly relevant for early modern English studies, a
field that remains structurally indebted to Shakespeare's foundational status
in the English canon. After all, the origins of English as an academic disci-
pline in the late nineteenth century are inextricable from the rise of racialized
nationalism and eugenic pseudoscience. The rationale for shifting university
study from classical to modern languages derived in part from the notion
that, as Robert Irvine argues, "the great literature of a language expressed the
unchanging spirit of the race that wrote it."[12] The canon of texts we read, write
about, and teach our students is still shaped by the structure of linguistic and
national isolationism inherited from a model of study built on explicitly eth-
nonationalist (and implicitly white) supremacy. Even as the content of much
literary study has become avowedly progressive in its aims, this isolationism
enables a series of crucial blind spots, particularly in the context of developing discourses of anti-Blackness in early modern England. It is difficult, for
example, to grapple with the extent to which slavery informs representations
of Blackness in early modern England without engaging with the transnational circulation of texts, bodies, and ideologies. In focusing on the idea of
Spain, as I have done here, I hope I have shown the extent to which English
literary studies remains haunted by its foundations in ethnic nationalism.

Survey of Black and Moorish Characters in English Plays

The plays listed below were written before the closing of the theaters in 1642, and all contain characters explicitly labeled as either "Moors" or "Black." In compiling this list I have drawn on Anthony Barthelemy, *Black Face, Maligned Race: The Representation of Blacks in English Drama from Shakespeare to Southerne* (Baton Rouge: Louisiana State University Press, 1987); Thomas L. Berger, William C. Bradford, and Sidney L. Sondergard, eds., *An Index of Characters in Early Modern English Drama: Printed Plays, 1500–1660* (Cambridge: Cambridge University Press, 1998); and Virginia Mason Vaughan, *Performing Blackness on English Stages, 1500–1800* (Cambridge: Cambridge University Press, 2005). I make no claims to presenting a complete list, but I hope it offers a sizeable representative survey. I have also included, where available, links to digitized open-access versions of these texts in the interest of demonstrating the availability of these often-understudied plays. Peer-reviewed scholarly editions of plays I discuss in detail are cited in the foot-notes of the chapters in which they appear.

Plays with Characters Labeled as Moors

1. Anonymous, *The Famous History of the Life and Death of Captain Thomas Stukely* (1596, published 1605).
   Setting: Ireland, Portugal, Alcazar.
   Characters: Muly Mahamet, wife Calipolis, various unnamed Moors.
      Multiple references to Islam; no character is described as Black.

Full text available: https://www.google.com/books/edition/_
/YrIzAQAAMAAJ?hl=en&sa=X&ved=2ahUKEwi4tcyzku
DuAhXRFFkFHTduDfAQre8FMA56BAgTEAQ.

2. Anonymous (published under names of John Webster and William Rowley), *The Thracian Wonder*. Composition date unknown (published 1661).
Setting: Thrace.
Characters: Alcade, "King of the Moors"; daughter Lillia Guida,
   described as a "white Moor" (5.1); several unnamed Moors as
   minor characters. "Moors" as a group are described as Black except
   for Lillia Guida and are not linked with Islam but rather vow *not* to
   take up arms against the religion of "Christendom" (3.2).
Full text available: https://quod.lib.umich.edu/e/eebo/A62477.0001.001
   /1:4?rgn=div1;view=fulltext.

3. Francis Beaumont and John Fletcher (also attributed to Fletcher alone,
and Philip Massinger and Fletcher), *Four Plays or Moral Representations
in One* (1608–13, published 1647).
Setting: Portugal.
Character: The personification of Honor enters in a chariot "drawn by
   two Moors."
Full text available: https://www.google.com/books/edition/The_Works
   _of_Beaumont_and_Fletcher_Four/7fAtAAAAYAAJ?hl=en
   &gbpv=1.

4. Francis Beaumont and John Fletcher (also attributed to Philip Massinger
and Fletcher), *The Spanish Curate* (1622, published 1647).
Setting: Spain.
Character: listed as "A woman Moore, servant to Amaranthe." In service
   but not enslaved; not connected to Islam.
Full text available: http://www.gutenberg.org/files/12141/12141-h/12141-h
   .htm.

5. Dabridgcourt Belchier, *Hans Beer-Pot his inuisible comedie, of see me, and
see me not: Acted in the Low Countries, by an honest company of health-
drinkers* (1618).
Setting: Low Countries.
Character: Adidnaraes Quixot, a "tawny Moor." Discussed in Chapter 4.

Full text available: https://quod.lib.umich.edu/e/eebo/A07637.0001.001
?c=eebo;c=eebo2;g=eebogroup;rgn=full+text;view=toc;xc=1;ql=
hans+beer-pot.

6. William Berkeley, *The Lost Lady* (1638).
Setting: Greece.
Character: Acanthe (Milesia in blackface disguise), presented in
imagined backstory as daughter of a Greek merchant and Egyptian
woman. No references to Islam; neither in service nor enslaved.
Full text available: https://quod.lib.umich.edu/e/eebo/A08731.0001.001
?view=toc.

7. Richard Brome, *The Novella* (1632, published 1653).
Setting: Italy.
Character: Jaconetta (later revealed to be the eunuch Jacomo),
described as a "Moor" and a "Blackamore," in service to protagonist Victoria. Not explicitly described as enslaved but described as
"given" to protagonist by her brother; no references to Islam.
Full text available: https://quod.lib.umich.edu/e/eebo/A77565.0001.001
/1:16?rgn=div1;view=fulltext.

8. Richard Brome, *The English Moor* (1640, published 1659).
Setting: England.
Character: Millicent, disguised in blackface as Catalina. In service, not
explicitly described as enslaved, although Quicksand's describes
"borrowing other moors of merchants that trade in Barbary" for
a performance, which may imply enslavement; no references to
Islam.
Full text available: https://www.dhi.ac.uk/brome/viewTranscripts.jsp
?play=EM&type=MOD&act=4&speech=719.

9. George Chapman, *The Memorable Masque of the Middle Temple and Lincoln's Inn* (1613).
Setting: Virginia.
Characters: Description mentions that every horse is accompanied with
"two moores, attired like Indian slaves"; no references to Islam.
Full text available: https://quod.lib.umich.edu/e/eebo/A18416.0001.001
/1:3?rgn=div1;view=fulltext.

10. Thomas Dekker, John Day, and William Haughton, *Lust's Dominion* (1600, published 1657).
    Setting: Spain.
    Characters: Eleazar, prince of Fez; Zarack; and Balthazar. Discussed in detail in Chapter 4.
    Full text available: https://extra.shu.ac.uk/emls/iemls/renplays /lustsdominion.htm.

11. John Fletcher, *Monsieur Thomas* (1614–17, published 1639).
    Setting: France.
    Character: Minor character, Kate, listed in stage directions as a "Black More," substituted for white woman in bed trick. In service to female protagonist, Mary; no references to Islam.
    Digitized first quarto available: https://archive.org/details /monsieurthomasco00flet/page/n83/mode/2up.

12. John Fletcher, also attributed to Nathan Field and Philip Massinger, *The Knight of Malta* (1616–19, published 1679).
    Setting: Malta
    Character: Zanthia (at times named in text Abdella), labeled "a more servant"; not linked with Islam. Discussed at length in Chapter 5.
    Full text available: https://www.gutenberg.org/files/47156/47156-h/47156 -h.htm.

13. John Fletcher, *The Island Princess* (1619–21, published 1647).
    Setting: Moluccan Islands.
    Characters: Characters labeled as "1 Moor" and "2 Moor" appear as prison guards; the Governor disguises himself "like a Moor priest." No references to Blackness vis-à-vis Moors. Discussed in Chapter 4.
    Full text available: https://emed.folger.edu/sites/default/files/folger _encodings/html/EMED-IP-3.html.

14. Samuel Harding, *Sicily and Naples* (1638, published 1640).
    Setting: Italy.
    Character: Zisco, a white nobleman in disguise as a Moor. In invented backstory, he is not enslaved or in service but a warrior who has "lately turn'd Christian" and fought against the Turks; he is frequently described as Black in the text.

Full text available: https://quod.lib.umich.edu/e/eebo2/A02629.0001.001
/1:12?rgn=div1;view=fulltext.

15. Thomas Heywood, *The Fair Maid of the West, Part I* (1600, published 1631).
Setting: England, Fez.
Characters: Mullisheg, King of Fez; various Moors. Discussed at length
in Chapter 4.

16. Thomas Heywood, *The Fair Maid of the West, Part II* (1630, published 1631).
Settings: Fez, Italy.
Characters: Mullisheg; his wife, Tota (described as a "negro"); Bashaw
Joffer Alcade. Discussed in Chapter 4.

17. Christopher Marlowe, *Tamburlaine the Great, Part I.*
Setting: Scythia and various locations.
Characters: "Moors" listed as a group in cast of characters; the Kings
of Fez, Morocco, and Arabia appear but are not labeled as Moors.
Two "Moors" described in stage directions carrying Bajazeth in a
cage. "Moors" are not explicitly linked either to Islam or color here;
we may be able to infer these Moors are black based on description
of "coal-black" Moors in part II; similarly, the world of the play is
largely Islamic with multiple references to Mohamed.
Full text available: https://www.gutenberg.org/files/1094/1094-h/1094-h
.htm.

18. Christopher Marlowe, *Tamburlaine the Great, Part II.*
Setting: Various, see above.
Characters: The king of Fez presents Tamburlaine with an army of
Moors with "coal-black faces"; several references to "Moors" as part
of Tamburlaine's army.
Full text available: https://www.gutenberg.org/files/1589/1589-h/1589-h
.htm.

19. Christopher Marlowe, *The Jew of Malta* (1592, published 1633).
Setting: Malta.
Character: An unnamed "Moor" for sale in a slave market, part of a
group of "Afric Moors" for sale alongside of Thracians and Turks.
No specific reference is made to either Blackness or Islam.

Full text available: https://www.gutenberg.org/files/901/901-h/901-h
.htm.

20. Philip Massinger, *The Parliament of Love* (1624; MS only).
    Setting: France.
    Characters: Beaupre, white woman disguised "like a more" to redeem
    her reputation. Her invented backstory is of enslavement, though
    she is described as a "maid" rather than as enslaved within France;
    no references to Islam.

21. George Peele, *The Battle of Alcazar* (1588–89, published 1594).
    Setting: Alcazar, Portugal.
    Characters: Muly Hamet, a Black Moor, a number of other characters
    termed "Moors" but not described in terms of color. Discussed in
    Chapter 4.
    Full text available: http://elizabethandrama.org/the-playwrights/george
    -peele/battle-alcazar-george-peele/.

22. George Peele, *The Famous Chronicle of King Edward I* (1590–93, pub-
    lished 1593).
    Setting: England.
    Characters: The wicked Queen Elinor of Spain is carried in her litter by
    "foure negro Moores."
    Full text available: https://quod.lib.umich.edu/e/eebo/A09224.0001.001
    /1:2?rgn=div1;view=fulltext.

23. William Rowley, *All's Lost by Lust* (1618–20, published 1633).
    Setting: Spain.
    Characters: Mully Moomen, "King of Africa"; Fidella, labeled "a Moore,"
    waiting woman to female protagonist; various unnamed "Moors."
    Discussed in Chapter 4.
    Full text available: https://quod.lib.umich.edu/cgi/t/text/text-idx?c=
    eebo;idno=A11155.0001.001.

24. William Shakespeare, *Titus Andronicus* (1594).
    Setting: Ancient Rome.
    Character: Aaron the Moor. Discussed in Chapter 4.
    Full text available: https://shakespeare.folger.edu/shakespeares-works
    /titus-andronicus/.

25. William Shakespeare, *Love's Labour's Lost* (1595–96; published 1598).
    Setting: Navarre.
    Characters: Stage direction calls for "blackamoors with music."
    Full text available: https://shakespeare.folger.edu/shakespeares-works
    /loves-labors-lost/.

26. William Shakespeare, *The Merchant of Venice* (1596, published 1600).
    Setting: Venice.
    Characters: Morocco, the "Moor" impregnated by Launcelot (discussed
    but not shown on stage). Discussed in Chapters 4 and 5.
    Full text available: https://shakespeare.folger.edu/shakespeares-works
    /the-merchant-of-venice/.

27. William Shakespeare, *Othello, The Moor of Venice* (1604, published 1622).
    Setting: Venice, Cyprus.
    Character: Othello. Discussed in Chapter 4.
    Full text available: https://shakespeare.folger.edu/shakespeares-works
    /othello/.

28. Thomas Lodge, *The Wounds of Civil War* (1594).
    Setting: Ancient Rome.
    Characters: Dictator Scilla enters in a chariot "drawn by four Moors."
    Full text available: https://archive.org/details
    /woundsofcivilwar00lodguoft/page/viii/mode/2up.

29. John Webster, *The White Devil* (1612).
    Setting: Italy.
    Characters: Zanche, a Moor, servant to female protagonist; Mulinassar
    (blackface disguise of the nobleman Francisco); a Moor described
    as a Christian who served against the Turks (5.1). Discussed in
    Chapter 4.
    Full text available: https://www.gutenberg.org/files/12915/12915-8.txt.

30. John Webster, *The Devil's Law-Case* (ca. 1619, published 1623).
    In the play's final scene, one of the female characters appears in disguise
    dressed as a nun, with her "face colored like a Moor," and gives a
    speech about the whiteness of her soul and virtue.
    Full text available: https://ota.bodleian.ox.ac.uk/repository/xmlui
    /handle/20.500.12024/0607.

Plays with Characters Described as Black but not as Moors

1. George Chapman, *The Blind Beggar of Alexandria* (1596, published 1598).
    Setting: Egypt.
    Character: Porus, King of Ethiopia. Chosen for marriage by white
        female character who declares "in my mind now the blackest is the
        fairest" (line 1592).
    Full text available: https://babel.hathitrust.org/cgi/pt?id=ucl.b4597332&
        view=1up&seq=21&q1=blackest.

2. John Gough, *The Strange Discovery* [adaption of Heliodorus' *Aethiopika*]
    (1640).
    Setting: Ethiopia, Athens, various settings.
    Characters: King and Queen of Ethiopia, Sisimethres, and Legate of
        Ethiopia, all described as Black and as "Aethiopes." No references to
        slavery or to Islam (also set in ancient world).
    Full text available: https://quod.lib.umich.edu/e/eebo/A01989.0001.001
        ?rgn=main;view=fulltext.

3. Ben Jonson, *The Masque of Blackness* (1605, published 1608).
    Setting: Niger.
    Characters: Niger and his twelve daughters, called "negroes" and
        "Aethiops." No references to either Islam or slavery.
    Full text available: http://www.luminarium.org/editions/maskblack.htm.

4. John Marston, *The Wonder of Women, or Sophonisba* (published 1606).
    Setting: Carthage.
    Character: Vangue, listed as "an Aethiopian slave," also referred to in
        the text as a "negro."
    Full text available: https://www.gutenberg.org/files/46311/46311-h/46311
        -h.htm#Page_231.

APPENDIX 2

Further Details on Black and
Moorish Characters

Moors, Blackness, and Islam

Total number of plays with characters labeled as Moors: **30** (see Appendix 1)

Total number of plays in which Moorish characters are described as Muslim: **6**

Of these, **4** plays contain characters described as both Muslim and Black (*The Fair Maid of the West, Parts I and II, All's Lost by Lust, Hans Beer-Pot*)

2 plays contain characters described as Moors but not as Black (*The Famous History of the Life and Death of Captain Thomas Stukely, The Battle of Alcazar*)

Total number of plays with characters labeled as Moors and not linked with Islam: **24**

Of these, **15** plays contain characters either described as Black Moors or as white characters disguised as Black Moors (*The Thracian Wonder, The Spanish Curate, The Lost Lady, The Novella, The English Moor, Lust's Dominion, Monsieur Thomas, The Knight of Malta, Sicily and Naples, The Parliament of Love, Titus Andronicus, The Merchant of Venice, Othello, The White Devil, The Devil's Law-Case*)

1 play contains characters labeled as Moor with no explicit mention of either their color or connections to Islam (*The Island Princess*)

6 plays call for "Moors" in non-speaking parts, with no mention of color (*Four Plays or Moral Representations in One, The Memorable Masque of the Middle Temple and Lincoln's Inn, Tamburlaine the Great, Parts I and II, The Jew of Malta, The Wounds of Civil War*)

2 plays call for "Black Moors" in non-speaking parts: *The Famous Chronicle of King Edward I, Love's Labour's Lost*

Moors, Blackness and Slavery

Total number of plays with characters labeled as Black or as Moors: **34** (see Appendix 1)

NB: Several of the plays I cite are listed twice here, because they contain multiple characters labeled as Black or as a Moor in different social positions.

Of these, **7** feature characters described as enslaved (*The Jew of Malta, The Wonder of Women or Sophonisba, The Parliament of Love, The Novella, The English Moor, The Masque of the Middle Temple, Lust's Dominion* [Zarack and Baltazar]) **5** feature Black characters carrying chairs or litters, a task associated with enslavement (*Four Plays or Moral Representations in One, Tamburlaine the Great Parts I and II, The Famous Chronicle of King Edward I, The Wounds of Civil War*)

10 contain Black characters in positions of service (*The White Devil, The Knight of Malta, All's Lost by Lust, Titus Andronicus, The Spanish Curate, Monsieur Thomas, Love's Labour's Lost, The Merchant of Venice* [the "Moor" impregnated by Launcelot], *Hans Beer-Pot*)

8 feature royal Black characters (*The Thracian Wonder, The Blind Beggar of Alexandria, The Masque of Blackness, The Merchant of Venice* [Morocco], *The Strange Discovery, The Fair Maid of the West Parts I and II*

2 feature royal Moors described as Muslim but not Black (*The Famous History of the Life and Death of Captain Thomas Stukely, The Battle of Alcazar*)

2 feature characters linked with both royalty and enslavement (*Lust's Dominion* [Eleazar], *Othello*)

2 feature white male characters in disguise as Black Moorish warriors (*Sicily and Naples, The White Devil*)

2 feature white female characters disguised in blackface and not in slavery or service (*The Devil's Law-Case; The Lost Lady*)

NOTES

Introduction

1. Nicholas Casey, "Spain Pledged Citizenship to Sephardic Jews. Now They Feel Betrayed," *New York Times*, July 24, 2021, final edition, via nytimes.com.

2. Nicholas Wade, "Gene Test Shows Spain's Jewish and Muslim Mix," *New York Times*, December 4, 2008, final edition, via nytimes.com.

3. This second case, as reported by the *Times*, immediately raises a significant question: Why assume that people living in Morocco and the Western Sahara now are the descendants of the relatives of the army that invaded Spain in 711?

4. This frozen temporality resonates with Hortense Spillers's discussion of the concept of "ethnicity" as used in the Moynihan Report: "Ethnicity in this case freezes in meaning, takes on constancy, assumes the look and affects of the Eternal. We could say, then, that in its powerful stillness, 'ethnicity,' from the point of view of the 'Report,' embodies nothing more than a mode of memorial time" ("Mama's Baby, Papa's Maybe: An American Grammar Book," *Diacritics* 17 [1987]: 66).

5. José Luis Cortes López calculates that there were 57,582 enslaved people in Spain in the sixteenth century, of whom roughly 65 percent were Black (although this latter calculation in particular seems to be quite speculative) (*La esclavitud negra en la España peninsular del siglo XVI* [Salamanca: Universidad de Salamanca, 1989], 196–204). In his seminal 1952 essay, Antonio Domínguez Ortíz estimates 100,000 (reprinted in *La esclavitud en Castilla en la edad moderna y otros estudios de marginados* [Granada: Editorial Comares, 2003], 9). Enslaved people also included Slavs, Circassians, and Tartars captured from along the Black Sea who came through Italian markets into Spain; the conquest of the Canary Islands brought enslaved *guanches*; later in the sixteenth century, thousands of Spanish *moriscos* were enslaved; and Portuguese imperial ventures brought enslaved people from as far afield as Goa and Kozhikode. See Alessandro Stella, *Histoires d'esclaves dans la péninsule ibérique* (Paris: Éditions de l'École des hautes études en sciences sociales, 2000), 58–74.

6. In addition to the scholars discussed below, see, among others, Barbara Everett, "'Spanish' Othello: The Making of Shakespeare's Moor," in *Shakespeare and Race*, ed. Catherine M.S. Alexander and Stanley Wells (Cambridge: Cambridge University Press, 2000), 64–81; Ania Loomba's chapter on *The Merchant of Venice* in her *Shakespeare, Race, and Colonialism* (Oxford: Oxford University Press, 2002), 135–60, esp. 147; Mary Janell Metzger, "'Now by My Hood, a Gentle and No Jew': Jessica, *The Merchant of Venice*, and the Discourse of Early Modern English Identity," *PMLA* 113 (1998): 52–63; and James Shapiro, *Shakespeare and the Jews* (New York: Columbia University Press, 1997).

7. Kim F. Hall and Peter Erickson, "A New Scholarly Song: Rereading Early Modern Race," *Shakespeare Quarterly* 67 (2016): 6.

8. The bibliography on this topic is too extensive to list in full here. In addition to the texts discussed below, some examples include Étienne Balibar, "Is There a Neo-racism?," in *Race, Nation, Class: Ambiguous Identities*, ed. Étienne Balibar and Immanuel Wallerstein (New York: Verso, 1992), 17–28, esp. 23–24; George M. Fredrickson, *Racism: A Short History* (Princeton, N.J.: Princeton University Press, 2002), 31–47; Ivan Hannaford, *Race: The History of an Idea in the West* (Washington, D.C.: Woodrow Wilson Center Press, 1996), 100–126; and Benzion Netanyahu, *The Origins of the Inquisition in Fifteenth-Century Spain*, 2nd ed. (New York: New York Review Books, 2001). For a particularly nuanced discussion of both what is compelling and what is troubling about this particular genealogy of race and racism, see David Nirenberg, "Race and the Middle Ages: The Case of Spain and its Jews," in *Rereading the Black Legend: The Discourses of Religious and Racial Difference in the Renaissance Empires*, ed. Margaret R. Greer, Maureen Quilligan, and Walter D. Mignolo (Chicago: University of Chicago Press, 2008), 71–87.

9. María Elena Martínez, *Genealogical Fictions: Limpieza de Sangre, Religion, and Gender in Colonial Mexico* (Stanford, Calif.: Stanford University Press, 2008), 9.

10. See, for example, Fredrickson, *Racism: A Short History*: "Closer to modern racism [than early modern slavery], arguably its first real anticipation, was the treatment of Jewish converts to Christianity in fifteenth- and sixteenth-century Spain. *Conversos* were identified and discriminated against because of the belief held by some Christians that the impurity of their blood made them incapable of experiencing a true conversion" (31).

11. Christopher Marlowe, *The Jew of Malta*, ed. James R. Siemen, 2nd ed. (New York: Norton New Mermaids Series, 1995), 2.1.41.

12. See Lynda E. Boose, "The Getting of a Lawful Race: Racial Discourse in Early Modern England and the Unrepresentable Black Woman," in *Women, "Race," and Writing in the Early Modern Period*, ed. Margo Hendricks and Patricia Parker (New York: Routledge, 1994), 39.

13. See Eric Griffin, "*Othello*'s Spanish Spirits: Or, Unsainting James," in *English Renaissance Drama and the Specter of Spain* (Philadelphia: University of Pennsylvania Press, 2009), 168–206.

14. Edmund Campos, "Jews, Spaniards and Portingales: Ambiguous Identities of Portuguese Marranos in Elizabethan England," *ELH* 69 (2002): 599–616.

15. Barbara Fuchs, *Exotic Nation: Maurophilia and the Construction of Early Modern Spain* (Philadelphia: University of Pennsylvania Press, 2009); Griffin, *English Renaissance Drama*.

16. On the historical presence of Jews in early modern London, see Shapiro, *Shakespeare and the Jews*, 62–76.

17. For a detailed study of the Black Legend, see Greer, Quilligan, and Mignolo, *Rereading the Black Legend*, and Griffin, *English Renaissance Drama*.

18. Barbara Fuchs, *Mimesis and Empire: The New World, Islam, and European Identities* (Cambridge: Cambridge University Press, 2001), and Barbara Fuchs, *The Poetics of Piracy: Emulating Spain in English Literature* (Philadelphia: University of Pennsylvania Press, 2013).

19. Fuchs, *Mimesis and Empire*.

20. Jerome J. Friedman, "Jewish Conversion, the Spanish Pure Blood Laws and Reformation: A Revisionist View of Racial and Religious Anti-Semitism," *Sixteenth Century Journal* 18 (1987): 27.

21. Marc Shell makes a similar argument, stating that "Spain at the time of the Reconquest plays a central role in the European history of the idea of caste or race," and going on to assert: "transformed to suit contemporary ideologies of social class in subsequent centuries,

Pure Blood eventually informed the rhetoric of German Nazis and Spanish fascists" ("Marranos [Pigs], or from Coexistence to Toleration," *Critical Inquiry* 17 [1991]: 309, 311–12).

22. Janet Adelman, *Blood Relations: Christian and Jew in the Merchant of Venice* (Chicago: University of Chicago Press, 2008), 78.

23. Michael Neill, "'Mulattos,' 'Blacks,' and 'Indian Moors': Othello and Early Modern Constructions of Human Difference," *Shakespeare Quarterly* 49 (1998): 365–66.

24. As Kaplan writes, "Most critics have relied on the work of Jerome Friedman, who argues that the institution of Spanish pure blood laws created an early modern racial definition of Jewish identity. However, no one offers contemporary English sources addressing Jewish race in the context of Spanish laws" ("Jessica's Mother: Medieval Constructions of Jewish Race and Gender in "The Merchant of Venice," *Shakespeare Quarterly* 58 [2007]: 1–2).

25. Hall and Erickson, "A New Scholarly Song," 2. There are by now far too many monographs on race in early modern literature to include a full list here. Key works include Patricia Akhimie, *Shakespeare and the Cultivation of Difference: Race and Conduct in the Early Modern World* (New York: Routledge, 2018); Anthony Barthelemy, *Black Face, Maligned Race: The Representation of Blacks in English Drama from Shakespeare to Southerne* (Baton Rouge: Louisiana State University Press, 1987); Dennis Britton, *Becoming Christian: Race, Reformation and Early Modern English Romance* (New York: Fordham University Press, 2014); Joyce Green, *Women and Race in Early Modern Texts* (Cambridge: Cambridge University Press, 2002); Kim F. Hall, *Things of Darkness: Economies of Race and Gender in Early Modern England* (Ithaca, N.Y.: Cornell University Press, 1995); Hendricks and Parker, *Women, "Race," and Writing in the Early Modern Period;* Sujata Iyengar, *Shades of Difference: Mythologies of Skin Color in Early Modern England* (Philadelphia: University of Pennsylvania Press, 2005); Ania Loomba, *Gender, Race, Renaissance Drama* (Manchester, UK: Manchester University Press, 1989); an Smith, *Barbarian Errors: Race and Rhetoric in Early Modern England* (New York: Palgrave Macmillan, 2009); Ayanna Thompson, *Performing Race and Torture on the Early Modern Stage* (New York: Routledge 2008); and Virginia Mason Vaughan, *Performing Blackness on English Stages, 1500–1800* (Cambridge: Cambridge University Press 2005).

26. Peter Erickson, "Representations of Blacks and Blackness in the Renaissance," *Criticism* 35 (1993): 503.

27. Gustav Ungerer, *The Mediterranean Apprenticeship of British Slavery* (Madrid: Editorial Verbum, 2008); Imtiaz Habib, *Black Lives in the English Archives, 1500–1677: Imprints of the Invisible* (Burlington, Vt.: Ashgate Publishing, 2008).

28. Michael Neill, introduction to *Othello*, by William Shakespeare, ed. Michael Neill (Oxford: Oxford University Press, 2006), 124–25. I discuss this quotation and other critics who share such views in detail at the beginning of Chapter 4.

29. Although Heng's discussion focuses on race in the medieval period rather than the early modern, the dynamic she describes of refusing to see race outside the "modern" applies to Neill's reading. Geraldine Heng, "The Invention of Race in the European Middle Ages I: Race Studies, Modernity, and the Middle Ages," *Literature Compass* 8 (2011): 320.

30. As Ania Loomba argues (addressing the field more broadly rather than Griffin specifically), "I am unable to dismiss the forceful colour-coding of the play or the passionate repetition of explicitly colour-based image of monstrosity, too well known to require repetition here" ("'Delicious Traffick': Racial and Religious Differences on Early Modern Stages," in *Shakespeare and Race*, ed. Catherine M. S. Alexander and Stanley Wells [Cambridge: Cambridge University Press, 2000], 206).

31. On representations of Blackness and slavery in the Spanish comedia, see John Beusterien, *An Eye on Race: Perspectives from Theater in Imperial Spain* (Lewisburg, Pa.: Bucknell University Press, 2006); Nicholas R. Jones, *Staging* Habla de Negros: *Radical Performances of the African Diaspora in Early Modern Spain* (University Park: Pennsylvania State University Press, 2019); and Baltasar Fra Molinero, *La imagen de los negros en el teatro del Siglo de Oro* (Madrid: Siglo Veintiuno Editores, 1995).

32. Michael Omi and Howard Winant, *Racial Formations in the United States from the 1960s to the 1990s* (New York: Routledge, 1994), 4. On intersectionality, see Kimberlé Crenshaw, *On Intersectionality: Selected Writings* (New York: New Press, 2017).

33. In *An Eye on Race* John Beusterien articulates a similar dynamic in his reading of race in the comedia, in which he describes representations of religious difference as "narrativized" and of Blackness as "denarrativized" vision.

34. Hall, *Things of Darkness*; Loomba, *Shakespeare, Race, and Colonialism*.

35. Geraldine Heng, *The Invention of Race in the European Middle Ages* (Cambridge: Cambridge University Press, 2018), 19.

36. Urvashi Chakravarty, *Fictions of Consent: Slavery, Servitude and Free Service in Early Modern England* (Philadelphia: University of Pennsylvania Press, 2022), 13.

37. Robert Hornback, *Racism and Early Blackface Comic Traditions: From the Old World to the New* (New York: Palgrave Macmillan, 2019).

38. Noémie Ndiaye, "'Come Aloft, Little Jack-Ape!': Race and Dance in *The Spanish Gypsie*," *English Literary Renaissance* 51 (2020): 123. Ndiaye's monograph was published as this book was going into proofs, so I have not had the opportunity to cite from it, but it is certain to be an important intervention in comparative early modern race studies. See *Scripts of Blackness: Early Modern Performance Culture and the Making of Race* (Philadelphia: University of Pennsylvania Press, 2022).

39. Christina Sharpe describes the particular difficulty of teaching the traumatic afterlives of slavery in the United States today in the context of a course on the histories of slavery and the Holocaust: "I have found that I have had to work very hard with students when it comes to thinking through slavery and its afterlives. When I taught the course chronologically, I found that many, certainly well meaning, students held onto whatever empathy they might have for reading about the holocaust but not for North American slavery" Christina Sharpe, *In the Wake: On Blackness and Being* (Durham, N.C.: Duke University Press, 2016),16.

40. See Walter Cohen, *Drama of a Nation: Public Theater in Renaissance England and Spain* (Ithaca, N.Y.: Cornell University Press, 1985).

41. Thompson, *Performing Race and Torture on the Early Modern Stage*, 4.

42. Christina Lee, *The Anxiety of Sameness in Early Modern Spain* (Manchester: Manchester University Press, 2016), 3.

43. Boose, "The Getting of a Lawful Race."

Chapter 1

1. Félix Lope de Vega, *La villana de Getafe*, ed. José María Díez Borque (Madrid: Editorial Origenes, 1990), 3.3215–18. All further citations from the play are from this edition and will be cited parenthetically in the body of the text. This and all following translations are my own unless otherwise noted.

2. For a detailed discussion of critics who address purity of blood and the history of race, see the introduction.

3. I borrow the phrase from Judith Butler's discussion of drag as gender performance in *Gender Trouble: Feminism and the Subversion of Identity* (New York: Routledge, 1990), 175.

4. For a detailed list of the range of institutions that demanded proof of purity of blood, see James S. Amelang, *Historias paralelas: Judeoconversos y moriscos en la España moderna* (Salamanca: Ediciones Akal, 2011), 115–18.

5. David Nirenberg, "Race in the Middle Ages: The Case of Spain and Its Jews," in *Rereading the Black Legend: The Discourses of Religious and Racial Difference in the Renaissance Empires*, ed. Margaret Greer, Maureen Quilligan, and Walter Mignolo (Chicago: University of Chicago Press, 2008), 80.

6. On the local nature of the statutes, see Henry Kamen, *The Spanish Inquisition: A Historical Revision* (New Haven, Conn.: Yale University Press, 1999), 230–54.

7. Albert Sicroff, *Los estatutos de limpieza de sangre: controversias entrelos siglos XV y XVII* (Madrid: Taurus Ediciones, 1985). For the Seville statute, see 120; for the Cuenca statute, see 127 n. 9. The first was imposed in 1516 and extended one generation in 1532, while the second was imposed in 1537.

8. Christina Lee, *The Anxiety of Sameness in Early Modern Spain* (Manchester: Manchester University Press, 2016), 4.

9. For tensions between higher-ranking nobles and Old Christian local gentry, see Sicroff, *Los estatutos*, 51–56; Lee, *The Anxiety of Sameness in Early Modern Spain*, 23–46.

10. *Documentos referentes al estatuto de la Santa Iglesia de Toledo* MS 13043, undated (seventeenth century), Biblioteca Nacional de España, Madrid Cited in Juan Hernández Franco and José Javier Ruiz Ibáñez, "Conflictividad social en torno a la limpieza de sangre en la españa moderna," *Investigaciones históricas: Época moderna y contemporánea*, 23 (2003): 35.

11. On the interlude's satire on purity of blood, see Enrique Martínez López, "Mezclar berzas con capochas: Armonía y guerra de castas en el 'Entremes del retablo de las maravillas' de Cervantes," *Boletin de la Real Academia Española* 72 (1992): 67–171; and Bruce W. Wardropper, "The Butt of the Satire in *El retablo de las maravillas*," *Bulletin of the Cervantes Society of America* 4 (1984): 25–33.

12. Noël Salomon, *Lo villano en el teatro del Siglo de Oro* (Madrid: Castalia, 1985), 109–20, 684–702.

13. Several manuscript proofs of purity have been digitized by the University of Pennsylvania's Special Collections and can be viewed at https://www.library.upenn.edu/search/openn?q=limpieza+de+sangre (accessed January 2021).

14. On the process of collecting and receiving petitions, see M. del Val González de la Peña, "La tramitación de los expedientes de limpieza de sangre del monasterio de bernardas de Alcalá de Henares," *Revista de Historia de la Cultura Escrita*, no. 5 (1998): 187–96; Lee, *The Anxiety of Sameness*, 109–12.

15. See, for example, Amelang, *Historias paralelas*, 177: "No es de sorprender que la letra de la ley prohibiera por igual a judíos y a musulmanes accede a una amplia variedad de puestos oficiales de la sociedad cristiana. El hecho de que se aplicara mucho mas en el caso de los judíos que en el de los musulmanes demuestra una vez más la mayor movilidad social de aquéllos. A fin de cuentas, eran muy pocos los moriscos que intentaban acceder a los Colegios Mayores de las universidades o que reivindicaban un lugar propio en los consejos municipales, en los cabildos catedralicios o en las órdenes militares." [It is not surprising that the letter of the law would have prohibited Jews and Muslims equally from acceding to a wide variety of official positions in Christian society. The fact that they were applied much more often in the case of Jews than

of Muslims demonstrates once more the greater social mobility of (the former group). At the end of the day, there were very few Moriscos who attempted to enter the *colegios mayores* of the universities, or to reclaim their own space on municipal councils, in cathedral councils or in military orders.] For a general comparison between converts from Judaism and Islam in early modern Spain, see Amelang, *Historias paralelas*, 173–79.

16. The bibliography on the history of Moriscos in Spain is too extensive to cite in its entirety here. In addition to Amelang, *Historias paralelas*, some notable works include Antonio Domínguez Ortiz and Bernard Vincent, *Historias de los moriscos: Vida y tragedia de una minoría* (Madrid: Alianza Editorial, 1979); and L. P. Harvey, *Muslims in Spain: 1500–1614* (Chicago: University of Chicago Press, 2005). The most stringent prohibitions were passed in 1566 (though not enforced until 1567): Moriscos of Granada were prohibited from wearing traditional clothing, speaking Arabic, and using communal baths, among many other regulations. See Barbara Fuchs, *Exotic Nation: Maurophilia and the Construction of Early Modern Spain* (Philadelphia: University of Pennsylvania Press, 2009), 23.

17. On the intermarriage of high-ranking Moriscos with Old Christian nobility in Granada, see Amelang, *Historias paralelas*, 177; for the assimilation of Morisco elites into Old Christian communities, see Harvey, *Muslims in Spain*, 37–44, 252–54.

18. For Moriscos' international alliances, see Harvey, *Muslims in Spain*, 332–52; on the difference between Moriscos and conversos more generally, see Amelang, *Historias paralelas*, 173–79.

19. Harvey, *Muslims in Spain*, 234–38.

20. The play was first printed in 1620 but composed several years earlier; on the range of composition dates and its chronological alignment with the expulsion of the Moriscos from Spain, see Borque's introduction to *La villana de Getafe*, 53–54.

21. Adolphe Coster provides a French translation of the ordinance in his study of Fray Luis de León. He cites from the University of Salamanca's *Libro de claustro*, which records a 1572 assembly of faculty to address "issues concerning the holy office [i.e., the Inquisition], where an official of the inquisition notified the faculty of the following: "ordonnons á l'Illustrisme Recteur et aux tres magnifiques et reverends Maîtres et Docteurs en théologie et autres facultés de l'Université, de quelque état ou condition qu'ils soient, de ne pas soutenir, ni permettre que l'on traite ni discute en aucune maniere, publiquement ni secretemente, dans des sermons ni en aucune autre maniere, en forme de dispute, la question de savoir si les descendants de juifs ou de maures ne doivent pas être exclus des Colleges, Congrégations, Ordres ou dignités; et que les personnes qui president ces disputes ne permettent pas qu'on traite ou discute cette question, comme il est dit, en aucune maniere, sous peine d'excommunication majeure *latae sententiae* et de cinq cents ducats pour les dépenses extraordinaire du Saint-Office . . . Valladolid, le 22 février 1572." [We command the Illustrious Rector, and the most magnificent and reverend Masters and Doctors of the University, in theology and in other departments, of whatever degree or condition they may be, to neither support nor permit in any way that people treat or discuss, either publicly or in secret, in sermons or in any other way, in the form of a dispute, the question of knowing whether or not the descendants of Jews and Moors should not be excluded from Colleges, Congregations, Orders and other dignities; and that the people who preside over debates shall not permit others to treat or discuss such questions, as we have said, in any form, under pain of automatic excommunication and of five hundred ducats for the extraordinary expenses of the Holy Office . . . (resolved in) Valladolid, 1572]. Cited in Adolphe Coster, *Luis de Léon*, vol. 1 (Paris: Extrait de la *Revue Hispanique*, 1921), 26 n. 3.

22. On the library's acquisition, see http://www.bne.es/es/Colecciones/FondoGeneral /Fondos/ (accessed January 15, 2010). The manuscript's first page describes the family of Pablo de Santa María, a famous convert from Judaism, and says: "se convirtio de su propia autoridad el ano de 1390 que avra agora dozientos y seis años" [he converted by his own authority in the year of 1390 and it has now been two hundred and six years since then], which gives the composition date of 1596.

23. Fernández de Córdoba is mentioned by name in Alonso Morgado's 1587 *Historia de Sevilla*, reprinted in facsimile (Seville: Archivo Hispalense, 1887), 196–201, and in Cristóbal de Chaves's undated (but post-1585) *Relación de la cárcel de Sevilla*, printed in Bartolomé José Gallardo, *Ensayo de una biblioteca española de libros raros y curiosos* (Madrid: M. Rivadeneyra, 1863; reprinted 1968).

24. Fernando Bouza, *Communication, Knowledge, and Memory in Early Modern Spain*, trans. Sonia López and Michael Agnew (Philadelphia: University of Pennsylvania Press, 2004), 54. On the same page, Bouza notes that another much-copied text also appears in the manuscript volume I discuss here, a set of instructions on how to rule given to Prince Philip II by his father Charles V, traveled as far as England; Queen Elizabeth had a copy in her library.

25. Sebastián de Covarrubias Orozco, *Tesoro de la lengua castellana o española*, ed. Manuel Camarero (Madrid: Castalia, 1994), s.v. "raza."

26. On the comparison to horse breeding, see *Papeles referentes al Estatuto de limpieza de sangre de la Iglesia de Toledo, hecho siendo Arzobispo D. Juan Martínez Silíceo*, MS 13038, undated (eighteenth century), Biblioteca Nacional de España, Madrid, 80–81v; on comparison to a poisoned fountain, 77v–78.On imbibing evil through milk, see *Documentos referentes al estatuto de la Santa Iglesia de Toledo*, MS 13043, undated (seventeenth century), Biblioteca Nacional de España, Madrid.

27. *Tratado de los statutos* [*sic*] *de limpieza—de su justificacion y conveniencia* [Treatise on the (pure) blood statutes—of their justification and utility]. MS 1320, undated (seventeenth century), Ordenes Militares Archivo Histórico Nacional, Madrid. Another copy appears in an untitled miscellany of manuscripts related to the Inquisition, MS 6157, undated (seventeenth century), Biblioteca Nacional de España Madrid, ff. 188–257.

28. A protest against Toledo's 1449 pure blood statute, Fernan Díaz de Toledo's *Instrucción del Relator para el obispo de Cuenca, a favor de la nación Hebrea*, uses the Santa María family as an example of the impracticality of pure blood statutes and lists the nobles with whom they intermarried. Cited in Sicroff, *Los estatutos*, 60 n. 53.

29. *Estatuto de la Santa Iglesia de Toledo*, MS 11211, undated (sixteenth century) Biblioteca Nacional de España, Madrid, 11v.

30. Ibid., 3r.

31. Francisco Cantera Burgos transcribes much of this brief, which can also be found in a manuscript copy in the Biblioteca Nacional, in *Alvar García de Santa María y su familia de conversos* (Madrid: Instituto Arias Montano, 1952), 280–84. This copy was apparently in the possession of a potential father-in-law of one of Pablo de Santa María's descendants; a marginal note reads: "Aqui esta la declaracion de su Santidad y de su Magestad en el negocio del Sr. D. Pedro Osorio de Velasco que se me dio para que lo viese quando se trato el casamiento con Doña Costanza, mi hija." [Here is the declaration of his Holiness and his Majesty regarding the business of Señor Don Pedro Osorio de Velasco, which he gave me to see when the marriage of my daughter, Doña Costanza, was discussed.] Cited in Cantera Burgos, *Alvar García de Santa María*, 280.

32. The Latin reads "origenis ab Haebrai macula nullatenus notari debeant." Cited in Cantera Burgos, *Alvar García de Santa María*, 283.

33. *Estatuto de la Santa Iglesia de Toledo*, MS 11211, 10v.

34. "Acception of persons" and "distributive justice" are both legal terms; the Real Academia Española defines *acepción de personas* as "acción de favorecer o inclinarse a unas personas más que a otras por algún motivo o afecto particular, sin atender al mérito o a la razón" [the action of favoring or inclining toward some people more than others for some personal motive or affinity, without attending to reason or merit]; and *justicia distributiva* as "la que establece la proporción con que deben distribuirse las recompensas y los castigos" [that which establishes the proportions in which rewards and punishments should be distributed].

35. Karoline P. Cook describes the fascinating history of Diego Romero, an encomendero living in Santa Fe, New Granada, who was accused in 1554 of being a Morisco. After years of legal disputes, which involved gathering testimonies from Spain about his origins, the case was dismissed. Karoline Cook, "'Moro de linaje y nación': Religious Identity, Race and Status in New Granada," in *Race and Blood in the Iberian World*, ed. Max S. Hering Torres, María Elena Martínez, and David Nirenberg (Berlin: Lit Verlag, 2012), 81–97.

36. Fuchs, *Exotic Nation*, 88–114; Israel Burshatin, "Playing the Moor" Parody and Performance in Lope de Vega's *El primer Fajardo*," *PMLA* 107 (1992): 566–81.

37. It is important to note here that anxieties about Moorish difference are by and large not focused on color. As Deborah Root notes, *mudejares* (Spanish Muslims) "were as indigenously 'Spanish' as the Christian population. . . . Centuries of coexistence had resulted in a certain ethnic homogeneity" ("Speaking Christian: Orthodoxy and Difference in Sixteenth-Century Spain, *Representations* 23 [1988]: 122–23). Thus, while on some occasions Moriscos are represented as having darker skin than Spanish Christians, they are most often not described in terms of color. On the ethnicity of Moriscos, see also Harvey, *Muslims in Spain*, 7–10.

38. The most detailed study of the play, which I will discuss below, is Francisco Márquez Villanueva's chapter "Lope, infamado de morisco" in his monograph *Lope: Vida y valores* (San Juan: Editorial de la Universidad de Puerto Rico, 1988). This essay emphatically denies that the play engages with questions of purity of blood in any meaningful way. Other critical studies that address the play, aside from those discussed here, include Victor Dixon, "Lope's *La villana de Getafe* and the Myth of Phaethon; or, the Coche as Status Symbol," in *What's Past Is Prologue: Essays in Honour of L. J. Woodward* (Edinburgh: Scottish Academic Press, 1974), which discusses the play's use of classical imagery. There are also two studies that use the play to discuss Lope de Vega's own biography, which are not particularly relevant to the close reading I perform here. Andrew Herscovits uses the play to discuss whether Lope was an anti-Semite in *The Positive Image of the Jew in the Comedia* (Bern, Switzerland: Peter Lang, 2005), 269–319. Dian J. Pamp, in *Lope de Vega ante el problema de limpieza de sangre* (Northampton: Smith College, 1968), argues that the play is evidence of Lope's own converso origins, an argument that has not been given credence by most scholars.

39. Georgina Dopico Black, *Perfect Wives, Other Women: Adultery and Inquisition in Early Modern Spain* (Durham, N.C.: Duke University Press, 2001), 109–65; John Beusterien, *An Eye on Race: Perspectives on Theater in Imperial Spain* (Lewisburg, Pa.: Bucknell University Press, 2006), 58–100; Melveena McKendrick, "Honour/Vengeance in the Spanish Comedia: A Case of Mimetic Transference?," *Modern Language Review* 79 (1984): 313–35.

40. See, for example, Israel Burshatin, "Playing the Moor"; Thomas Case, "Lope and the Moriscos," *Bulletin of the Comediantes* 44, no. 2 (1992): 195–216; Antonio Sánchez Jiménez, "'Segunda Cava en España': Moro, morisco y venganza en tres comedias de Lope de Vega,"

Bulletin of the Comediantes 55 (2003): 117–32; Ricardo Krauel, "Tradición literaria y otredad: La representación del árabe en *La desdicha por la deshonra* de Lope de Vega," *Dactylus* 15 (2006): 44–57; and Anjela María Mescall, "Staging the Moor: Turks, Moriscos, and Antichrists in Lope de Vega's *El Otomano famoso*," *Renaissance Drama* 39 (2011): 37–67. Thomas Case does briefly quote from *La villana* on page 205 but offers very little analysis. The other essays I cite here do not mention the play at all.

41. Fuchs frames her discussion of the play with the question: "If, in the poems [*romances moriscos*] Spaniards essentially pass as Moors, could not historical *moriscos* pass as Spaniards?" She observes that we do not have the same historical evidence for the assimilation of Moriscos that we do for the assimilation of conversos, but offers up Lope's play instead as a "powerful literary representation of the problem" ("Maurophilia and the Moorish Subject," in *The Conversos and Moriscos in Late Medieval Spain and Beyond*, vol. 1, edited by Kevin Ingram [Leiden: Koninklijke Brill, 2009], 283).

42. On the importance of Getafe both to Lope himself and as a stopping point between Madrid and Seville, see Márquez Villanueva, "Lope, Infamado de Morisco," 333–58.

43. This passage offers one indication that the play was composed after the expulsion of the Moriscos had begun, since Lope and Félix will be expelled from Spain if their Moorish descent is proven. *Melcochas*, or taffies, were a popular candy in Andalucía. Félix's grandfather's presumed occupation as candymaker serves as proof that he is not noble.

44. *Romances moriscos* are a fascinating genre of poetry that circulated in sixteenth- and seventeenth-century Spain, which revolve largely around the romantic difficulties of noble Moors and their ladies. Fuchs, *Exotic Nation*, especially chapter 4, "Playing the Moor."

45. Márquez Villanueva, "Lope, infamado de morisco," 304–5.

46. Ibid., 306.

47. See Barbara Fuchs's brief discussion of the play: "And while the *comedia* dispels the possible libel of Moorish ancestry, it tells us nothing about the opposite situation: the actual Moriscos' ability to pass, constructing themselves as fully Old-Christian subjects" ("Maurophilia and the Moorish Subject," 284).

48. For example, when Lope comes to tell doña Ana that his master, Félix, is on the way, Ana refers to Lope as the star that presages Félix's coming. Lope replies: "Si hay estrellas de azabache / bien lo puedo parecer" [If there are stars made of jet, I could well seem like one] (2.1291–92).

49. *Primo* can refer to a first cousin or more generally to a relative. At no point does the play suggest that a relationship between the two of them would be problematically incestuous; nonetheless, the emphasis once again demonstrates the ease with which blood ties can be falsely impersonated.

50. My analysis of the invisibility of whiteness draws on Richard Dyer, *White* (New York: Routledge, 1997). On the power of whiteness see Cheryl Harris, "Whiteness as Property," *Harvard Law Review* 106 (1993): 1707–91.

Chapter 2

1. Mateo Alemán, *Guzmán de Alfarache*, ed. José Maria Micó (Madrid: Editorial Cátedra, 2001), vol. 1, 415. All further citations are taken from this edition and cited parenthetically in the text. Unless otherwise noted, this and all other translations are my own.

2. Mateo Alemán, *The Rogue, or the Life of Guzmán de Alfarache*, trans. James Mabbe, ed. James Fitzmaurice-Kelly (1924; reprinted New York: AMS Press, Tudor Translation Series, 1967), vol. 2, 187. All further citations are from this edition and are cited parenthetically within the text.

3. I discuss my decision to retain the term *Gypsy* in reference to fictional characters in the introduction. I use the term *Roma* later in the chapter when making reference to the Romani people.

4. Antoine Arnauld, *The Coppie of the Anti-Spaniard made at Paris by a French Man, a Catholique. Wherein is Directly Proued how the Spanish King is the Onely Cause of all the Troubles in France. Translated Out of French into English* (London, 1590. Early English Books Online).

5. Cited in Rica Amran, "Juan de Vergara y el estatuto de limpieza de sangre de la Catedral de Toledo," *Ehumanista* 33 (2016): 413.

6. *The apologie or defence of the most noble Prince William, by the grace of God, Prince of Orange . . . against the proclamation and edict, published by the King of Spaine, by which he proscribeth the saide lorde prince, whereby shall appeare the sclaunders and false accusations conteined in the said proscription, which is annexed to the end of this apologie / presented to my lords the Estates Generall of the Lowe Countrie, together with the said proclamation or prescription; printed in French and in all other languages* (Delft, 1581. Early English Books Online).

7. Edwin Sandys, *A relation of the state of religion and with what hopes and pollicies it hath beene framed, and is maintained in the severall states of these westerne parts of the world* (Long, 1605, Early English Books Online).

8. Edmund Spenser, *A View of the Present State of Ireland* (Dublin, 1633; University of Oregon, Renascence Editions, 1997), n.p.

9. On the mythologization of Gothic ancestry in Spain, see Kevin Ingram, "Historiography, Historicity and the Conversos," in *The Conversos and Moriscos in Late Medieval Spain and Beyond*, vol. 1, *Departures and Change*, ed. Kevin Ingram (Leiden: Brill: 2009), 335–56.

10. José María Micó, introduction to *Guzmán de Alfarache*, vol. 1, 79. The book was popular enough to inspire a spurious sequel in 1602.

11. See James Fitzmaurice Kelly's introduction to *The Rogue*, xxx.

12. Thomas Coryat, *The Odcombian Banquet: Dished Foorth by Thomas the Coriat, and Serued in by a Number of Noble Wits in Prayse of His Crudities and Crambe Too. Asinus Portans Mysteria* (London, 1611, Early English Books Online).

13. Sir William Cornwallis, *Essayes of Certaine Paradoxes* (London, 1617, Early English Books Online).

14. James Fitzmaurice-Kelley plausibly speculates that Mabbe initially only had access to the second part of Guzmán in the Italian, but then later checked his translation against a Spanish text he acquired before publishing it. In any case, the ordering of some episodes in part 2 of Mabbe's translation follows that of the Italian translation, which deviates from the Spanish (xxxv).

15. Despite his popularity in the period, Mabbe's translation of Guzmán has received relatively little critical attention in recent years, and much of it has focused on whether Mabbe's expansive prose stylings render him a "good" translator or not. See, for example, Nicholas G. Round, "What Makes Mabbe So Good?," *Bulletin of Hispanic Studies* 78 (2001): 145–66; and John R. Yamamoto-Wilson, "James Mabbe's Achievement in His Translation of 'Guzmán de Alfarache,'" *Translation and Literature* 8 (1999): 137–56.

16. Barbara Fuchs, *The Poetics of Piracy: Emulating Spain in English Literature* (Philadelphia: University of Pennsylvania Press, 2013), 10.

17. Ben Jonson declares of Guzmán: "For though Spaine gave him his first ayre and vogue / He would be call'd, henceforth, the English-Rogue" (vol. 1, 31). Fuchs discusses this prefatory poem (though not Mabbe's translation itself) in *The Poetics of Piracy*, 32–38.

18. Dale B. J. Randall, *The Golden Tapestry: A Critical Survey of Non-chivalric Spanish Fiction in English Translation* (Durham, N.C.: Duke University Press, 1963), 172.

19. To give just one example of this interest in Spain: in 1615–25, the decade in which the marriage seemed most likely, over sixty translations of nonfiction works alone appeared in English, a third of all of those produced in the years 1600–1660. J. N. Hillgarth, *The Mirror of Spain, 1500–1700* (Ann Arbor: University of Michigan Press, 2000), 451.

20. Of course, the archetypal picaresque novel is the anonymous *Lazarillo de Tormes* (1554), which also had early and widespread success in English translation. While *Lazarillo's* protagonist is similarly concerned with social mobility, that text does not engage as explicitly with questions of purity of blood as does *Guzmán de Alfarache*. Further, while David Rowland's 1576 English translation does contain thirty-four footnotes (some fourteen of them borrowed from a French translation), none of them allude to Spain's Jewish or Moorish heritage.

21. Yirmiyahu Yovel, *The Other Within: The Marranos; Split Identity and Emerging Modernity* (Princeton, N.J.: Princeton University Press, 2009), 271. The term "Old Christian" or *cristiano viejo* refers to Spaniards of "pure" descent, whose ancestors did not intermarry with converted Jews or Moors.

22. While scholars such as Judith A. Whitenack and Benito Brancaforte argue that Guzmán's repentance is entirely strategic, Enrique Moreno Báez and Alexander A. Parker assert that Guzmán's repentance is an example of the universality of Grace. Mabbe's translation of Guzmán's conversion does not deviate significantly from the Spanish text. While a detailed discussion of this issue is outside of the scope of this essay, it is worth noting that the English text's omission of ambivalent representations of converso identity, discussed above, removes an important substratum of critique and parody, which might have the effect of producing a more sincerely repentant narrator for English readers. For an overview of this debate, see Deborah Skolnik Rosenberg, "The Converso and the Spanish Picaresque Novel," in *Marginal Voices: Studies in Converso Literature of Medieval and Golden Age Spain*, ed. Amy Aronson-Friedman and Gregory Kaplan (Leiden: Brill, 2012), 194–95.

23. Carroll Johnson provides a compelling list of reasons to read Guzmán as possessing "racial heritage as a New Christian or Converso" (*Inside Guzmán de Alfarache* [Berkeley: University of California Press, 1978], 165–214). Anne J. Cruz qualifies this assessment, concluding that his characterization both evokes and exceeds the position of the converso: "[Guzmán] is, instead, an overdetermined status, one that encompasses all the dubious circumstances of the 'other'" (*Discourses of Poverty: Social Reform and the Picaresque Novel in Early Modern Spain* [Toronto: University of Toronto Press, 1999], 100).

24. On the mule as a figure for the converso, see Rosenberg, "The Converso and the Spanish Picaresque Novel," 194–95.

25. For example, in his monumental 1611 Spanish dictionary (to which Mabbe frequently alludes in his footnotes), Covarrubias, in his definition of *limpio*, specifies "limpio se dize comunmente el hombre cristiano viejo sin raza de moro, ni judio" [*limpio* is commonly used (to describe) an Old Christian without a trace of Moorish or Jewish ancestry]. Sebastián de Covarrubias Orozco, *Tesoro de la lengua castellana o española*, ed. Manuel Camarero (Madrid: Castalia, 1994), s.v. "limpio."

26. Ryan Giles, "Picaresque Fatherhood: Racial and Literary Heritage in Guzmán de Alfarache 1.1," *Neohelicon* 40 (2013): 243.

27. Barbara Fuchs, *Exotic Nation: Maurophilia and the Construction of Early Modern Spain* (Philadelphia: University of Pennsylvania Press, 2009).

28. Fuchs, *Exotic Nation*, 132, 133.

29. These are just a few examples among many. Other examples of footnotes that highlight words of Arabic origin can be found in vol. 1, 89, and in vol. 2, 22, 38, 91101, 134, 145, 150, 154, and 236.

30. Cited from James Shapiro, "Shakespeare and the Jews," in *The Merchant of Venice: Texts and Contexts* ed. Martin Coyle (New York: Palgrave Macmillan, 1998), 73.

31. Covarrubias's entry begins: "Marrano, es el recien convertido al Christianismo, y tenemos ruin concepto, del, por haverse convertido fingidamente. Diego Velazquez en un librito que hizo intitulado Defensio statuti Tolesani, dize asi: Sed eos Hispani Marranos Vocare Solemos, & baptizati ficti christiani sunt. Quando en Castilla se convirtieron los Judios que en ella quedaron, una de las condiciones que pidieron, fue, que por entonces no les forcassen a comer la carne del Puerco: lo cual protestaban no hazerlo por guardar la ley de Moysen, sino tan solamente por tenerla en uso, y causarlas nausea y fastidio." [Marrano is a recent convert to Christianity, and we have a terrible opinion of them for having feigned conversion. Diego Velazquez, in a little book called Defensio statuti Tolesani Sed, says this: eos Hispani Marranos Vocare Solemos, & baptizati ficti christiani sunt. When the Jews who remained in Castile converted (after the expulsion), one of the conditions they asked was that they be allowed to not eat pork from then on: which they asserted they did not wish to do not to keep the law of Moses, but only because they were accustomed to doing so, and it irritated them and caused them nausea.] Covarrubias, *Tesoro*, s.v. "Marrano."

32. Just as *marrano* is defined as a convert from Islam and *levantisco* as an "Easterling" as well as a Jew, at least one reference to converted Jews is completely elided from the text. In Alemán's novel, Guzmán goes to a "platero confeso" [converso silversmith] to sell a jewel. Mabbe's Guzmán, by contrast, goes to a "goldsmith" who is described only as "a rich man, and a great Usurer" (vol. 2, 119). Similarly, in a note about the term *Old Christian* Mabbe tells the reader, "Old Christians in Spain are counted the best, by way of difference from the Moores, whom they call new Christians, as being but lately converted," with no mention of Jews at all (vol. 1, 128 n. 1). Compare this to Mabbe's frequent source Covarrubias, who defines *cristiano viejo* as "el hombre limpio que no tiene raza de moro, ni de judio [the pure man who has no trace of either Moorish or Jewish descent]. Covarrubias, *Tesoro*, s.v. "Cristiano Viejo."

33. See Fuchs, *Exotic Nation*, 135.

34. *Thomas Middleton and Early Modern Textual Culture: A Companion to the Collected Works*, ed. Gary Taylor and John Lavagnino (Oxford: Oxford University Press, 2007), 1107.

35. Barbara Fuchs discusses a number of these plays in "Beyond the Missing Cardenio: Anglo-Spanish Relations in Early Modern Drama," *Journal of Medieval and Modern Philology* 39 (2009): 143–60.

36. For more on how the prefatory material glorifies the "Englishing" of Guzmán, see Barbara Fuchs, "Pirating Spain: Jonson's Commendatory Poetry and the Translation of Empire," *Modern Philology* 99 (2002): 341–56.

37. See Taylor and Lavagnino, *Thomas Middleton and Early Modern Textual Culture: A Companion to the Collected Works*, 866.

38. Thomas Middleton, *Thomas Middleton: The Collected Works*, ed. Gary Taylor et al. (Oxford: Clarendon, 2007). All further citations are taken from this text and cited parenthetically by line and scene number.

39. As Suzanne Gossett points out in her introduction to the play, this is the first representation of rape on the English stage in which neither perpetrator nor victim knows the other. In

The Collected Works of Thomas Middleton, ed. Gary Taylor and John Lavagnino (Oxford: Oxford University Press, 2007), 1723.

40. This and all other citations from the novella are taken from Miguel De Cervantes Saavedra, ed. Harry Sieber, *Novelas ejemplares II*, 23rd ed. (Madrid: Catedra, 2006). All further citations appear parenthetically in the body of the text.

41. See, for example, Suzanne Gossett, "Best Men Are Molded out of Faults: Marrying the Rapist in Elizabethan Drama," *English Literary Renaissance* 14 (1984): 305–27; and Karen Bamford, "Rape and Redemption in The Spanish Gypsy," in *Women, Violence, and English Renaissance Literature: Essays Honoring Paul Jorgensen*, ed. Linda Woodbridge and Sharon Beehler (Tempe: Arizona Center for Medieval and Renaissance Studies, 2003), 29–49.

42. Suzanne Gossett also comments on this, calling the "development of the rapist" the "most striking change" between the original and the adaptation ("Best Men Are Molded out of Faults," 323).

43. He tells Clara, "So much am I the executioner / Of my own trespass that I have no heart / Nor reason to disclose my name or quality; / You must excuse me that" (3.1.79–82).

44. Karen Bamford also discusses the difference between Roderigo and Rodolfo, arguing that "while Rodolfo shows no sign of penitence or growth," the English play "transform[s] this amoral tale into a moral exemplum" ("Rape and Redemption in The Spanish Gypsy," 35).

45. Shakespeare's poem *The Rape of Lucrece* and Middleton and Rowley's *The Changeling* (also set in Spain) are two examples among many of texts that describe illegitimate sexual congress as a "stain" on the blood.

46. The first quote is from Robert Ashley, translator (from French; original author not identified),*A Comparison of the English and Spanish Nation: Composed by a French Gentleman Against those of the League in Fraunce, which Went about to Perswade the King to Breake His Alliance with England, and to Confirme it with Spaine. by Occasion Whereof, the Nature of both Nations is Liuely Decyphered. Faithfully Translated, Out of French, by R.A.* (London, 1589, Early English Books Online). The second is from Antoine Arnauld, *The Coppie of the Anti-Spaniard.*

47. See, among many others, Albert Sicroff, *Los estatutos de limpieza de sangre: controversias entrelos siglos XV y XVII* (Madrid: Taurus Ediciones, 1985), and Georgina Dopico-Black, *Perfect Wives, Other Women: Adultery and Inquisition in Early Modern Spain* (Durham, N.C.: Duke University Press, 2001). I also discuss this phenomenon in greater detail in my first chapter.

48. For more on this reading, see Keith Whitlock, "*The Spanish Gypsy* under Spanish Eyes," *Sederi* 6 (1996): 218.

49. In this vein, William H. Clamurro argues that "the almost complete lack of conscience or moral responsibility on Rodolfo's part produces a feeling of incompleteness and undermines our sense of true or complete justice in this same happy conclusion" (*Beneath the Fiction: The Contrary Worlds of Cervantes's Novelas ejemplares* [New York: Peter Lang, 1997], 150–51).

50. Many critics have weighed in on this question. Alban Forcione reads the story as a Catholic allegory of redemption, with Luisico's innocent blood reminiscent of the blood spilled by Christ. Alban K. Forcione, *Cervantes and the Humanist Vision: A Study of Four Exemplary Novels* (Princeton, N.J.: Princeton University Press, 1983). Theresa Ann Sears, by contrast, argues that "la fuerza de la sangre" is "the father's law writ in blood that joins three generations, grandfather to father to son, and that elides, that denies the truth of the virgin blood shed by Leocadia, as well as the force that shed it" (*A Marriage of Convenience: Ideal and Ideology in the Novelas ejemplares* [New York: Peter Lang, 1993], 157).

51. Eric Griffin, *English Renaissance Drama and the Specter of Spain* (Philadelphia: University of Pennsylvania Press, 2009), 186–88.

52. Ashley, *A Comparison of the English and the Spanish Nation* n.p.

53. Taylor notes: "The word 'Madrid' occurs ten times in the dialogue; in no other English play performed before 1642 does it appear more than three times, and in all other English plays of the period the word is spoken altogether only ten times. That is, this single play, written while Charles was in Madrid, contains half of the dramatic references to Madrid in the entire period from 1580 to 1642." Taylor, "Historicism, Presentism and Time: Middleton's *The Spanish Gypsy* and *A Game at Chess*," *Sederi* 18 (2008): 155.

54. See Griffin, *English Renaissance Drama and the Specter of Spain*, chap. 1, "From Ethos to Ethnos," 27–48.

55. Whitlock, for example, in "*The Spanish Gypsy* under Spanish Eyes," argues that "whereas Cervantes, against the background of racism peculiar to Spain at that time, treats blood as the carrier of both social status and racial purity, the dramatisation against the English background of great social change and new money, betrays anxiety at 'disparagement' alone, that is marrying downward in the social class structure" (218). I do not wish to suggest that Spaniards were not also attentive to questions of New World money and social mobility (as they certainly were), but merely that such questions are not central to this particular novella.

56. Taylor, "Historicism, Presentism and Time," 154. He further expands on this issue in the context of the title: "The play could have been called 'The Fair Gypsy' or 'The Little Gypsy Girl,' but instead it advertises its Spanishness. It does so in the very months when the English people were obsessed with what was happening or might happen in Madrid. The change in the title, and its effect, can hardly be accidental. Moreover, the altered title loses the specificity of the original: there is only one 'little female gypsy' or 'beautiful female gypsy' in the novella, and consequently there is no ambiguity about the protagonist of the story. But which gypsy is 'The Spanish Gypsy'? Preciosa? Alvarez? Don Juan? All the play's Gypsies are Spanish" (154).

57. For the evolution of this phenomenon, see Lou Charnon-Deutsch, *The Spanish Gypsy: The History of a European Obsession* (University Park: Pennsylvania State University Press, 2004).

58. See Dale B. J. Randall, *Jonson's Gypsies Unmasked: Background and Theme of the Gypsies Metamorphos'd* (Durham, N.C.: Duke University Press, 1975), 48–49.

59. Cited in *Race in Early Modern England: A Documentary Companion*, ed. Ania Loomba and Jonathan Burton (New York: Palgrave Macmillan, 2007), 169–70.

60. For an overview of the complex position of the Romani or "Gypsies" in medieval and early modern Europe, see Geraldine Heng, *The Invention of Race in the European Middle Ages* (Cambridge: Cambridge University Press 2018), 417–57.

61. Randall, *Jonson's Gypsies Unmasked*, 49.

62. Ben Jonson, *Masques of Difference: Four Court Masques by Ben Jonson*, ed. Kristen McDermott, annotated edition (Manchester: Manchester University Press, 2008).

63. Gary Taylor provides a lengthy list of correspondences between historical events and the action of the play in "Historicism, Presentism and Time," 147–70.

64. Taylor, "Historicism, Presentism and Time," 151.

65. Noémie Ndiaye, "'Come Aloft, Little Jack-Ape!' Race and Dance in The Spanish Gypsie," *ELR* 51 (2020): 129.

66. As Eric Griffin argues, "the tendency to identify modern racism's roots in Iberia may itself be a 'Black Legend' inheritance. For to ascribe Spanish origins to such a pernicious

phenomenon as the racist 'structure of feeling' is to locate a cultural impulse in others when, like so many inquisitional practices . . . it may have been far more widespread" (*English Renaissance Drama*, 10).

Chapter 3

1. Andrés de Claramonte, *El valiente negro en Flandes*, ed. Alfredo Rodríguez López Vázquez (Alcalá: Universidad de Alcalá, 1997), 23. All further citations are from this edition and will be cited parenthetically in the body of the text. As this edition does not contain line numbers, I have cited by page number.

2. On the "notorious indeterminacy" of the term *Moor*, see Emily Bartels, *Speaking of the Moor, from Alcazar to Othello* (Philadelphia: University of Pennsylvania Press, 2009), 3–4; and Ambereen Dadabhoy, "Barbarian Moors: Documenting Racial Formation in Early Modern England," in *The Cambridge Companion to Shakespeare and Race*, ed. Ayanna Thompson (Oxford: Oxford University Press, 2021), 30–46.

3. It is important to note that Muslim ancestry is often not associated with phenotypical difference in early modern Spain. See John Beusterien in *An Eye on Race*, who notes, "the Moor is not necessarily associated with color. In turn, the *negro* is a set category" (*An Eye on Race: Perspectives from Theater in Imperial Spain* [Lewisburg: Bucknell University Press, 2006], 109). Barbara Fuchs similarly argues, "Even if outside Spain skin color is enlisted to essentialize difference, blackness emphatically does not equal Moorishness within Spain. Instead, Spanish racial hysteria focused on covert cultural and religious practices" ("The Spanish Race," in *Rereading the Black Legend: The Discourses of Religious and Racial Difference in the Renaissance Empires*, ed. Margaret R. Greer, Maureen Quilligan, and Walter D. Mignolo [Chicago: University of Chicago Press, 2007], 95. There are characters on the Spanish stage who are explicitly described as *moros negros* or Black Moors. Nonetheless, these two categories neither automatically nor necessarily overlap.

4. Chloe Ireton, "'They Are Blacks of the Caste of Black Christians': Old Christian Black Blood in the Sixteenth- and Early Seventeenth-Century Iberian Atlantic," *Hispanic American Review* 97 (2017): 580.

5. See, for example, Herman Bennett, *Colonial Blackness: A History of Afro-Mexico* (Bloomington: Indiana University Press, 2009); Larissa Brewer-García, *Beyond Babel: Translations of Blackness in Colonial Peru and New Granada* (Cambridge: Cambridge University Press, 2020); and Ann Twinam, *Purchasing Whiteness: Pardos, Mulattos, and the Quest for Social Mobility in the Spanish Indies* (Stanford, Calif.: Stanford University Press, 2016).

6. My approach draws on David Theo Goldberg's formulation of relational studies of race in comparative literature. "The Comparative and the Relational: Meditations on Racial Methods," in *A Companion to Comparative Literature*, ed. Ali Behdad and Dominic Thomas (Chichester: Wiley-Blackwell, 2011), 357–68.

7. Alessandro Stella, *Histoires d'esclaves dans la Péninsule Ibérique* (Paris: Éditions de l'École des hautes études en sciences sociales, 2000), 58–74. See also Aurelia Martín Casares, *La esclavitud en la Granada del siglo XVI: Género, raza y religion* (Granada: University of Granada, 2000), 65–68.

8. Debra Blumenthal, *Enemies and Familiars: Slavery and Mastery in Fifteenth-Century Valencia* (Ithaca, N.Y.: Cornell University Press, 2009), 267.

9. Ibid., 2.

10. Cited in William D. Phillips, *Historia de la esclavitud en España* (Madrid: Editorial Playor, 1990), 236. José Luis Cortes López calculates that there were 57,582 slaves in Spain in

the sixteenth century, of whom roughly 65 percent were Black (although this latter calculation in particular seems to be quite speculative). See *La esclavitud negra en la España Peninsular del siglo XVI* (Salamanca: Universidad de Salamanca, 1989), 196–204. In his seminal 1952 essay, Antonio Domínguez Ortíz estimates 100,000. See *La esclavitud en Castilla en la edad moderna y otros estudios de marginados* (Granada: Editorial Comares, 2003), 9.

11. Enslaved people included Slavs, Circassians, and Tartars captured from along the Black Sea who came through Italian markets into Spain; the conquest of the Canary Islands brought enslaved *guanches*; later in the sixteenth century, thousands of Spanish Moriscos were enslaved; and Portuguese imperial ventures brought slaves from as far afield as Goa and Kozhikode. Stella, *Histoires d'esclaves*, 58–74.

12. On the predominance of enslaved Black Africans in Extremadura, see Rocío Periáñez Gómez, whose analysis of records of sale shows that enslaved Black people were the majority of those sold in every decade from 1550 to 1700, except for the years 1640–60, when Spain was at war with Portugal. *Negros, Mulatos y Blancos: Los esclavos en Extremadura durante la edad moderna* (Badajoz: Diputación de Badajoz, 2010), 91–93. In a detailed analysis of the slave trade in Seville from 1560 to 1580, Manuel F. Fernández Chaves and Rafael M. Pérez García remark on "el hecho de que la mayoría de esa población esclava fuese de procedencia (directa o en segunda generación) africana y de color negro" [the fact that the majority of this slave population was of African provenance (either directly or second-generation) and black in color]. "Las redes de la trata negrera: Mercaderes portugueses y tráfico de esclavos en Sevilla (c. 1560–1580)," in *La esclavitud negroafricana en la historia de España, siglos XVI y XVII*, ed. Aurelia Martín Casares and Margarita García Barranco (Granada: Editorial Comares, 2010), 9.

13. Martín Casares, *La esclavitud en la Granada*, 94–97.

14. James H. Sweet, "The Iberian Roots of American Racist Thought," *William and Mary Quarterly: A Magazine of Early American History and Culture* 54 (1997): 164.

15. Martín Casares observes, "Los términos 'negro' o 'negra' se empleaban habitualmente como sinónimo de esclavo y esclava en la España del siglo XVI. No me refiero únicamente al uso popular de estos vocablos, sino también, al lenguaje de la legislación y de los documentos notariales o eclesiásticos. Los casos son inumerable." [The terms *negro* or *negra* were habitually used as synonyms for slave in sixteenth-century Spain. I do not only refer to popular usage of the term, but also to the language of legislation and of ecclesiastical and notarial documents. The cases are innumerable]. Casares, *La esclavitud en Granada*, 145.

16. Alessandro Stella, "'Negres de sa Majeste': A propos du rôle de l'esclavage en Andalousie au siècle d'or," in *Actas del II congreso de historia de Andalucía* (Córdoba: Publicaciones de la Consejería de Cultura de Andalucía, 1995), vol. 7, 617–35.

17. Cited in Juan R. Castellano, "El negro esclavo en el entremés del Siglo de Oro," *Hispania* 44 (1961): 55.

18. Nicholas R. Jones, *Staging* Habla de Negros: *Radical Performances of the African Diaspora in Early Modern Spain* (University Park: Pennsylvania State University Press, 2019), 11.

19. Baltasar Fra Molinero, *La imagen de los negros en el teatro del Siglo de Oro* (Madrid: Siglo Veintiuno Editores, 1995); Jones, *Staging* Habla de Negros.

20. On associations of Blackness with evil in English drama, see Anthony Barthelemy, *Black Face, Maligned Race* (Baton Rouge: Louisiana State University Press, 1987), 72; see also Virginia Mason Vaughan, *Othello: A Contextual History* (Cambridge: Cambridge University Press, 1996), 52. On associations of Blackness with slavery, see note 5 above.

21. Antiobo inherits his Blackness from his mother, who is an Ethiopian princess. In Spanish plays of the period, North Africans are not necessarily represented as Black. See note 38 below.

22. Lope de Vega, *El negro del major amo*, in *Comedias*, vol. 11 (Madrid: Biblioteca Castro, 1993), 473.

23. Jones does cite two examples of Black performers at a court masque in Portugal in the sixteenth century, and circumstantial evidence that may link a Black woman to comedia performance. See *Staging* Habla de Negros, 30–31.

24. See Jones, *Staging* Habla de Negros, 45–46, for records of blackface cosmetics and costumes.

25. Lope de Vega, *La limpieza no manchada*, ed. Fernando R. de Flor (Salamanca: University of Salamanca Press, 2018), 3.653–54.

26. Manuel Olmedo Gobante, "'El mucho número que hay dellos': *El valiente negro en Flandes* y los esgrimistas afrohispanos de Grandezas de la espada," *Bulletin of the Comediantes* 70 (2018): 71–72.

27. The play has proved difficult to date precisely. It was not published until 1652, though its author died in 1634. It is estimated to have been composed between 1610 and 1621. See Henry Louis Gates and Maria Wolff, "An Overview of Sources on the Life and Work of Juan Latino, the 'Ethiopian Humanist,'" *Research in African Literatures* 29 (1998): 36.

28. Elizabeth Wright's excellent monograph offers a detailed analysis of the life and work of the historical Juan Latino. See *The Epic of Juan Latino: Dilemmas of Race and Religion in Renaissance Spain* (Toronto: University of Toronto Press, 2016). See also Gates and Wolff, "An Overview of Sources"; and V. B. Spratlin, *Juan Latino: Slave and Humanist* (New York: Spinner Press, 1938).

29. Fernando, too, is based on a historical figure, the Morisco nobleman Fernando de Valor, who returned to Islam, took the name Abenhumeya, and helped to lead the rebellion in the Alpujarras. See Spratlin, *Juan Latino*, 207–8.

30. Fra Molinero, *La imagen de los negros*, 139.

31. See John Beusterien, who argues, "In this play Juan defines himself as Black, a category for him that excludes his possibility of being a Moor or having Moorish blood. In this society, the *newest* Christians are not New Christians [i.e., converts from Judaism and Islam and their descendants] since the mark of their Black skin grants them acceptance from the point of view of blood purity by the Old Christian" (*An Eye on Race*, 112). See also Fra Molinero, *La imagen de los negros*, 125–62.

32. All citations are from Diego Ximénez de Enciso, *El encubierto y Juan Latino*, ed. Eduardo Julia Martínez (Madrid: Aldus, 1951). Further citations appear parenthetically in the body of the text. As this edition does not list line numbers, I have cited by page number throughout. All translations are my own.

33. Compare this discussion of Juan's "pure" soul, for example, to the Duke of Sesa's dismissal of Fernando: "Leyéndolo estoy el alma. / En fin, moro" [I'm reading his soul. In short, he's Moorish] (174). Similarly, Fernando is described in a prophecy about the man who will lead the *morisco* uprising: "Hereje de su ley será primero, / habido exteriormente por cristiano; / mas en lo interior y verdadero / será en linaje y fe mahometano" [First he must be a heretic from his religion; A Christian on the outside, in truth and on the inside he will be Mahometan, in lineage and in faith] (231).

34. See, for example, Gates and Wolff: "Latino's marriage can allow us to infer that he gained his freedom at some point during this period, although no evidence is given as to the certainty of such an event" ("An Overview of Sources," 19). Elizabeth Wright, in a later article, refers to Latino as a "freedman" without further elaboration. Elizabeth Wright, "Narrating the Ineffable Lepanto: The *Austrias Carmen* of Joannes Latinus (Juan Latino)," *Hispanic Review* 77, no. 1 (2009): 71–92.

35. Sebastián de Covarrubias Orozco, *Tesoro de la lengua castellana o española*, ed. Manuel Camarero (Madrid: Castalia, 1994), s.v. "negro," "blanco."

36. Richard Dyer, *The Matter of Images: Essays on Representation* (New York: Routledge, 2002), 127.

37. See, among others, Kim F. Hall, *Things of Darkness: Economies of Race and Gender in Early Modern England* (Ithaca, N.Y.: Cornell University Press, 1995); Sujata Iyengar, *Shades of Difference: Mythologies of Skin Color in Early Modern England* (Philadelphia: University of Pennsylvania Press, 2005); and Cord Whitaker, *Black Metaphors: How Modern Racism Emerged from Race Thinking* (Philadelphia: University of Pennsylvania Press, 2019).

38. For a sustained discussion of this trope, see Hall, *Things of Darkness*, 107–15; and Melissa Sanchez, "Transdevotion: Race, Gender and Christian Universalism," *Journal for Early Modern Cultural Studies* 19 (2019): 94–115.

39. Lope de Vega, *El prodigio de Etiopia*, in *Obras de Lope de Vega IV: Comedias de los santos*, ed. Cayetano Alberto de la Barrera y Leirado (Madrid: Real Academia Española, 1894), 121–50; Lope de Vega, *El santo negro Rosambuco de la ciudad de Palermo*, in Barrera y Leirado, 362–92; Antonio Mira de Amescua, *El negro del mejor amo* (Barcelona: Red Ediciones 2012); Rodrigo Pacheco, *El negro del Serafín* in *Comedias famosas compuestos por Don Rodrigo Pacheco, Lusitano, vecino de la ciudad de Granada.* (Madrid: Biblioteca Nacional de España MS 14824, 1642), 167–87.

40. Ana Ogallas Moreno catalogs six unbound versions (*pliegos*) from the seventeenth century and five additional versions, both in loose-leaf and codex form, from the eighteenth.

41. *Sublimación* in Spanish can mean either sublimation in the psychological sense or exaltation. The context suggests to me that Moreno means the latter. Andrés de Claramonte, *El valiente negro en Flandes*, ed. Ana Ogallas Moreno (Madrid: Clásicos Hispánicos, 2016), 17.

42. Fra Molinero, *La imagen de los negros*, 189–90. It is difficult to discern here the relationship between lack of awareness of the predominance of the play's interracial marriage and an unwillingness to entertain the possibility that it may not have been quite as taboo as these authors suggest. I have been able to draw on the open-access digitization of manuscripts and early print editions that has only been undertaken in recent years in Spain, which makes it easy to compare multiple early editions simply by searching a few databases. Fra Molinero in particular, who cites the 1888 edition of the play in his bibliography, may have been made aware of the alternate ending only after completing his analysis, which relies on Juan's exclusion.

43. Fra Molinero, *La imagen de los negros*, 189–90. Javier Irigoyen-García's excellent reading of Juan as a postcolonial subject does not mention the marriage at all, despite the fact that the essay focuses on Juan's social ascent. However, since his bibliography cites only the 1888 edition, he may not have been aware of it. See Javier Irigoyen Garcia, "Ascensión social y enfrentamiento entre negros en *El valiente negro en Flandes* de Andres de Claramonte: Una aproximación postcolonial," *Afro-Hispanic Review* 24 (2005): 151–64.

44. Beusterien, *An Eye on Race*, 101, 157.

45. See, for example, Olga Barrios: "los dramaturgos del Siglo de Oro . . . dejaron patente su crítica contra la esclavitud" [the playwrights of the Golden Age . . . make their critique of slavery obvious] ("Entre la esclavitud y el ensalzamiento: La presencia africana en la sociedad y en el teatro del Siglo de Oro español," *Bulletin of the Comediantes* 54 [2002]: 304). See also José Fradejas Lebrero: "Y esto solo ha podido ocurrir en un pueblo: El hispano. Sin duda el único pueblo, que por su condición católica, construido por un conglomerado étnico, que ha aceptado los matrimonios mixtos." [And this only could have occurred in one community: Spanish. It is doubtless that it is the only community, because of its Catholic nature and multi-ethnic makeup, to accept mixed marriages] ("Notas sobre la relación de 'El valiente negro en Flandes' de A. Claramonte," *Murgetana* 119 [2008]: 99).

46. For a list of early modern English translations from Spanish, see Dale Randall, *The Golden Tapestry: A Critical Survey of Non-Chivalric Spanish Fiction in Translation, 1543–1657* (Durham, N.C.: Duke University Press, 1963), 234–40.

47. On England's relationship with the Afro-Iberian slave trade, see Emily Weissbourd, "'Those in Their Possession': Race, Slavery, and Queen Elizabeth's 'Edicts of Expulsion,'" *Huntington Library Quarterly* 78 (2015): 1–19.

Chapter 4

1. Samuel Taylor Coleridge, "Comments on Othello." Cited in William Shakespeare, *Othello*, ed. Edward Pechter (New York: Norton, 2004), 230.

2. Thomas Rymer, *A Short View of Tragedy*, 1693. Cited in William Shakespeare, *Othello*, ed. Edward Pechter (New York: Norton, 2004), 201.

3. William Shakespeare, *Othello*, ed. Edward Pechter (New York: Norton, 2004), 1.3.136–37. All further citations are taken from this edition and will be cited parenthetically in the body of the text.

4. See, for example, Emily Bartels on literary criticism focused on race in early modern England: "In general this work tends to start with struggle and work backward—to read identity through conflict, cross-cultural encounters through conquest, race through racism. When the history of Africa is brought into the picture, what gets prominence is the development of the Atlantic slave trade, which feeds neatly into a history of racism but which would not come to define England's relation to Africa until the Restoration" ("Othello and Africa: Postcolonialism Reconsidered," *William and Mary Quarterly* 54 [1997]: 45–64, 47).

5. The opening words of Daniel Vitkus's "Turning Turk in *Othello*: The Conversion and Damnation of the Moor" are "The tragedy of *Othello* is a drama of conversion" (*Shakespeare Quarterly* 48 [1997]: 145–76, 145). Similarly, Julia Reinhardt Lupton argues that "disclosing the play's reliance on the Pauline division of nations necessarily reorients the current color-based approach to the play, in which the scandal of 'monstrous' miscegenation inherited from the nineteenth-century racial Imaginary has come to govern *Othello*'s economy of differences" ("Othello Circumcised: Shakespeare and the Pauline Discourse of Nations," *Representations* 57 [1997]: 73–89, 74). See also Jonathan Burton, *Traffic and Turning: Islam and English Drama, 1579–1624* (Newark: University of Delaware Press, 2005).

6. Michael Neill, introduction to *Othello*, by William Shakespeare, ed. Michael Neill (Oxford: Oxford University Press, 2006), 124–25.

7. Kim F. Hall, "Othello and the Problem of Blackness," in *A Companion to Shakespeare's Works: The Tragedies*, ed. Richard Dutton and Jean Howard (Hoboken, N.J.: Wiley-Blackwell, 2005), 358.

8. On scholarly resistance to engaging with anti-Black racism in early modern texts, see, among others, Arthur Little, "Re-historicizing Race, White Melancholia, and the Shakespearean Property," *Shakespeare Quarterly* 67 (2016): 84–103; and Ian Smith, "We Are Othello: Speaking of Race in Early Modern Studies," *Shakespeare Quarterly* 67 (2016): 104–24.

9. Emily Bartels, *Speaking of the Moor: From Alcazar to Othello* (Philadelphia: University of Pennsylvania Press, 2009), 5.

10. In addition to the works cited in note 5 above, Nabil Matar offers a particularly nuanced assessment of the triangulation of the Christian, Moor, and Turk in *Othello* in the context of early modern Anglo-Islamic relations. See *Britain and Barbary, 1589–1689* (Gainesville: University of Florida Press, 2005), 24–33.

11. It is worth noting that this pattern seems to be less true of medieval texts, where "Saracens" are often represented as Black. See Geraldine Heng, *The Invention of Race in the European Middle Ages* (Cambridge: Cambridge University Press, 2018), 110–62.

12. William Harrison, *The Description of England*, in Raphael Holinshed, *The First and Second Volumes of Chronicles Comprising 1 the Description and Historie of England, 2 the Description and Historie of Ireland, 3 the Description and Historie of Scotland* (London, 1587, Early English Books Online), 163.

13. Gustav Ungerer, *The Mediterranean Apprenticeship of British Slavery* (Madrid: Editorial Verbum, 2008); Imtiaz Habib, *Black Lives in the English Archives, 1500–1677: Imprints of the Invisible* (Burlington, Vt.: Ashgate Publishing, 2008).

14. Habib, *Black Lives*, 70.

15. For a discussion of this case see Ungerer, *The Mediterranean Apprenticeship of British Slavery*, 93–94. A transcription of the petition can be found at https://www.runnymedetrust.org /blog/africans-in-tudor-england.

16. Miranda Kaufmann, *Black Tudors: The Untold Story* (London: OneWorld, 2017), 264.

17. Ungerer offers a detailed breakdown of this dynamic in *The Mediterranean Apprenticeship of British Slavery*. For the relationships among the English, Spanish, and Black Africans in the Atlantic world, see Matthieu Chapman, *Anti-Black Racism in Early Modern England: The Other "Other"* (New York: Routledge, 2017), 125–37; Michael Guasco, *Slaves and Englishmen: Human Bondage in the Early Atlantic World* (Philadelphia: University of Pennsylvania Press, 2014), 80–120; and Cassander L. Smith, *Black Africans in the British Imagination: English Narratives of the Early Atlantic World* (Baton Rouge: Louisiana State University Press, 2016), especially 1–29.

18. Miguel Cervantes Saavedra, *The First Part of the Delightful History of the Most Ingenious Knight Don Quixote of the Mancha*, trans. Thomas Shelton (London, 1612, Early English Books Online), 308.

19. *The pleasaunt historie of Lazarillo de Tormes a Spaniarde wherein is conteined his marueilous deedes and life. With the straunge aduentures happened to him in the seruice of sundrie masters*, trans. David Rowland, chapter 1, "Lazaro declareth his life, and whose son he was" (London, 1586, Early English Books Online).

20. Ibid.

21. Mateo Alemán, *Guzmán de Alfarache*, vol. 2, ed. José Maria Micó (Madrid: Editorial Cátedra, 2001), 316. Mateo Alemán, *The Rogue, or the Life of Guzmán de Alfarache*, trans. James Mabbe, ed. James Fitzmaurice-Kelly (1924; reprinted New York: AMS Press, Tudor Translation Series, 1967), vol. 4, 52.

22. Alemán, *Guzmán*, 316; Mabbe, *The Rogue*, vol. 4, 287.

23. Neill, introduction to *Othello*, 124–25.

24. See Appendix 1 for a full list of the plays I consider.

25. Matar, *Britain and Barbary*, 28–29. For differences between costuming and use of cosmetics for Moors and Turks, see Virginia Mason Vaughan, "'Enter Three Turks and a Moor': Signifying the 'Other' in Early Modern English Drama," in *Speaking Pictures: The Visual/Verbal Nexus of Dramatic Performance*, ed. Jacquelyn Bessell, Fernando Cioni and Virginia Mason Vaughan(Madison, NJ: Fairleigh Dickinson University Press, 2010), 119–38.

26. On the genre of the "Turk play," see, among others, Jonathan Burton, *Traffic and Turning*, and "English Anxiety and the Muslim Power of Conversion: Five Perspectives on 'Turning Turk' in Early Modern Texts," *Journal for Early Modern Cultural Studies* 2 (2002): 35–67; Jane Degenhardt, *Islamic Conversion and Christian Resistance on the Early Modern Stage* (Edinburgh: Edinburgh University Press, 2010); Nabil Matar, *Turks, Moors, and Englishmen in the Age of Discovery* (New York: Columbia University Press, 1999); and Daniel J. Vitkus, *Turning Turk: English Theater and the Multicultural Mediterranean 1579–1630* (New York: Palgrave Macmillan, 2003.

27. On the absence of references to Morocco's religion, see Jack D'Amico, *The Moor in English Renaissance Drama* (Tampa: University of South Florida Press, 1991), 170.

28. See Anthony Barthelemy, *Black Face, Maligned Race: The Representation of Blacks in English Drama from Shakespeare to Southerne* (Baton Rouge: Louisiana State University Press, 1987), 1–17; and Vaughan, *Performing Blackness*, 18–24. Robert Hornback usefully complicates this model by demonstrating that not only Judeo-Christian associations between Blackness and evil but also classical associations between Blackness and foolishness in stage tradition. See Robert Hornback, *Racism and Early Blackface Comic Traditions: From the Old World to the New* (New York: Palgrave Macmillan, 2018), 1–34.

29. Noémie Ndiaye, "'Come Aloft, Little Jack-Ape!' Race and Dance in *The Spanish Gypsie*," *ELR* 51 (2020): 147–48.

30. Degenhardt, *Islamic Conversion and Christian Resistance*, 143–44.

31. Dabridgcourt Belchier, *Hans Beer-Pot his inuisible comedie, of see me, and see me not: Acted in the Low Countries, by an honest company of health-drinkers* (London, 1618, Early English Books Online). All further citations are from this edition.

32. William Rowley, *A Tragedy Called All's Lost by Lust*, ed. Edgar C. Morris (Lexington, Mass.: D.C. Heath, 1908), 4.1.182–83. Pejorative terms used to describe the Moors are in 1.1.20, 30, 33, 84, and elsewhere throughout the play.

33. Thomas Heywood, *The Fair Maid of the West, Parts I and II*, ed. Robert K. Turner (Lincoln: University of Nebraska Press, Regents Renaissance Drama, 1967).

34. The stage directions simply read "pulls his beard and hair off." John Fletcher, *The Island Princess*, ed. Clare McManus (New York: Bloomsbury Press, Arden Shakespeare, 2013), 5.5.55.

35. The play makes one reference to "maumet gods" (4.5.116), which some (including McManus) have taken as a reference to Mohammed, a reading that originates in Alexander Dyce's edition (1843–46). Jonathan Gil Harris, however, persuasively argues that the term is more accurately glossed as "puppet" and refers to idolatry rather than Islam (particularly in anti-Catholic polemic).

36. McManus, introduction to *The Island Princess*, 1.

37. Jonathan Gil Harris, "Alien Heat," *London Review of Books* 38 (2016), n.p., https://www.lrb.co.uk/the-paper/v38/n06/jonathan-gil-harris/alien-heat.

38. I am not, in distinguishing between Blackness and Islam, suggesting the absolute separation Matthieu Chapman posits between Blackness and Moorishness in his Afropessimist approach to early modern drama, *Anti-Black Racism in Early Modern England*. Chapman

positions Othello, for example, as not Black because he is a Moor, whereas I focus on how a single character may inhabit multiple identity categories. For a full list of these plays, see Appendix 1.

39. Vaughan, *Performing Blackness*, has one chapter entitled "Royal Slaves," but this focus on Restoration and eighteenth-century texts.

40. This moment is discussed in Vaughan, *Performing Blackness*, 36.

41. Kim F. Hall, *Things of Darkness: Economies of Race and Gender in Early Modern England* (Ithaca, N.Y.: Cornell University Press, 1995), 211–53.

42. John Fletcher et al., *The Knight of Malta*, in *The Dramatic Works in the Beaumont and Fletcher Canon*, vol. 8, ed. Fredson Bowers (Cambridge: Cambridge University Press 1992), 3.2.80–81.

43. Noémie Ndiaye, "Race, Capitalism, and Globalization in *Titus Andronicus*," in *The Cambridge Companion to Shakespeare and Race*, ed. Ayanna Thompson (Cambridge: Cambridge University Press, 2020), 162.

44. William Shakespeare, *Titus Andronicus*, ed. Jonathan Bate, 2nd ed. (New York: Bloomsbury Press, Arden Shakespeare, 2018), 2.1.517, 514. Further citations are from this edition and will be cited parenthetically in the body of the text.

45. The play was written before the historic expulsion of Spain's Moriscos. Emily Bartels has linked these lines to the expulsion of Moriscos, speculating that they might have been a later addition. Given the composition date of the play and the fact that the 1492 expulsion of Spain's Moors is much more frequently referenced in early modern England than that of the Moriscos, I believe it is more likely a reference to the earlier expulsion. See Bartels, *Speaking of the Moor*, 120.

46. *Lust's Dominion* was not published until 1657 but has been associated with Dekker, Day, and Haughton's *Spanish Moor's Tragedy*, composed in 1600. Recent studies include Bartels, *Speaking of the Moor*; Barthelemy, *Black Face, Maligned Race*, 103–23; and Claire Jowitt, "Political Allegory in Late Elizabethan and Early Jacobean Turk Plays: *Luste's Dominion* and *The Turke*," *Comparative Drama* 36 (2002): 411–43.

47. In *The Dramatic Works of Thomas Dekker*, vol. 4, ed. Fredson Bowers (Cambridge: Cambridge University Press, 1961), 115–230, 1.2.68. All further citations are from this edition and will be cited parenthetically.

48. English plays that focus on Islamic difference, and particularly conversion, tend to revolve around Turks rather than Moors. For a list of representative works, see note 28 above.

49. See Eric Griffin, *English Renaissance Drama and the Specter of Spain: Ethnopoetics and Empire* (Philadelphia: University of Pennsylvania Press, 2009), as well as "From Ethos to Ethnos: Hispanizing 'the Spaniard' in the Old World and the New," *New Centennial Review* 2 (2002): 69–116. Griffin does not provide any statistics documenting precisely how widely read these pamphlets were, but he does note that an anonymous Catholic tract complains that printers divulge "numbers of false and defamatorie libels" against Spain. See Griffin, "From Ethos to Ethnos," 97–98.

50. Antoine Arnauld, *The Coppie of the Anti-Spaniard made at Paris by a French Man, a Catholique. Wherein is Directly Proued how the Spanish King is the Onely Cause of all the Troubles in France. Translated Out of French into English* (London, 1590, Early English Books Online).

51. Anonymous, *A Comparison of the English and Spanish Nation: Composed by a French Gentleman Against those of the League in Fraunce, which Went about to Perswade the King to Break His Alliance with England, and to Confirme it with Spaine. by Occasion Whereof, the*

Nature of both Nations is Liuely Decyphered, trans. Robert Ashley (London: 1589, Early English Books Online), 2, 19.

52. Bartels, *Speaking of the Moor*, 135.

53. Vitkus, "Turning Turk in *Othello*," 145.

54. Dennis Britton, *Becoming Christian: Race, Reformation and Early Modern English Romance* (New York: Fordham University Press, 2014), 113.

55. Ibid., 114.

56. Nabil Matar also notes that these lines do not position Othello as the Turk. Intriguingly, he suggests that the "Turk" Othello refers to may be Iago, because of his lies (*Britain and Barbary*, 32).

57. Griffin, *English Renaissance Drama and the Specter of Spain*, 178–79.

58. See, for example, Vitkus, "Turning Turk in *Othello*": "When Othello tells 'Of being taken by the insolent foe / And sold to slavery; of my redemption thence' (1.3.136–37), are we to understand that he was a Christian Moor taken captive by Islamic corsairs, perhaps the renegades of Barbary, and then 'redeemed' by Christians? Or did his 'redemption' involve a conversion from Islam to Christianity?" (162).

59. Shylock defends his position in *The Merchant of Venice*'s trial scene by arguing that Antonio's flesh is his property just as slaves are the property of many Venetians: "You have among you many a purchas'd slave / Which like your asses, and your dogs and mules / You use in abject and in slavish parts, / Because you bought them" (4.1.90–93). Lars Engle suggests that these lines may be intended to resonate with the unnamed "Moor" in Portia's household whom Launcelot Gobbo is accused of impregnating: "Black servants in aristocratic Christian households in the Renaissance were often slaves. . . . One of the points of the suggestive exchange between Lorenzo and Launcelot may be to prepare us for the lack of any rebuttal to Shylock's comments about slavery in the next scene" (*Shakespearean Pragmatism* [Chicago: University of Chicago Press, 1993], 101–2).

60. Alessandro Serpieri, "Othello and Venice: Discrimination and Projection," in *Visions of Venice in Shakespeare*, ed. Laura Tosi and Shaul Bassi (Burlington, Vt.: Ashgate, 2011), 187.

61. Michael Neill, "'His Master's Ass': Slavery, Service, and Subordination in *Othello*," in *Shakespeare and the Mediterranean*, ed. Susan Brock, Tom Clayton and Vicente Forés (Newark: University of Delaware Press, 2004), 217.

62. Determined via "The Collected Works of Shakespeare Search Engine," http://sydney.edu.au/engineering/it/~matty/Shakespeare/test.html (accessed May 20, 2013).

63. For example, the OED gives as the second definition of *slave*: "Used as a term of contempt. Now arch." *Oxford English Dictionary Online*, s.v. "slave," www.oed.com (accessed May 20, 2020).

64. On the pervasive theme of service in *Othello*, see Neill, "'His Master's Ass'"; and Mark Rose, "Othello's Occupation: Shakespeare and the Romance of Chivalry," *English Literary Renaissance* 15 (1985): 293–311.

65. Benjamin Braude, "The Sons of Noah and the Construction of Ethnic and Geographical Identities in the Medieval and Early Modern Periods," *William and Mary Quarterly* 54 (1997): 103–42.

66. Ibid., 133.

67. On Othello's, Eleazar's, and Aaron's lack of active sexual desire in the context of geohumoralism, see Mary Floyd Wilson, *English Ethnicity and Race in Early Modern Drama* (Cambridge: Cambridge University Press, 2003), 43–44.

Chapter 5

1. The play was first published in 1618. As with many early modern plays, its composition and initial performance dates are unknown. For a discussion of possible dates, see the introduction to Lope de Vega, *Servir a señor discreto*, ed. Frida Weber de Kurlat (Madrid: Castalia, 1975).

2. Cited in Alberto del Campo Tejedor, "El estigma oscuro: La caracterización estereotípica del negroafricano hace medio milenio," in *Aulas abiertas, Tomo III: Inmigración, raíces e inclusión social*, ed. Edileny Tomé da Mata and Álvaro Rodríguez Camacho (Madrid: Dykinson, S.L., 2020), 79–137, 127.

3. Fredson Bowers, ed., *The Dramatic Works in the Beaumont and Fletcher Canon*, vol. 8 (Cambridge: Cambridge University Press 1992), 453.

4. See, among others, Celia Daileader, *Racism, Misogyny, and the Othello Myth* (Cambridge: Cambridge University Press, 2005); Arthur Little, *Shakespeare Jungle Fever: National Imperial Re-visions of Race, Rape, and Sacrifice* (Stanford, Calif.: Stanford University Press, 2000); and Ania Loomba, *Gender, Race, Renaissance Drama* (Manchester: Manchester University Press, 1989).

5. Ania Loomba, "'Delicious Traffick': Racial and Religious Difference on Early Modern Stages," in *Shakespeare and Race*, ed. Catherine M. S. Alexander and Stanley Wells (Cambridge: Cambridge University Press, 2000), 203–24.

6. Lynda E. Boose, "'The Getting of a Lawful Race': Racial Discourse in Early Modern England and the Unrepresentable Black Woman," in *Women, 'Race,' and Writing in the Early Modern Period*, ed. Margo Hendricks and Patricia Parker (London: Routledge, 1994), 46.

7. For a more recent and nuanced approach to racial mixing in early modern England, see Kyle Grady, "Emphasis and Elision: Early Modern English Approaches to Racial Mixing and their Afterlives," *New Literary History* 52 (2021): 585–604.

8. A number of Lope de Vega's plays feature characters labeled as *mulatas*. In addition to the two plays I discuss here, *El premio del bien hablar, El arenal de sevilla, La octava maravilla*, and *La victoria de la honra* stage romances between an enslaved mixed-race woman and a white Spaniard; *El amante agradecido* also stages an enslaved mixed-race female character. I have not found references to other Spanish playwrights from this period who represent mixed-race female characters as Lope does, but this may be a function of the fact that his plays are more frequently studied and printed. For information on the plays I cite above, see Frida Weber de Kurlat, "El tipo del negro en el teatro de Lope de Vega: Tradición y creación," *Nueva Revista de Filología Hispanica* 19 (1970): 337–59; and Antonio M. Rueda, "From *Bozal* to *Mulata*: A Sociolinguistic Analysis of the Black African Slave in Early Modern Spanish Theater," *Critical Multilingualism Studies* 5 (2017): 87–110.

9. Baltasar Fra Molinero discusses this dynamic in *La imagen de los negro en el teatro del Siglo de Oro* (Madrid: Siglo Veintiuno Editores, 1995), 26–31.

10. Cited from the digital edition produced by the Biblioteca Virtual Miguel de Cervantes, http://www.cervantesvirtual.com/obra-visor/comedia-eufemia--0/html/fef90722-82b1-11df-acc7-002185ce6064_1.htm (accessed January 2021).

11. Nicholas R. Jones, *Staging Habla de Negros: Radical Performances of the African Diaspora in Early Modern Spain* (University Park: Pennsylvania State University Press, 2019), 119–58.

12. I discuss this subgenre in greater detail in Chapter 3.

13. The oldest extant manuscript dates from 1643, though it was most likely written earlier, as Mira de Amescua died in 1644; the play was first published in 1653. I also discuss this play in Chapter 3.

14. Lope de Vega, *Obras de Lope de Vega, Tomo IV* (Madrid: Real Academia Española, 1894), 359–92, 370. All other citations are from this edition and are cited parenthetically in the text. As this edition does not contain line numbers, I have cited by page.

15. Mira de Amescua, *El negro del mejor amo* (Barcelona: Red Ediciones 2012), 1.463–64. All further citations are from this edition and will be cited parenthetically in the text.

16. On representations of Black women as lustful and bodily, see, among others, Daileader, *Racism, Misogyny, and the Othello Myth*, 14–49; Kim F. Hall, *Things of Darkness: Economies of Race and Gender in Early Modern England* (Ithaca, N.Y.: Cornell University Press, 1995), 62–122; and Virginia Mason Vaughan, *Performing Blackness on English Stages, 1500–1900* (Cambridge: Cambridge University Press, 2005), 74–92. On such representations in Spanish poetry, see Mar Martínez Góngora, "La invención de la 'blancura': El estereotipo y la mímica en 'Boda de negros' de Francisco de Quevedo," *Modern Language Notes* 120 (2005): 262–86.

17. Lope de Vega, *Amar, servir e esperar* (Middleton, Del.: BiblioBazaar, 2007), 63. All further citations are from this edition and will be cited parenthetically in the body of the text. I cite by page since this edition does not include line numbers

18. See Chapter 3 for a detailed discussion of this dynamic.

19. On the composition date of the play, see Frida Weder de Kurlat, ed., introduction to Lope de Vega, *Servir a señor discreto* (Madrid: Castalia, 1975), 17–26. All further references to the play are from this edition and will be cited parenthetically in the text.

20. The Real Academia Española defines *indiano*: "Dicho de una persona: Que vuelve rico de América" [when said of a person: one who returns from America rich]. *Diccionario de la lengua española*, s.v. "indiano," def. 3, dle.rae.es (accessed December 1, 2017).

21. On the distinction between *hidalgo* and *caballero*, see Christina Lee, *The Anxiety of Sameness in Early Modern Spain* (Manchester: Manchester University Press 2016), 25–34.

22. It is important to note, as I discuss in previous chapters, that Muslim ancestry is often not associated with phenotypical difference in early modern Spain. John Beusterien notes, "the Moor is not necessarily associated with color. In turn, the *negro* is a set category" (*An Eye on Race: Perspectives from Theater in Imperial Spain* [Lewisburg, Pa.: Bucknell University Press, 2006], 109). Barbara Fuchs similarly argues, "Even if outside Spain skin color is enlisted to essentialize difference, blackness emphatically does not equal Moorishness within Spain. Instead, Spanish racial hysteria focused on covert cultural and religious practices" ("The Spanish Race," in *Rereading the Black Legend: Discourses of Religious and Racial Difference in the Renaissance Empires*, ed. Margaret R. Greer, Maureen Quilligan, and Walter D. Mignolo [Chicago: University of Chicago Press, 2007], 88–98, 95). There are characters on the Spanish stage who are explicitly described as *moros negros* or Black Moors. Nonetheless, these two categories are neither automatically nor necessarily overlapping.

23. See note 5 above.

24. William Shakespeare, *The Merchant of Venice*, ed. Leah S. Marcus (New York: Norton, 2006), 3.5.28–30. All other citations are from this edition.

25. Kim F. Hall, "Guess Who's Coming to Dinner? Colonization and Miscegenation in *The Merchant of Venice*," *Renaissance Drama* 23 (1992): 87–111, 89.

26. Ibid., 105.

27. My analysis draws on Gayle Rubin's crucial essay "The Traffic in Women: Notes on the 'Political Economy' of Sex" in *Toward an Anthropology of Women*, ed. Rayna R. Raiter (New York: Monthly Review Press, 1975), 157–210. On the traffic in women in *The Merchant of Venice*, see Karen Newman, "Portia's Ring: Unruly Women and Structures of Exchange in *The Merchant of Venice*," *Shakespeare Quarterly* 38 (1987): 19–33.

28. For Portia's manipulation of rules and "law," see, among others, Amanda Bailey, *Of Bondage: Debt, Property, and Personhood in Early Modern England* (Philadelphia: University of Pennsylvania Press, 2013), 70–74.

29. See Jean Howard, "An English Lass amid the Moors: Gender, Race, Sexuality, and National Identity in Heywood's *The Fair Maid of the West*," in *Women, "Race," and Writing in the Early Modern Period*, ed. Margo Hendricks and Patricia Parker (New York: Routledge, 1994), 101–17.

Conclusion

1. My approach to this topic is in part a response to Arthur Little's important question: "Is Shakespeare or the Renaissance/early modern period white property?" In "Re-historicizing Race, White Melancholia, and the Shakespearean Property," *Shakespeare Quarterly* 67, no. 1 (2016): 93.

2. William Shakespeare, *Titus Andronicus*, ed. Jonathan Bate, 2nd ed. (New York: Bloomsbury Press, Arden Shakespeare, 2018), 286, n. 27.

3. William Shakespeare, *Titus Andronicus*, ed. Eugene M. Waith, 2nd ed. (1984; reissue, Oxford: Oxford University Press, 2008), 170, n. 27.

4. "Marion Carter," http://www.legacy.com/obituaries/washingtonpost/obituary.aspx?fhid =4278&n=marion-carter&pid=113125127 (accessed May 28, 2022).

5. "Getting Word: African American Oral History Project," https://www.monticello.org /getting-word/people/marion-elizabeth-carter (accessed May 28, 2022).

6. Arthur (Arturo) Schomburg, "Juan Latino, Magister Latinus," in *Ebony and Topaz*, ed. Charles Spurgeon Johnson (New York: Books for Libraries Press, 1971; first printed 1927), 69–71. On Schomburg's journey to Spain, see Elizabeth Wright, *The Epic of Juan Latino: Dilemmas of Race and Religion in Renaissance Spain* (Toronto: University of Toronto Press, 2016), 181–83.

7. Beatrice Fleming and Marion Pryde, *Distinguished Negroes Abroad* (Washington, D.C.: Associated Publishers, 1946).

8. W. Napoleon Rivers, "Why Negroes Should Study Romance Languages and Literature," *Journal of Negro History* 19, no. 2 (April 1934): 119.

9. Robert F. Reid-Pharr, *Archives of Flesh: African America, Spain, and Post-humanist Critique* (New York: New York University Press, 2016), 43.

10. Frantz Fanon, *Black Skin, White Masks*, trans. Richard Philcox (New York: Grove Press, 2008), 188.

11. William Childers, *Transnational Cervantes* (Toronto: University of Toronto Press, 2006), 237–38.

12. Robert Irvine, "English Literary Studies: Origin and Nature," in *The Edinburgh Introduction to Studying English Literature*, 2nd ed., ed. Dermot Cavanagh, Alan Gillis, Michelle Keown, James Loxley, Randall Stevenson (Edinburgh: Edinburgh University Press, 2014), 19.

BIBLIOGRAPHY

Adelman, Janet. *Blood Relations: Christian and Jew in the Merchant of Venice*. Chicago: University of Chicago Press, 2008.

Akhimie, Patricia. *Shakespeare and the Cultivation of Difference: Race and Conduct in the Early Modern World*. New York: Routledge, 2018.

Alemán, Mateo. *Guzmán de Alfarache*. 2 vols., edited by. José Maria Micó. Madrid: Editorial Cátedra, 2001.

Alemán, Mateo. *The Rogue, or the Life of Guzmán de Alfarache*, trans. James Mabbe, ed. James Fitzmaurice-Kelly. 4 vols. 1924. Reprint, New York: AMS Press, Tudor Translation Series, 1967.

Amelang, James S. *Historias paralelas: Judeoconversos y moriscos en la España moderna*. Salamanca: Ediciones Akal, 2011.

Amran, Rica. "Juan de Vergara y el estatuto de limpieza de sangre de la Catedral de Toledo." *Ehumanista* 33 (2016): 402–24.

Anonymous. *Documentos referentes al estatuto de la Santa Iglesia de Toledo*. MS 13043, undated (seventeenth century), Biblioteca Nacional de España, Madrid.

———. *Estatuto de la Santa Iglesia de Toledo*. MS 11211, undated (sixteenth century), Biblioteca Nacional de España, Madrid.

———. *[Papeles de Inquisición]*. MS 6157, undated (seventeenth century), ff. 188–257. Biblioteca Nacional de España, Madrid.

———. *Papeles referentes al Estatuto de limpieza de sangre de la Iglesia de Toledo, hecho siendo Arzobispo D. Juan Martínez Silíceo*, MS 13038, undated (eighteenth century), Biblioteca Nacional de España, Madrid.

———. *Tratado de los statutos* [sic] *de limpieza—de su justificacion y conveniencia*. MS 1320, undated (seventeenth century). Ordenes Militares, Archivo Histórico Nacional, Madrid.

Arnauld, Antoine. *The Coppie of the Anti-Spaniard made at Paris by a French Man, a Catholique. Wherein is Directly Proued how the Spanish King is the Onely Cause of all the Troubles in France. Translated Out of French into English*. London, 1590. Early English Books Online.

Ashley, Robert, translator. *A Comparison of the English and Spanish Nation*. London: 1589. Early English Books Online.

Bailey, Amanda. *Of Bondage: Debt, Property, and Personhood in Early Modern England*. Philadelphia: University of Pennsylvania Press, 2013.

Balibar, Etienne. "Is There a Neo-racism?" In *Race, Nation, Class: Ambiguous Identities*, edited by Étienne Balibar and Immanuel Wallerstein, 17–28. New York: Verso, 1992.

Bamford, Karen. "Rape and Redemption in The Spanish Gypsy." In *Women, Violence, and English Renaissance Literature: Essays Honoring Paul Jorgensen*, edited by Linda

Woodbridge and Sharon Beehler, 29–49. Tempe: Arizona Center for Medieval and Renaissance Studies, 2003.

Bartels, Emily. "Othello and Africa: Postcolonialism Reconsidered." *William and Mary Quarterly* 54 (1997): 45–64.

———. *Speaking of the Moor, from Alcazar to Othello.* Philadelphia: University of Pennsylvania Press, 2009.

Barthelemy, Anthony. *Black Face, Maligned Race: The Representation of Blacks in English Drama from Shakespeare to Southerne.* Baton Rouge: Louisiana State University Press, 1987.

Barrios, Olga. "Entre la esclavitud y el ensalzamiento: La presencia africana en la sociedad y en el teatro del Siglo de Oro español." *Bulletin of the Comediantes 54 (2002): 287–311.*

Beaumont, Francis, and John Fletcher. *The Knight of Malta.* In *The Dramatic Works in the Beaumont and Fletcher Canon,* vol. 8, edited by Fredson Bowers. Cambridge: Cambridge University Press 1992.

Bennett, Herman. *Colonial Blackness: A History of Afro-Mexico.* Bloomington: Indiana University Press, 2009.

Beusterien, John. *An Eye on Race: Perspectives from Theater in Imperial Spain.* Lewisburg, Pa.: Bucknell University Press, 2006.

Belchier, Dabridgcourt. *Hans Beer-Pot his inuisible comedie, of see me, and see me not: Acted in the Low Countries, by an honest company of health-drinkers.* London, 1618. Early English Books Online.

Blumenthal, Debra. *Enemies and Familiars: Slavery and Mastery in Fifteenth-Century Valencia.* Ithaca, N.Y.: Cornell University Press, 2009.

Boose, Lynda E. "The Getting of a Lawful Race: Racial Discourse in Early Modern England and the Unrepresentable Black Woman." In *Women, "Race," and Writing in the Early Modern Period,* edited by Margo Hendricks and Patricia Parker, 35–54. New York: Routledge, 1994.

Bouza, Fernando. *Communication, Knowledge, and Memory in Early Modern Spain,* trans. Sonia López and Michael Agnew. Philadelphia: University of Pennsylvania Press, 2004.

Braude, Benjamin. "The Sons of Noah and the Construction of Ethnic and Geographical Identities in the Medieval and Early Modern Periods." *William and Mary Quarterly* 54 (1997): 103–42.

Brewer-García, Larissa. *Beyond Babel: Translations of Blackness in Colonial Peru and New Granada.* Cambridge: Cambridge University Press, 2020.

Britton, Dennis. *Becoming Christian: Race, Reformation and Early Modern English Romance.* New York: Fordham University Press, 2014.

Burshatin, Israel. "Playing the Moor" Parody and Performance in Lope de Vega's *El primer Fajardo." PMLA* 107 (1992): 566–81.

Burton, Jonathan. "English Anxiety and the Muslim Power of Conversion: Five Perspectives on 'Turning Turk' in Early Modern Texts." *Journal for Early Modern Cultural Studies* 2 (2002): 35–67.

———. *Traffic and Turning: Islam and English Drama, 1579–1624.* Newark: University of Delaware Press, 2005.

Burton, Jonathan, and Ania Loomba, eds. *Race in Early Modern England: A Documentary Companion.* New York: Palgrave Macmillan, 2007.

Butler, Judith. *Gender Trouble: Feminism and the Subversion of Identity.* New York: Routledge, 1990.

Campo Tejedor, Alberto del. "El estigma oscuro: La caracterización estereotípica del negroafricano hace medio milenio." In *Aulas abiertas, Tomo III: Inmigración, raíces e inclusión social*, edited by Edileny Tomé da Mata and Álvaro Rodríguez Camacho, 79–137. Madrid: Dykinson, S.L., 2020.

Campos, Edmund. "Jews, Spaniards and Portingales: Ambiguous Identities of Portuguese Marranos in Elizabethan England." *ELH* 69 (2002): 599–616.

Cantera Burgos, Francisco. *Alvar García de Santa María y su familia de conversos*. Madrid: Instituto Arias Montano, 1952.

Case, Thomas. "Lope and the Moriscos." *Bulletin of the Comediantes* 44 (1992): 195–216.

Castellano, Juan R. "El negro esclavo en el entremés del Siglo de Oro." *Hispania* 44 (1961): 55–65.

Cervantes Saavedra, Miguel De. *The First Part of the Delightful History of the Most Ingenious Knight Don Quixote of the Mancha*, translated by Thomas Shelton. London, 1612. Early English Books Online.

———. *Novelas ejemplares*. 2 vols., 23rd edition, edited by Harry Sieber. Madrid: Cátedra, 2006.

Chakravarty, Urvashi. *Fictions of Consent: Slavery, Servitude and Free Service in Early Modern England*. Philadelphia: University of Pennsylvania Press, 2022.

Chapman, Matthieu. *Anti-Black Racism in Early Modern England: The Other "Other."* New York: Routledge 2017.

Charnon-Deutsch, Lou. *The Spanish Gypsy: The History of a European Obsession*. University Park: Pennsylvania State University Press, 2004.

Chaves, Cristóbal de. *Relación de la cárcel de Sevilla*, printed in Bartolomé José Gallardo, *Ensayo de una biblioteca española de libros raros y curiosos*. 1863. Reprint, Madrid: M. Rivadeneyra, 1968.

Childers, William. *Transnational Cervantes* Toronto: University of Toronto Press, 2006.

Clamurro, William H. *Beneath the Fiction: The Contrary Worlds of Cervantes's Novelas ejemplares*. New York: Peter Lang, 1997.

Claramonte, Andrés de. *El valiente negro en Flandes*, edited by Alfredo Rodríguez López Vázquez. Alcalá: Universidad de Alcalá, 1997.

Cohen, Walter. *Drama of a Nation: Public Theater in Renaissance England and Spain*. Ithaca, N.Y.: Cornell University Press, 1985.

Cook, Karoline. "'Moro de linaje y nación': Religious Identity, Race and Status in New Granada." In *Race and Blood in the Iberian World*, edited by Max S. Hering Torres, María Elena Martínez, and David Nirenberg, 81–97. Berlin: Lit Verlag, 2012.

Cortes López, José Luis. *La esclavitud negra en la España peninsular del siglo XVI*. Salamanca: Universidad de Salamanca, 1989.

Coster, Adolphe. *Luis de Léon*, vol. 1. Paris: Extrait de la *Revue Hispanique*, 1921.

Covarrubias Orozco, Sebastián de. *Tesoro de la lengua castellana o Española*, edited by Manuel Camarero. Madrid: Castalia, 1994.

Cornwallis, William. *Essayes of Certaine Paradoxes*. London: 1617. Early English Books Online.

Coryat, Thomas. *The Odcombian Banquet: Dished Foorth by Thomas the Coriat, and Serued in by a Number of Noble Wits in Prayse of His Crudities and Crambe Too. Asinus Portans Mysteria*. London: 1611. Early English Books Online.

Crenshaw, Kimberlé. *On Intersectionality: Selected Writings*. New York: New Press, 2017.

Cruz, Anne J. *Discourses of Poverty: Social Reform and the Picaresque Novel in Early Modern Spain*. Toronto: University of Toronto Press, 1999.

Dadabhoy, Ambereen. "Barbarian Moors: Documenting Racial Formation in Early Modern England." In *The Cambridge Companion to Shakespeare and Race*, edited by Ayanna Thompson, 30–46. Oxford: Oxford University Press, 2021.

Daileader, Celia. *Racism, Misogyny, and the Othello Myth: Inter-racial Couples from Shakespeare to Spike Lee*. Cambridge: Cambridge University Press, 2005.

D'Amico, Jack. *The Moor in English Renaissance Drama*. Tampa: University of South Florida Press, 1991.

Degenhardt, Jane. *Islamic Conversion and Christian Resistance on the Early Modern Stage*. Edinburgh: Edinburgh University Press, 2010.

[Dekker, Thomas, et al.] *Lust's Dominion, or the Lascivious Queen*. In *The Dramatic Works of Thomas Dekker*, vol. 4, edited by Fredson Bowers, 115–230. Cambridge: Cambridge University Press, 1961.

Dixon, Victor. "Lope's *La villana de Getafe* and the Myth of Phaethon; or, the Coche as Status Symbol." In *What's Past Is Prologue: Essays in Honour of L. J. Woodward*, edited by Salvador Bacarisse, Bernard Bentley, Mercedes Clarasó, and Douglas Gifford, 33–45. Edinburgh: Scottish Academic Press, 1984.

Domínguez Ortíz, Antonio. *La esclavitud en Castilla en la edad moderna y otros estudios de marginados*. 1952. Reprint, Granada: Editorial Comares, 2003.

Domínguez Ortiz, Antonio and Bernard Vincent, *Historias de los moriscos: Vida y tragedia de una minoría*. Madrid: Alianza Editorial, 1979.

Dopico Black, Georgina. *Perfect Wives, Other Women: Adultery and Inquisition in Early Modern Spain*. Durham, N.C.: Duke University Press, 2001.

Dyer, Richard. *The Matter of Images: Essays on Representation*. New York: Routledge, 2002.

———. *White: Essays on Race and Culture*. New York: Routledge, 1997.

Engle, Lars. *Shakespearean Pragmatism: Market of His Time*. Chicago: University of Chicago Press, 1993.

Erickson, Peter. "Representations of Blacks and Blackness in the Renaissance." *Criticism* 35 (1993): 499–527.

Erickson, Peter and Kim F. Hall. "A New Scholarly Song: Rereading Early Modern Race." *Shakespeare Quarterly* 67 (2016): 1–13.

Everett, Barbara. "'Spanish' Othello: The Making of Shakespeare's Moor." In *Shakespeare and Race*, edited by Catherine M. S. Alexander and Stanley Wells, 64–81. Cambridge: Cambridge University Press, 2000.

Fanon, Frantz. *Black Skin, White Masks*, translated by Richard Philcox. New York: Grove Press, 2008.

Fernández Chaves, Manuel F. and Rafael M. Pérez García. "Las redes de la trata negrera: Mercaderes portugueses y tráfico de esclavos en Sevilla (c. 1560–1580)." In *La esclavitud negroafricana en la historia de España, siglos XVI y XVII*, ed. Aurelia Martín Casares and Margarita García Barranco, 5–34. Granada: Editorial Comares, 2010.

Fleming, Beatrice, and Marion Pryde. *Distinguished Negroes Abroad* . Washington, D.C.: Associated Publishers, 1946.

Fletcher, John. *The Island Princess*, edited by Clare McManus. New York: Bloomsbury Press, Arden Shakespeare, 2013.

Fletcher, John, et al. *The Knight of Malta*. In *The Dramatic Works in the Beaumont and Fletcher Canon*, vol. 8, edited by Fredson Bowers. Cambridge: Cambridge University Press, 1992.

Forcione, Alban K. *Cervantes and the Humanist Vision: A Study of Four Exemplary Novels.* Princeton, N.J.: Princeton University Press, 1983.

Fradejas Lebrero, José. "Notas sobre la relación de 'El valiente negro en Flandes' de A. Claramonte." *Murgetana* 119 (2008): 95–114.

Fra Molinero, Baltasar. *La imagen de los negros en el teatro del Siglo de Oro.* Madrid: Siglo Veintiuno Editores, 1995.

Fredrickson, George M. *Racism: A Short History.* Princeton, N.J.: Princeton University Press, 2002.

Friedman, Jerome J. "Jewish Conversion, the Spanish Pure Blood Laws and Reformation: A Revisionist View of Racial and Religious Anti-Semitism." *Sixteenth Century Journal* 18 (1987): 3–30.

Fuchs, Barbara. "Beyond the Missing Cardenio: Anglo-Spanish Relations in Early Modern Drama." *Journal of Medieval and Modern Philology* 39 (2009): 143–60.

——. *Exotic Nation: Maurophilia and the Construction of Early Modern Spain.* Philadelphia: University of Pennsylvania Press, 2009.

——. "Maurophilia and the Moorish Subject." In *The Conversos and Moriscos in Late Medieval Spain and Beyond*, vol. 1, edited by Kevin Ingram, 269–85. Leiden: Koninklijke Brill, 2009.

——. *Mimesis and Empire: The New World, Islam, and European Identities.* Cambridge: Cambridge University Press, 2001.

——. *The Poetics of Piracy: Emulating Spain in English Literature.* Philadelphia: University of Pennsylvania Press, 2013.

——. "The Spanish Race." In *Rereading the Black Legend: The Discourses of Religious and Racial Difference in the Renaissance Empires*, edited by Margaret R. Greer, Maureen Quilligan, and Walter D. Mignolo, 88–98. Chicago: University of Chicago Press, 2007.

Gates, Henry Louis and Maria Wolff. "An Overview of Sources on the Life and Work of Juan Latino, the 'Ethiopian Humanist.'" *Research in African Literatures* 29 (1998): 14–51.

Giles, Ryan. "Picaresque Fatherhood: Racial and Literary Heritage in *Guzmán de Alfarache* 1.1." *Neohelicon* 40 (2013): 227–44.

González de la Peña, M. del Val. "La tramitación de los expedientes de limpieza de sangre del monasterio de bernardas de Alcalá de Henares." *Revista de Historia de la Cultura Escrita* 5 (1998): 187–96.

Gossett, Suzanne. "Best Men Are Molded out of Faults: Marrying the Rapist in Elizabethan Drama." *English Literary Renaissance* 14 (1984): 305–27.

——. Introduction to *The Spanish Gypsy*, by Thomas Middleton. In *The Collected Works of Thomas Middleton*, edited by John Lavagnino and Gary Taylor, 1723–27. Oxford: Oxford University Press, 2007.

Goldberg, David Theo. "The Comparative and the Relational: Meditations on Racial Methods." In *A Companion to Comparative Literature*, edited by Ali Behdad and Dominic Thomas, 357–68. Chichester: Wiley-Blackwell, 2011.

Grady, Kyle. "Emphasis and Elision: Early Modern English Approaches to Racial Mixing and their Afterlives." *New Literary History* 52 (2021): 585–604.

Green, Joyce. *Women and Race in Early Modern Texts.* Cambridge: Cambridge University Press, 2002.

Greer, Margaret R, Maureen Quilligan, and Walter D. Mignolo, eds. *Rereading the Black Legend: The Discourses of Religious and Racial Difference in the Renaissance Empires.* Chicago: University of Chicago Press, 2007.

Griffin, Eric. *English Renaissance Drama and the Specter of Spain: Ethnopoetics and Empire.* Philadelphia: University of Pennsylvania Press, 2009.

———. "From Ethos to Ethnos: Hispanizing 'the Spaniard' in the Old World and the New." *New Centennial Review* 2 (2002): 69–116.

Guasco, Michael. *Slaves and Englishmen: Human Bondage in the Early Atlantic World.* Philadelphia: University of Pennsylvania Press, 2014.

Habib, Imtiaz M. *Black Lives in the English Archives, 1500–1677: Imprints of the Invisible.* Burlington, Vt.: Ashgate Publishing, 2008.

Hall, Kim F. "Guess Who's Coming to Dinner? Colonization and Miscegenation in *The Merchant of Venice.*" *Renaissance Drama* 23 (1992): 87–111.

———. "Othello and the Problem of Blackness." In *A Companion to Shakespeare's Works: The Tragedies,* edited by Richard Dutton and Jean Howard, 357–74. Hoboken, N.J.: Wiley-Blackwell, 2005.

———. *Things of Darkness: Economies of Race and Gender in Early Modern England.* Ithaca, N.Y.: Cornell University Press, 1995.

Hannaford, Ivan. *Race: The History of an Idea in the West.* Washington, D.C.: Woodrow Wilson Center Press, 1996.

Harris, Cheryl I. "Whiteness as Property." *Harvard Law Review* 106 (1993): 1707–91.

Harrison, William. *The Description of England.* In Raphael Holinshed, *The First and Second Volumes of Chronicles Comprising 1 the Description and Historie of England, 2 the Description and Historie of Ireland, 3 the Description and Historie of Scotland.* London, 1587. Early English Books Online.

Harvey, L. P. *Muslims in Spain: 1500–1614.* Chicago: University of Chicago Press, 2005.

Hendricks, Margo and Patricia Parker, eds. *Women, "Race," and Writing in the Early Modern Period.* New York: Routledge, 1994.

Heng, Geraldine. *The Invention of Race in the European Middle Ages.* Cambridge: Cambridge University Press, 2018.

———. "The Invention of Race in the European Middle Ages I: Race Studies, Modernity, and the Middle Ages." *Literature Compass* 8 (2011): 320.

Herscovits, Andrew. *The Positive Image of the Jew in the Comedia.* Bern, Switzerland: Peter Lang, 2005.

Heywood, Thomas. *The Fair Maid of the West, Parts I and II,* edited by Robert K. Turner. Lincoln: University of Nebraska Press, Regents Renaissance Drama, 1967.

Hillgarth, J. N. *The Mirror of Spain, 1500–1700: The Formation of a Myth.* Ann Arbor: University of Michigan Press, 2000.

Hornback, Robert. *Racism and Early Blackface Comic Traditions: From the Old World to the New.* New York: Palgrave Macmillan, 2019.

Howard, Jean. "An English Lass amid the Moors: Gender, Race, Sexuality, and National Identity in Heywood's *The Fair Maid of the West.*" In *Women, "Race," and Writing in the Early Modern Period,* edited by Margo Hendricks and Patricia Parker, 101–17. New York: Routledge, 1994.

Ingram, Kevin. "Historiography, Historicity and the Conversos." In *The Conversos and Moriscos in Late Medieval Spain and Beyond,* vol. 1, *Departures and Change,* ed. Kevin Ingram, 335–56. Leiden: Brill, 2009.

Ireton, Chloe. "'They Are Blacks of the Caste of Black Christians': Old Christian Black Blood in the Sixteenth- and Early Seventeenth-Century Iberian Atlantic." *Hispanic American Review* 97 (2017): 579–612.

Irigoyen Garcia, Javier. "Ascensión social y enfrentamiento entre negros en *El valiente negro en Flandes* de Andres de Claramonte: Una aproximación postcolonial." *Afro-Hispanic Review* 24 (2005): 151–64.

Irvine, Robert. "English Literary Studies: Origin and Nature." In *The Edinburgh Introduction to Studying English Literature*, edited by Dermot Cavanagh, Alan Gillis, Michelle Keown, James Loxley, and Randall Stevenson, 2nd ed. Edinburgh: Edinburgh University Press, 2014.

Iyengar, Sujata. *Shades of Difference: Mythologies of Skin Color in Early Modern England*. Philadelphia: University of Pennsylvania Press, 2005.

Johnson, Carroll. *Inside Guzmán de Alfarache*. Berkeley: University of California Press, 1978.

Jones, Nicholas R. *Staging Habla de Negros: Radical Performances of the African Diaspora in Early Modern Spain*. University Park: Pennsylvania State University Press, 2019.

Jonson, Ben. *Masques of Difference: Four Court Masques by Ben Jonson*, edited by Kristen McDermott. Manchester: Manchester University Press, 2008.

Jowitt, Claire. "Political Allegory in Late Elizabethan and Early Jacobean Turk Plays: *Luste's Dominion* and *The Turke*." *Comparative Drama* 36 (2002): 411–43.

Kamen, Henry. *The Spanish Inquisition: A Historical Revision*. New Haven, Conn.: Yale University Press, 1999.

Kaplan, M. Lindsay. "Jessica's Mother: Medieval Constructions of Jewish Race and Gender in 'The Merchant of Venice.'" *Shakespeare Quarterly* 58 (2007): 1–30.

Kaufmann, Miranda. *Black Tudors: The Untold Story*. London: OneWorld Publications, 2017.

Krauel, Ricardo. "Tradición literaria y otredad: La representación del árabe en La desdicha por la deshonra de Lope de Vega." *Dactylus* 15 (2006): 44–57.

Lavagnino, John and Gary Taylor, eds. *Thomas Middleton and Early Modern Textual Culture: A Companion to the Collected Works*. Oxford: Oxford University Press, 2007.

Lebrero, José Fradejas. "Notas sobre la relación de 'El valiente negro en Flandes' de A. Claramonte." *Murgetana* 119 (2008): 95–114.

Lee, Christina. *The Anxiety of Sameness in Early Modern Spain*. Manchester: Manchester University Press, 2016.

Little, Arthur. *Shakespeare Jungle Fever: National Imperial Re-visions of Race, Rape, and Sacrifice*. Stanford, Calif.: Stanford University Press, 2000.

———. "Re-historicizing Race, White Melancholia, and the Shakespearean Property." *Shakespeare Quarterly* 67 (2016): 84–103.

Loomba, Ania. "'Delicious Traffick': Racial and Religious Differences on Early Modern Stages." In *Shakespeare and Race*, edited by Catherine M. S. Alexander and Stanley Wells, 203–24. Cambridge: Cambridge University Press, 2000.

———. *Gender, Race, Renaissance Drama*. Manchester: Manchester University Press, 1989.

———. *Shakespeare, Race, and Colonialism*. Oxford: Oxford University Press, 2002.

Lupton, Julia Reinhardt. "Othello Circumcised: Shakespeare and the Pauline Discourse of Nations." *Representations* 57 (1997): 73–89.

Marlowe, Christopher. *The Jew of Malta*, edited by James R. Siemen, 2nd ed. New York: Norton New Mermaids Series, 1995.

Márquez Villanueva, Francisco. *Lope: Vida y valores*. San Juan: Editorial de la Universidad de Puerto Rico, 1988.

Martín Casares, Aurelia. *La esclavitud en la Granada del siglo XVI: Género, raza y religion*. Granada: University of Granada, 2000.

Martínez Góngora, Mar. "La invención de la 'blancura': El estereotipo y la mímica en 'Boda de negros' de Francisco de Quevedo." *Modern Language Notes* 120 (2005): 262–86.

Martínez López, Enrique. "Mezclar berzas con capochas: Armonía y guerra de castas en el 'Entremes del retablo de las maravillas' de Cervantes." *Boletin de la Real Academia Española* 72 (1992): 67–172.

Martínez, María Elena. *Genealogical Fictions: Limpieza de Sangre, Religion, and Gender in Colonial Mexico.* Stanford, Calif.: Stanford University Press, 2008.

Massinger, Philip. *The Parliament of Love*, edited by Kathleen Marguerite Lea and Francis Godolphin Waldron. Oxford: Malone Society, 1928.

Matar, Nabil. *Britain and Barbary, 1589–1689.* Gainesville: University of Florida Press, 2005.

———. *Turks, Moors, and Englishmen in the Age of Discovery.* New York: Columbia University Press, 1999.

McKendrick, Melveena. "Honour/Vengeance in the Spanish Comedia: A Case of Mimetic Transference?" *Modern Language Review* 79 (1984): 313–35.

Mescall, Anjela María. "Staging the Moor: Turks, Moriscos, and Antichrists in Lope de Vega's *El Otomano Famoso.*" *Renaissance Drama* 39 (2011): 37–67.

Metzger, Mary Janell. "'Now by My Hood, a Gentle and No Jew': Jessica, *The Merchant of Venice*, and the Discourse of Early Modern English Identity." *PMLA* 113 (1998): 52–63.

Middleton, Thomas. *Thomas Middleton: The Collected Works*, edited by John Lavagnino and Gary Taylor. Oxford: Clarendon Press, 2007.

Mira de Amescua, Antonio. *El negro del mejor amo.* Barcelona: Red Ediciones 2012.

Morgado, Alonso. *Historia de Sevilla.* 1587. Reprinted in facsimile. Seville: Archivo Hispalense, 1887.

Ndiaye, Noémie. "'Come Aloft, Little Jack-Ape!': Race and Dance in *The Spanish Gypsie.*" *English Literary Renaissance* 51 (2020): 121–51.

———. "Race, Capitalism, and Globalization in *Titus Andronicus.*" In *The Cambridge Companion to Shakespeare and Race*, edited by Ayanna Thompson, 158–74. Cambridge: Cambridge University Press, 2020.

———. *Scripts of Blackness: Early Modern Performance Culture and the Making of Race.* Philadelphia: University of Pennsylvania Press, 2022.

Neill, Michael. "'His Master's Ass': Slavery, Service, and Subordination in *Othello.*" In *Shakespeare and the Mediterranean*, edited by Susan Brock, Tom Clayton and Vicente Forés, 215–29. Newark: University of Delaware Press, 2004.

———. "'Mulattos,' 'Blacks,' and 'Indian Moors': Othello and Early Modern Constructions of Human Difference." *Shakespeare Quarterly* 49 (1998): 361–74.

Netanyahu, Benzion. *The Origins of the Inquisition in Fifteenth-Century Spain*, 2nd ed. New York: New York Review Books, 2001.

Newman, Karen. "Portia's Ring: Unruly Women and Structures of Exchange in *The Merchant of Venice.*" *Shakespeare Quarterly* 38 (1987): 19–33.

Nirenberg, David. "Race and the Middle Ages: The Case of Spain and its Jews." In *Rereading the Black Legend: The Discourses of Religious and Racial Difference in the Renaissance Empires*, edited by Margaret R. Greer, Maureen Quilligan, and Walter D. Mignolo, 71–87. Chicago: University of Chicago Press, 2008.

Ogallas Moreno, Ana. Introduction to *El valiente negro en Flandes* by Andrés de Claramonte, edited by Ana Ogallas Moreno. Madrid: Clásicos Hispánicos, 2016.

Olmedo Gobante, Manuel. "'El mucho número que hay dellos': *El valiente negro en Flandes* y los esgrimistas afrohispanos de Grandezas de la espada." *Bulletin of the Comediantes* 70 (2018): 67–91.

Omi, Michael and Howard Winant, *Racial Formations in the United States from the 1960s to the 1990s*. New York: Routledge, 1994.

Pacheco, Rodrigo. *El negro del Serafín*. In *Comedias famosas compuestos por Don Rodrigo Pacheco, Lusitano, vecino de la ciudad de Granada*, 167–87. Madrid: Biblioteca Nacional de España MS 14824, 1642.

Pamp, Dian J. *Lope de Vega ante el problema de limpieza de sangre*. Northampton: Smith College, 1968.

Periáñez Gómez, Rocío. *Negros, Mulatos y Blancos: Los esclavos en Extremadura durante la edad moderna*. Badajoz: Diputación de Badajoz, 2010.

Phillips, William D. *Historia de la esclavitud en España*. Madrid: Editorial Playor, 1990.

Randall, Dale B. J. *The Golden Tapestry: A Critical Survey of Non-chivalric Spanish Fiction in English Translation*. Durham, N.C.: Duke University Press, 1963.

———. *Jonson's Gypsies Unmasked: Background and Theme of the Gypsies Metamorphos'd*. Durham, N.C.: Duke University Press, 1975.

Reid-Pharr, Robert F. *Archives of Flesh: African America, Spain, and Post-humanist Critique* New York: New York University Press, 2016.

Rivers, W. Napoleon. "Why Negroes Should Study Romance Languages and Literature." *Journal of Negro History* 19 (April 1934): 118–36.

Root, Deborah. "Speaking Christian: Orthodoxy and Difference in Sixteenth-Century Spain." *Representations* 23 (1988): 118–34.

Rose, Mark. "Othello's Occupation: Shakespeare and the Romance of Chivalry." *English Literary Renaissance* 15 (1985): 293–311.

Rosenberg, Deborah Skolnik. "The Converso and the Spanish Picaresque Novel." In *Marginal Voices: Studies in Converso Literature of Medieval and Golden Age Spain*, ed. Amy Aronson-Friedman and Gregory Kaplan, 183–206. Leiden: Brill, 2012.

Round, Nicholas G. "What Makes Mabbe So Good?" *Bulletin of Hispanic Studies* 78 (2001): 145–66.

Rowland, David, translator. *The pleasaunt historie of Lazarillo de Tormes a Spaniarde*. London, 1586. Early English Books Online.

Rowley, William. *A Tragedy Called All's Lost by Lust*, edited by Edgar C. Morris. Lexington, Mass.: D. C. Heath, 1908.

Rubin, Gayle. "The Traffic in Women: Notes on the 'Political Economy' of Sex." In *Toward an Anthropology of Women*, edited by Rayna R. Raiter, 157–210. New York: Monthly Review Press, 1975.

Rueda, Antonio M. "From *Bozal* to *Mulata*: A Sociolinguistic Analysis of the Black African Slave in Early Modern Spanish Theater." *Critical Multilingualism Studies* 5 (2017): 87–110.

Salomon, Noël . *Lo villano en el teatro del Siglo de Oro*. Madrid: Castalia, 1985.

Sánchez Jiménez, Antonio. "'Segunda Cava en España': Moro, morisco y venganza en tres comedias de Lope de Vega." *Bulletin of the Comediantes* 55 (2003): 117–32.

Sanchez, Melissa. "Transdevotion: Race, Gender and Christian Universalism." *Journal for Early Modern Cultural Studies* 19 (2019): 94–115.

Sandys, Edwin. *A relation of the state of religion and with what hopes and pollicies it hath beene framed, and is maintained in the severall states of these westerne parts of the world.* London, 1605. Early English Books Online.

Schomburg, Arthur (Arturo). "Juan Latino, Magister Latinus." In *Ebony and Topaz*, edited by Charles Spurgeon Johnson, 69–71. 1927. Reprint, New York: Books for Libraries Press, 1971.

Sears, Theresa Ann. *A Marriage of Convenience: Ideal and Ideology in the Novelas ejemplares.* New York: Peter Lang, 1993.

Serpieri, Alessandro. "Othello and Venice: Discrimination and Projection." In *Visions of Venice in Shakespeare*, edited by Laura Tosi and Shaul Bassi, 185–96. Burlington, Vt.: Ashgate, 2011.

Shakespeare, William. *The Merchant of Venice*, edited by Leah S. Marcus. New York: Norton, 2005.

———. *Othello*, edited by Michael Neill. Oxford: Oxford University Press, 2006.

———. *Othello*, edited by Edward Pechter. New York: Norton, 2004.

———. *Titus Andronicus*, edited by Jonathan Bate, 2nd ed. New York: Bloomsbury Press, Arden Shakespeare, 2018.

———. *Titus Andronicus*, edited by Eugene M. Waith, 2nd ed. Oxford: Oxford University Press, 2008.

Shapiro, James. *Shakespeare and the Jews.* New York: Columbia University Press, 1997.

Sharpe, Christina. *In the Wake: On Blackness and Being.* Durham, NC: Duke University Press, 2016.

Shell, Marc. "Marranos (Pigs), or from Coexistence to Toleration." *Critical Inquiry* 17 (1991): 306–35.

Sicroff, Albert. *Los estatutos de limpieza de sangre: controversias entre los siglos XV y XVII.* Madrid: Taurus Ediciones, 1985.

Smith, Cassander L. *Black Africans in the British Imagination: English Narratives of the Early Atlantic World.* Baton Rouge: Louisiana State University Press, 2016.

Smith, Ian. *Barbarian Errors: Race and Rhetoric in Early Modern England.* New York: Palgrave Macmillan, 2009.

———. "We Are Othello: Speaking of Race in Early Modern Studies." *Shakespeare Quarterly* 67 (2016): 104–24.

Spenser, Edmund. *A View of the Present State of Ireland.* Dublin, 1633. Digitized at University of Oregon, Renascence Editions, 1997, n.p.

Spillers, Hortense. "Mama's Baby, Papa's Maybe: An American Grammar Book." *Diacritics* 17 (1987): 64–81.

Spratlin, V. B. *Juan Latino: Slave and Humanist.* New York: Spinner Press, 1938.

Stella, Alessandro. *Histoires d'esclaves dans la Péninsule Ibérique.* Paris: Éditions de l'École des hautes etudes en Sciences Sociales, 2000.

———. "'Negres de sa Majeste': A propos du rôle de l'esclavage en Andalousie au siècle d'or." In *Actas del II congreso de historia de Andalucía*, vol. 7, 617–35. Cordoba: Publicaciones de la Consejería de Cultura de Andalucía, 1995.

Sweet, James H. "The Iberian Roots of American Racist Thought." *William and Mary Quarterly* 54 (1997): 143–66.

Taylor, Gary. "Historicism, Presentism and Time: Middleton's *The Spanish Gypsy and A Game at Chess*" *Sederi* 18 (2008): 147–70.

Thompson, Ayanna. *Performing Race and Torture on the Early Modern Stage*. New York: Routledge, 2008.

Twinam, Ann. *Purchasing Whiteness: Pardos, Mulattos, and the Quest for Social Mobility in the Spanish Indies*. Stanford, Calif.: Stanford University Press, 2016.

Ungerer, Gustav. *The Mediterranean Apprenticeship of British Slavery*. Madrid: Editorial Verbum, 2008.

Vaughan, Virginia Mason. "'Enter Three Turks and a Moor': Signifying the 'Other' in Early Modern English Drama." In *Speaking Pictures: The Visual/Verbal Nexus of Dramatic Performance*, edited by Jacquelyn Bessell, Fernando Cioni, and Virginia Mason Vaughan, 119–38. Madison, N.J.: Fairleigh Dickinson University Press, 2010.

———. *Othello: A Contextual History*. Cambridge: Cambridge University Press, 1996.

———. *Performing Blackness on English Stages, 1500–1800*. Cambridge: Cambridge University Press 2005.

Vega, Félix Lope de. *Amar, servir e esperar*. Middleton, Del.: BiblioBazaar, 2007.

———. *La limpieza no manchada*, edited by Fernando R. de Flor. Salamanca: University of Salamanca Press, 2018.

———. *El prodigio de Etiopia*. In *Obras de Lope de Vega IV: Comedias de los santos*, edited by Cayetano Alberto de la Barrera y Leirado, 121–50. Madrid: Real Academia Española, 1894.

———. *El negro del major amo*. In *Comedias*, vol. 11, edited by Jesús Gómez and Paloma Cuenca. Madrid: Biblioteca Castro, 1993.

———. *El santo negro Rosambuco de la ciudad de Palermo*. In *Obras de Lope de Vega IV: Comedias de los santos*, edited by Cayetano Alberto de la Barrera y Leirado, 362–92. Madrid: Real Academia Española, 1894.

———. *Servir a señor discreto*, edited by Frida Weber de Kurlat. Madrid: Castalia, 1975.

———. *La villana de Getafe*, edited by José María Díez Borque. Madrid: Editorial Origenes, 1990.

Vitkus, Daniel. *Turning Turk: English Theater and the Multicultural Mediterranean 1579–1630*. New York: Palgrave Macmillan, 2003.

———. "Turning Turk in *Othello*: The Conversion and Damnation of the Moor." *Shakespeare Quarterly* 48 (1997): 145–76.

Wardropper, Bruce W. "The Butt of the Satire in *El retablo de las maravillas*." *Bulletin of the Cervantes Society of America* 4 (1984): 25–33.

Weber de Kurlat, Frida. "El tipo del negro en el teatro de Lope de Vega: Tradición y creación." *Nueva Revista de Filología Hispanica* 19 (1970): 337–59.

Webster, John. *The White Devil*, edited by Lara Bovilsky. New York: Bloomsbury Press, New Mermaids, 2021.

Weissbourd, Emily. "'Those in Their Possession': Race, Slavery, and Queen Elizabeth's 'Edicts of Expulsion.'" *Huntington Library Quarterly* 78 (2015): 1–19.

Whitaker, Cord. *Black Metaphors: How Modern Racism Emerged from Race Thinking*. Philadelphia: University of Pennsylvania Press, 2019.

Whitlock, Keith. "*The Spanish Gipsy* under Spanish Eyes." *Sederi* 6 (1996): 215–27.

William of Orange. *The apologie or defence of the most noble Prince William, by the grace of God, Prince of Orange*. Delft, 1581. Early English Books Online.

Wilson, Mary Floyd. *English Ethnicity and Race in Early Modern Drama*. Cambridge: Cambridge University Press, 2003.

Wright, Elizabeth. *The Epic of Juan Latino: Dilemmas of Race and Religion in Renaissance Spain.* Toronto: University of Toronto Press, 2016.

———. "Narrating the Ineffable Lepanto: The *Austrias Carmen* of Joannes Latinus (Juan Latino)." *Hispanic Review* 77 (2009): 71–92.

Ximénez de Enciso, Diego. *El encubierto y Juan Latino*, edited by Eduardo Julia Martínez. Madrid: Aldus, 1951.

Yamamoto-Wilson, John R. "James Mabbe's Achievement in His Translation of 'Guzmán de Alfarache.'" *Translation and Literature* 8 (1999): 137–56.

Yovel, Yirmiyahu. *The Other Within: The Marranos; Split Identity and Emerging Modernity.* Princeton, N.J.: Princeton University Press, 2009.

INDEX

ACKNOWLEDGMENTS

I began this project almost fifteen years ago, and I have been lucky to have the help of colleagues and community at every step. It would be impossible to list everyone who has supported me along the way—but I'm going to do my best.

Thank you to the Seattle's Young Shakespeare Workshop, where I first learned to love close reading and early modern texts, and to Brown University's comparative literature department, especially the generous mentorship of Karen Newman. I am grateful for the support of the comparative literature program at the University of Pennsylvania throughout my graduate school years, and especially to Joanne Dubil, whose warmth made our program a community and whose administrative wizardry is unparalleled.

I am grateful to Ania Loomba, my dissertation advisor, for her guidance as this project first took shape, and for the example her scholarship set for my own. From wide-ranging conversations to careful close readings of many drafts, Ania pushed me to think more deeply and write more clearly at every step of the way. I am also grateful for her unflagging support through my many years on the academic job market.

Margreta De Grazia's generous feedback also helped me to articulate the stakes of my project. I am especially grateful to have learned from her example that the stories scholars tell about early modern texts—especially Shakespeare—can at times be as revealing as the texts themselves.

Barbara Fuchs mentored me throughout my dissertation and postdoctoral fellowship, and has since become a colleague, collaborator, and friend. Her support for my intellectual and professional development alike has been instrumental. I am immeasurably lucky to have benefited from her deep knowledge of the field, generosity to junior scholars, and keen intelligence.

I am grateful to the Ahmanson-Getty Postdoctoral fellowship program at UCLA for providing a vibrant academic community, especially fellow postdocs Andrew Devereux and the late Bill Goldman. The archival research that informs this book would not have been possible without support from the Huntington Library and the Phyllis Rackin Prize for feminist scholarship in the humanities. I also owe a huge debt of gratitude to John Pollack at Penn's Kislak Center, who first sparked my enthusiasm for archival work. Lehigh's Paul Franz, Jr. Fellowship allowed me much-needed time to finally finish this book.

Portions of this book contain material previously published in academic journals. A previous version of the first part of Chapter 2 was published as "Translating Spain: Purity of Blood and Orientalism in Mabbe's *Rogue* and *Guzmán de Alfarache*," in *Modern Philology* 114 (2017): 552–72. Sections of Chapters 3 and 4 were previously published as "'I Have Done the State Some Service': Reading Slavery in *Othello* through *Juan Latino*," in *Comparative Drama* 47 (2013): 529–51. My conclusion expands on work published as "Beyond *Othello*: Juan Latino in Black America" in *Journal of American Studies* 54 (2020): 59–65. My thanks to the editors of these journals for granting permission to reproduce this text, and to the anonymous peer reviewers for their helpful feedback.

This book has been shaped by both the work and fellowship of brilliant scholars in the field of early modern race studies. I am grateful to all the participants in the Folger Library's yearlong colloquium "Gender, Race, and Early Modern Studies," led by Kimberly Anne Coles and Ayanna Thompson, for stimulating conversations and crucial feedback on what became Chapter 5. The book's conclusion developed out of conversations in the incredible SAA seminar "Shakespeare and Black America," led by Kim F. Hall and Patricia Cahill. Conversations with Abdulhamit Arvas, Urvashi Chakravarty, and Noémie Ndiaye have made my work infinitely smarter. I am also grateful for the Shakespeare Without Borders Conference community, and to Rutgers's "Race in the Early Modern World" reading group. Special thanks to Patricia Akhimie for inviting me to join the group, and for creating such a vital intellectual community in the midst of COVID-19 lockdown. If I've done my job right, my debt to Kim F. Hall's pathbreaking scholarship is evident throughout this book. I also want to thank her for her unerring kindness and generosity, from taking time to have a coffee with me when I first approached her as an anxious graduate student, to emailing me with references to Juan Latino that she encountered in her own work. Many thanks to Jonathan Burton, Robert Hornback, Anna Klosowska, Christina Lee, and Elizabeth Wright for their support of my work.

I'm honored that my book is included in the Race B4 Race series, and grateful to Geraldine Heng and Ayanna Thompson for their vision, and for shepherding this project along from beginning to end. Many thanks to Jerome Singerman for his sage advice and editorial acumen when my book was first sent out to readers, and to Jenny Tan for her brilliance, patience, and kindness as she oversaw the manuscript's completion. I am also grateful to Noreen

O'Connor-Abel and Sara Lickey for their sharp attention to detail, to Rachel Shaw for her thoughtful index, and to the Penn Press design and marketing team. Many thanks, too, to friend and brilliant editor Thomas Lay, who gave me vital feedback on my book proposal before I sent it out into the world.

I am grateful to the Penn's Critical Writing Program and to its director Valerie Ross for giving me my first full-time teaching position. Nothing has taught me more about writing for clarity than teaching composition. Bryn Mawr's English department threw me a lifeline when I was on my way out of academia, and I am grateful for the welcoming community I found there.

Most of my best ideas have emerged out of conversations with my students at Penn, Bryn Mawr, and Lehigh. My thanks to all of them for helping me to see familiar texts with new eyes, and for reminding me that academic work can be joyful and exciting. Special thanks to the amazing graduate students in my "Early Modern Race and Empire" and "Shakespeare and Literary Theory" seminars at Lehigh.

I was fortunate to find a professional home in the English department at Lehigh. The department's commitment to literature and social justice has animated vibrant conversations and challenged me to think more clearly about the stakes of my work. Special thanks to Scott Gordon, Dawn Keetley, and Edward Whitley for their expert guidance navigating the logistics of the tenure track; Jenna Lay and Amardeep Singh for their kindness and boundless patience with my questions about graduate student mentorship; and Marilisa Jiménez Garcia for the shared pet stories and emotional support as we navigated our first years at Lehigh together. Suzanne Edwards, faculty mentor extraordinaire and friend, has saved the day more times than I can count, from dispensing practical wisdom to giving eleventh-hour feedback on a book chapter. Conversations with Kate Crassons have both made my work smarter and made me laugh until I cried. She also literally robbed her children to give me lunch money, for which I owe her many martinis. Beth Dolan gave me and my tiny dog Paula a home away from home in the Lehigh valley; her warmth, grace and generosity are unparalleled.

None of this would be possible without the support of my family and community, all of whom have submitted to learning more about early modern literature than anyone should have to with remarkable good grace. Thanks to my dad, for always believing I could do hard things. My mom's boundless intellectual curiosity has been a model for me for as long as I can remember. I am thankful to them both for their love and support. I am grateful every day for my friendship with my siblings. I am thankful to my brother

Ben for his fierce commitment to the people he loves, his unwavering belief in my capabilities, and our shared investment in long running inside jokes. My sister Jenny has talked with me through endless iterations of this project—not to mention the larger project of my life—on walks and at dive bars over many years. I am thankful without measure for her support, her humor, and her commitment to dressing up in costume whenever possible.

Endless thanks to all the friends who made Philadelphia (and, briefly, New York City) home during graduate school and beyond: Kate Aid, Asma Al-Naser, Derek Beaudry, Nesrine Chahine, Hilary Christensen, Megan Cook, Daniel Dewispelare, Sarah Dowling, Selma Feliciano Arroyo, Carolyn Fornoff, Ben Huberman, Ilinca Iurascu, Anna Maria Hong, Anna Knoell, Greta Lafleur, Grace Lavery, Thomas Lay, Edward Lybeer, Marla Pagan Mattos, Luci Morreale, Amy Paeth, Lisa Ruth Rand, Jessica Rosenberg, Poulomi Saha, Julia Verkholantsev, Rafael Walker, Thomas Ward, and Lucas Wood.

Matt Goldmark and I slogged side-by-side through the unglamorous process of wrestling years of dissertation-plus-articles into an actual book. He has read this book almost as many times as I have. I am thankful for his brilliant editorial eye, for his ability to convince me to keep writing when doing so seemed impossible, and most of all for his friendship.

John Hidalgo and I found each other at Shakespeare camp at high school, and I have been thankful for his friendship ever since. Thanks to Tatiana Homonoff, the world's best freshman roommate, for years of long talks about ideas, feelings, and reality TV. Niki Papadopoulos has been at my side through some of my greatest adventures and toughest times and writes the funniest emails of anyone I have ever met. Her friendship is a gift. Rebecca Sheehan has been my partner in crime through countless she(eha)nanigans. Thanks to Julia Bloch (and Rachel and Rafa Zolf!) for movie nights, holiday celebrations, and playground hangouts. I'm grateful to Emma Stapely for her wisdom, her commitment to queer sisterhood, and her willingness to spend hours rhapsodizing over YA fiction with me.

Meghan Teal, my partner and my heart, makes every day better. I am so grateful for the joy, care, and laughter she has brought into my life, and for the home we have made together with Paula the dog and Arthur the cat. I'm not sure which I am more in awe of: Meghan's brilliance or her deep capacity for love. I do know I am indescribably lucky to benefit from both.

Alicia Cedano helped to raise me, was the first person to speak Spanish with me, and always believed I would be a writer. This book is dedicated, with great love, to her memory.

CPSIA information can be obtained
at www.ICGtesting.com
Printed in the USA
BVHW032024120323
660194BV00001BA/20

9 781512 822908